Chance.

Beginnings

By

Roberts Essex

Dedication

I dedicate this work to my mother, the heart of our family, the single soul who has shaped who I am today.

She embodies strength and grace. Through every hardship, she stood tall—a beacon of resilience, unwavering in her love and devotion. She taught me that true strength isn't in never falling but in rising every time we do. Her wisdom, warmth, and kindness have been the guiding lights illuminating my path, even when the way seemed uncertain or unforgiving.

In her eyes, I saw the quiet strength of a woman who gave everything without asking for anything in return. Her sacrifices, though never spoken of, have never gone unnoticed. She has been my teacher, confidante, and greatest supporter. Above all, she has shown me the boundless capacity of a mother's love—the kind that asks for nothing but gives all.

She believed in me when I couldn't believe in myself. When I stumbled, she was always there with open arms, ready to lift me up and remind me of my worth. She taught me the importance of empathy, the beauty of selflessness, and the power of a kind word. She showed me what it means to live with purpose, to care deeply for others, and to never give up on my dreams.

This book reflects everything she instilled in me: the lessons, the love, the courage, and the undying belief that anything is possible with hard work, compassion, and faith. Because of my mom, I strive to be the best version of myself every day. Her example will forever be the blueprint for how I want to live—with integrity, grace, and an open heart.

Thank you for being my constant, my source of inspiration, and the greatest gift I could ever have received. I am proud to be your son, and I dedicate this work to you, Ma.

Epigraph

"Most of us are not raised to actively encounter our destiny. We may not know that we have one. As children, we are seldom told we have a place in life that is uniquely ours alone. Instead, we are encouraged to believe that our life should somehow fulfill the expectations of others, that we will (or should) find our satisfactions as they have found theirs.

Rather than being taught to ask ourselves who we are, we are schooled to ask others.

We are, in effect, trained to listen to others' versions of ourselves. We are brought up in our lives as told to us by someone else!

When we survey our lives, seeking to fulfill our creativity, we often see we had a dream that went glimmering because we believed, and those around us believed, that the dream was beyond our reach. Many of us would have been, or at least might have been, done, *tried something, if...*

If we had known who we really were."

— *Julia Cameron*

Table of Contents

Preface

In 1968, singer/songwriter Roger Miller wrote and recorded a soulful, heart-warming tune about the birth and early times of a little boy he called "Vance." Something about that song and that vignette inspired me to draft this story about the life and times of a boy with such a similar start, transforming over time into a man with such a full and fulfilling life. A life beyond even his imagination.

The story is not about a character like the fabled Forrest Gump. However, it does span several decades and recalls historical events that flavored or influenced the life of a simple man and his entire family. It's the chronicle of a man whose life was shaped by his choices and faith, with time and events naturally unfolding around him. This is the story of that man, his family, and his "real" life. Time and events occur around Chance in real time, usually uninfluenced by him but frequently affected by his incite or decision.

It's not an adventure through a romance comedy with characters like Huck Finn or Tom Sawyer. But traditions of the deep south will play a huge part in the culture and the upbringing of this boy, in the transformation of this man, in the choices and plethora of colors on his palate. It's a narrative rooted in truth, though some events may seem so extraordinary they could border on fiction. It is non-fiction, but, at times, some of the events or experiences of Chance and his cast of supporting life characters seem hard to believe or even conceive.

Here's a young fellow who grew up during a pretty wonderful time to be a child in America. The era offered simple joys; affordable housing, cheap gasoline, bold fashion trends, and unforgettable music. It was a time of penny candy and endless childhood wonder.

A time when neighbors could walk the streets in their suburbia day or night, completely at ease, without fear or apprehension of danger. Nobody was assaulted, sex crimes occurred on television or in true crime magazines, and most homeowners rarely even locked their doors. It was an almost make-believe time when the greatest caution was exercised for a child riding his bike on the sidewalk and a homeowner's cause for angst was acquiring a broken window from a kid's fly-ball or an occasional misguided stone.

Here is Georgia during the last half of the 20th century, a time of conflicting cultural stability and erratic social upheaval. Chance and his family are a living, breathing representation of Savannah during this era, embodying the city's essence and flavor.

This is the story of a devoutly Christian man who sometimes strays from the path of righteousness and his faith into the darkest recesses of lust and iniquity. A man whose mistakes often lead to profound realizations, bringing him closer to the faith he strayed from. He is a man who will occasionally, repeatedly falter and finally get knocked down to his very knees. Once there, he realizes that being on his knees was exactly where he needed to be most of them, and the rest of his life for that matter. His special relationship with Jesus Christ and his "guardian angel (we'll call "Earl" – and I'll explain that later) forged his very essence, his being, into a man of honor and integrity.

Chance is the story of a simple, humble servant of God, of his life and times. It's a compilation of stories of the man but also the character-building exploits and anecdotes of his family and friends.

The story spans a period in time from Presidents Kennedy to Carter, from Mercury 7 to reusable forms of space travel called "shuttles" we would come to know by the names of Columbia, Enterprise, and Challenger.

A period of time when a Cuban missile crisis between world powers nearly led to a disastrous outcome over nuclear weapons and the eventual escalation of a full-on, multi-national, post-WWII conflict we would call "Desert Storm."

It's an era where glass radio tubes evolved into transistors, transistors into microprocessors, and digital "chips" containing a million bits of information. Music shifted formats rapidly; from vinyl records to 8-track tapes, then cassettes, and eventually compact discs that changed the way we listened forever.

This concept was fairly short-lived due to a variety of issues with a more compact and more easily maintained product in the form of a cassette. Much smaller, much more easily transported, extremely lightweight and versatile, were cheaper to manufacture, could store more information than the bulky, and were easily breakable 8-track cartridges. Although less frequently damaged by the ever-increasing, readily-disposable-minded consumer, they still more frequently than not entangled and disabled the stereo equipment for which they were so highly valued.

Seemingly overnight, and right after the space shuttles were introduced, the cassette tape gave way to the unimaginably compacted and completely digitalized, laser-imprinted audio disks we refer to still as the "compact disc." I suppose one of the astronauts designed the concept with his "space pen" while encircling the earth at 3,000 mph in zero gravity. Pretty amazing either way.

In less than 20 years, literally, we found our technology had been fully transformed from leaded pencils and the written word to the insensitive, sterile, unapologetic, and completely paperless wonder now known as "electronic" or "e-mail." No longer was it necessary to lick a stamp and send a personal note to your friend or business associate, sending was simply a matter of striking a "lick" on the keyboard of your handy, dandy desktop computer.

It was an era when a gallon of regular, leaded gasoline priced at twenty-five cents became a carton of cigarettes for $20. Millions of lives were lost to senseless cancers from tar and nicotine, death, and disability due to traffic accidents and injury.

The time, the place, and the feeling were and are Mayberry and The Waltons, Green Acres, Dallas, Police Story, EMERGENCY, and

Peyton Place all mixed up and blended. Funny, frightening, surprising, and sometimes unbelievable tales and events that filled this character's life with joy and made every minute worth living; certainly, guaranteed his every day to be entertaining.

Chance embodies what every child deserves; what every young man hopes for; what middle-aged men long for when in desperation; and what elderly men pray to return to in the final throws of life. He is the aspiration of both the king and the pauper, a man every family wishes they had in their own lives.

Chance is also a collection of short stories and narratives of a life full of hope and wanderlust, of a man in the throes of enlightenment, fulfillment, and profound optimism.

From pleasure in one moment to regret the next, all human emotions we all live and die to end. A jack of all trades, literally, and a master of few, Chance lived the life most only dreamed of and experienced a loss that he would never curse against another living being.

And this is his story.

***

"Getting pushed down is pure incentive to simply do your best to get back up. By the same token, and to a much greater measure, being knocked on your ass is the greatest motivation from your guardian angel to get down on your knees."

Chance Brogdon, 2015

Introduction

We could start with a decade; I could give you a year.

Would it matter?

The Korean conflict had just ended. Eisenhower had dispatched "advisors" to South Vietnam to assist French occupiers as communist forces invading from the north began nipping at freedom's heels. It was a precarious time, with the United States emerging as a self-appointed guardian of liberty, stepping into its role as the world's protector. The nation was posturing as a 'big brother' under the *Truman Doctrine*; a promise from President Harry Truman guaranteeing Third World countries protection from communist threats whenever and wherever they arose as a clear and present danger.

War was coming again. What began as advisory missions would soon escalate into full-blown confrontations, culminating in a Cold

War that cast its ominous shadow over the globe. Despite the brewing tensions, life in America seemed to carry on with an almost idyllic normalcy.

American cars ran on regular, leaded gasoline and were adorned with tail fins; extravagant flourishes that served no purpose but to exude style and flair. Drive-ins, car hops, and those little tabletop jukeboxes were all the rage. They turned simple outings into iconic experiences, fueling a vibrant and carefree social life.

Television was just becoming the rage. Rabbit ears, three channels (if you were lucky) in black-and-white, the pledge of allegiance in the mornings, and the sound of the national anthem playing at 11 p.m. every night became staples of the American household. The glow of the screen brought families together, broadcasting a mix of entertainment and patriotism that helped shape a collective identity. Overnight, only a test pattern's lonely, droning tone filled the airwaves, a reminder of how technology was rapidly transforming daily life.

Rock 'n' roll dominated the airwaves, with the latest craze shifting from the homegrown charm of Elvis and Buddy Holly to a bolder, more electrifying beat from Britain, delivered by wild youngsters sporting peculiar haircuts. Meanwhile, the familiar crooners like Dean Martin and Frank Sinatra were gradually giving way to a revolutionary concept known as "album-oriented radio." In Music City, icons like Loretta Lynn, Conway Twitty, and Dolly Parton strolled its streets and lit up the stages of the Grand Ole Opry, shaping the soundtrack of an era. Music history wasn't just happening; it was exploding into a vibrant cultural phenomenon.

Roller skates and bicycles with long, padded banana-shaped seats were the ultimate symbols of cool. Bubblegum, moon pies, and Pepsi cola remained staples of childhood joy, while White Castle began yielding to the shiny new Krystal burger. Even the classic curbside carhop was being phased out, making room for the cheerful red-headed clown we'd come to know as Ronald McDonald.

Amidst these cultural shifts, a young and dynamic Presidential candidate was emerging; a military hero named Kennedy, promising a bold new vision for America. He would lead the nation through one of its most defining social struggles, while also championing a captivating distraction; a race to conquer space against the Soviet Union, America's greatest rival.

The shadow of the Cold War loomed large, with names like Castro and Khrushchev instilling unease across the nation. The terrifying possibility of global annihilation seemed just a button press or key turn away. Air raid drills became routine, civil defense posters hung like silent warnings, and the wail of sirens cut through daily life; annoying, but a stark reminder of the precarious times. These measures, inconvenient as they were, became a reluctant fixture of American resilience.

Gave it away, didn't I?

No big deal. Like I said, would it really matter?

Children didn't wear helmets or knee pads while riding their bicycles, and the idea of safety belts in cars was just beginning to catch on. Not everyone made the team, and only the best athletes earned trophies or recognition. Excellence wasn't a participation prize; it was a hard-won achievement. In school, grades were straightforward: an "A" for getting everything right, an "F" for getting it all wrong, and a solid "0" if you didn't bother turning in your assignment. Discipline was equally unambiguous; you got your fanny paddled for misbehaving at school and your backside whipped when you got home.

Values were ingrained early, and respect wasn't optional. Kids were taught to say "yes, sir" and "yes, ma'am," and they faced consequences if they dared to show disrespect to anyone. There was a structure to life, a clarity of right and wrong, and a no-nonsense approach to growing up that built character, even if it wasn't always gentle.

What happened to us?

My God.

It suffices to say that growing up in the southern U.S. during the 1960s was a journey all its own. While the same events unfolded in other parts of the country; and even the world; being a Southerner during that time meant you experienced turmoil in a way that was raw, visceral, and deeply ingrained in the everyday fabric of life.

The nation was finally reckoning with the overdue push for civil rights. Night after night, national television screens displayed scenes of state troopers in the Deep South turning vicious attack dogs on peaceful Black protesters in Alabama and Mississippi. It was impossible not to see it coming; the resurgence of the KKK; predictable, and yet no less horrifying when it arrived.

We witnessed the unthinkable: the assassination of our President, the silencing of one of the greatest civil rights leaders the world had ever known, and the extinguishing of hope with the loss of a man who might have carried forward the torch of progress and unity.

And then came Vietnam; a shadow looming over the next chapter of our lives, a conflict that would divide families, communities, and the nation itself.

Draft dodgers, social upheaval, and the public persecution of returning soldiers defined the era. These men came home battle-weary and broken, having fought in a war they neither believed in nor supported. Yet, instead of receiving the respect they deserved, they were ridiculed for sacrificing their lives and honor to a cause they had no choice but to serve.

Unlike the clear moral imperatives of World Wars I and II, or even the Korean conflict, Vietnam lacked a 'just cause' to rally behind. It was a conflict built on pretense, with the United States assuming the role of big brother to France over a small strip of land in Southeast Asia; South Vietnam. This wasn't about defending strategic interests in valuable resources, precious metals, oil, or agriculture. There were no endangered wildlife species or critical commodities at stake, only a vague promise of stemming the tide of communism.

The jungles of Southeast Asia, seared into the memory of millions through nightly news broadcasts, were an unforgiving expanse; stiflingly humid, relentlessly wet, and utterly untamable. For our soldiers and displaced allies, misery wasn't just common; it was the norm. Mosquito bites, venomous stings, and torrential downpours soaked their uniforms and spirits. Add to that the ever-present chaos of bullets, mortars, hidden traps, and the tragic sight of comrades' bodies scattered across the terrain. Each day brought them face-to-face with an enemy who seemed to rise from the very ground itself; small-framed but fierce fighters, camouflaged and entrenched in a labyrinth of underground tunnels and dens. Rifles, machetes, and grenades were their tools of warfare, honed to brutal precision.

The jungle floor was riddled with concealed death traps. Paths that seemed safe often hid lethal snares: punji sticks; long shards of bamboo coated in human waste and buried beneath the mud. These

6

grotesque weapons impaled unsuspecting soldiers in their feet, legs, or torsos, delivering not just excruciating pain but also swift and deadly blood poisoning. Death was not quick or kind; it was drawn out, agonizing, and cruel. A bullet, cold and final, might have been a mercy compared to this.

For those sent to fight, Vietnam was a living hell. Sons, daughters, brothers, and cousins were summoned to a war already lost before it began. They were deployed to protect a nation that neither sought freedom nor welcomed their sacrifice. This was not a crusade for justice or liberation; it was a theater of futile posturing, mired in inevitable defeat and the tragic surrender of lives to a cause that offered no gratitude, only anguish.

At home, our own national guardsmen; friends, neighbors, and kin; were called upon to take up arms against our youth, against students and young adults protesting a war they didn't believe in. Armed with rifles and tear gas, they confronted crowds of kids wielding nothing more than rocks, bottles, and conviction. It was a time of unthinkable insanity, a nation caught in a storm of its own making, where the lines between right and wrong blurred under the weight of political chaos.

The nuclear age had been born from the fires of Hiroshima and Nagasaki, its ungodly power unleashed as an unintended legacy of World War II. What began as unimaginable destruction had evolved into an equally unimaginable source of power and control. For decades, the United States and the Soviet Union stood locked in a relentless contest of strength, each side posturing, each side prepared to unleash devastation to prove its dominance.

"The bomb" became more than a weapon; it was a tool of manipulation, a means of bending nations; both allies and adversaries, to the will of the powerful. Smaller, undeveloped countries became unwilling pawns, caught between giants, their resistance crushed under the looming shadow of annihilation. And so began the era of the Cold War, a conflict without bullets, but no less devastating, where fear and intimidation ruled the day, and peace always hung by a thread.

Most prominently, the United States and the Soviet Union (USSR), known interchangeably as Russia, were locked in a relentless arms race for global dominance. Both sides remained maddeningly poised in a constant state of readiness, each prepared to strike first rather than face the unimaginable destruction of being caught off guard. There would be no victors in such a catastrophe, only the unfortunate survivors left to navigate a scorched and uninhabitable earth. Senseless.

Chance would always carry the memories of those endless nuclear drills, the ones meant to prepare but instead left a lasting impression of unease. "Duck and Cover," a simple and almost playful limerick, had been transformed into a national anthem of sorts; broadcast on TV and radio, drilled into kids and their parents as if the bright flash in the sky could somehow be survived with a crouch beneath a school desk. That little tune, absurdly upbeat for what it represented, had a way of sticking in the mind like bubblegum on a hot summer sidewalk.

The air raid sirens, blaring at all hours of the day and night, became a regular intrusion into daily life. The eerie test pattern with its grating, steady tone would cut through normal television programming without warning. And then, like clockwork, that cold, matter-of-fact voice would deliver its chilling message, a shard of fear slicing through the monotony of the day:

"This is a test of the Emergency Broadcast System. This is only a test. Beeeeeeeeep."

Those words were meant to reassure, but they didn't. The silence that followed carried more weight than the sound, a stark reminder of just how fragile everything had become.

There it was; on TV, in school films, and on AM radio; a persistent, looming threat of global catastrophe that threaded itself into the fabric of everyday life. It wasn't overt, but it didn't need to be. The undercurrent was always there, beneath the surface of the American ideal, a subliminal hum that was impossible to ignore and undeniably real.

In time, this constant tension seemed to drive a shift in the national psyche. Americans, desperate for escape or relief from the weight of war, economic uncertainty, pollution, and political and social discord, turned increasingly to substances; natural and synthetic. Pot, LSD, hashish, and heroin crept into the streets, homes, and daily lives of the people. America, in many ways, turned to drugs.

At the same time, a sexual revolution swept through the culture, preaching the gospel of "free love," communal living, and doing whatever felt good. It was liberating and unrestrained, a wild rebellion against convention. But with freedom came consequences, and soon a wave of sexually transmitted diseases swept through the population; gonorrhea, chlamydia, and the resurgence of syphilis among them.

Then, from the depths of Africa, a new and terrifying condition emerged, one that would devastate the gay community and beyond. The virus, first called HIV (Human Immunodeficiency Virus), brought with it the devastating disease known as AIDS (Acquired Immune Deficiency Syndrome). Within a decade, its reach was global, and its impact was both catastrophic and enduring, casting a long shadow over the LGBTQ community and society at large.

The 1960s were truly a coming of age; for the world, for the United States, and for a wide-eyed little boy growing up in the east Savannah suburbs, soaking it all in. By the 1970s, the world had changed dramatically. The decade ushered in profound cultural shifts, an end to an unpopular war, the disgrace of a Presidential resignation, and a new era in music and art. For that skinny, pimple-faced boy, now a young man, it was a time of transition. While his peers celebrated senior parties, he skipped the festivities, flipping pizzas for gas money and bracing himself for the challenges of adulthood.

Through the daily confusion, there was one source of trust and information during the early evening hours: the nightly news with Walter Cronkite. It was that one place of calm, trust, and absolute confidence that we came to rely on daily.

There, in a little haven of contentment, a little boy named Chance was learning living, and growing in a neighborhood called Avondale. As his Dad had hoped and his Mom predicted, he was a healthy young boy who would eventually come of age and evolve into a young man of means. It took these events, and many others, to build the character and stamina that a man like Chance would need to take him to a place of unimaginable happiness. These and a full conviction of faith and unyielding love for his Lord and Savior, Jesus Christ.

But Chance Brogdon would turn out to be anything but predictable. Faith and fate seemed destined to be one unexpected event after another. Although battered at birth, his life would now be a virtual kaleidoscope of wonder, enlightenment, a tragedy he could never have predicted, and eventual fulfillment beyond his dreams.

"There was never yet an un-interesting life.

Such a thing is an impossibil-ity.

Inside of the dullest exterior, there is a drama, a comedy, and a tragedy."

Mark Twain

Chapter One

———— ❖ ————

Into This World

The morning he was born was cold, and it was raining.

The chill of the early hour hung in the air, the kind that made you pull your coat a little tighter. The stars still shimmered in the dark sky, their light twinkling softly in the quiet before dawn. Raindrops fell steadily, their touch transforming into a delicate glaze of ice as they met the ground, the trees, and anything else in their path. Slowly, the world seemed to take on a shimmering stillness, wrapped in the quiet anticipation of a new beginning.

Did I say? It was cold and very wet.

It was the kind of rain that fell softly, almost gentle in its descent, yet managed to soak everything it touched. Chilly droplets, sharp as tiny needles, pricked at your skin and blurred your vision as they rolled off your lashes and traced a path down your upper lip. Without an umbrella or a hat, the rain had a way of finding every vulnerability; slipping past your collar, trickling down your back, and pooling in the most unwelcome places, leaving you cold and uncomfortable.

Outside, the freezing rain dripped steadily from the eaves of the little shack, forming delicate, crystalline icicles. They hung in quiet elegance, catching the faint glimmer of moonlight and adding a fragile beauty to the cold, damp night.

It was so cold that day, in that house, in the middle of nowhere.

It was a setting that could have been plucked straight from the pages of a storybook; a tiny house, almost more shack than home. The damp, dark walls carried the marks of time, weathered by years of dust, rain, and the smoke from old oak and yellow pine burning in the stone hearth. The floor, once gleaming tongue-and-groove oak, had long since lost its luster, leaving behind boards that now felt icy cold against the tender soles of bare feet.

"*So much warmer nearer the fire*," she mused to herself, longing for its comfort.

For hours, the cold of the room had been the last thing on her mind. The earlier contractions had been mild, sporadic, and at times strong enough to catch her breath, but still bearable. The warmth of the fire and the quiet joy of feeling the baby move beneath her hand had shielded her from the discomfort. But now, the intensity was growing, sharper and more insistent with every passing moment.

It's difficult to put into words the torment of those relentless waves of agony; something a man, or even a woman who hasn't endured it, might struggle to grasp. The raw, searing sensation of living tissues stretching beyond their limits to usher another life into the world is an indescribable intensity. By the time help finally arrived, she was on the brink of giving up. Six miles from the nearest town, twenty from the rural hospital in Screven, with no phone to call for assistance and no neighbors within shouting distance.

It felt almost like divine intervention, as though an angel had leaned down and given him a little "flick" on the ear, prompting the young father to come home just a little earlier than usual that morning.

Little Man

Mama sure had a time with this one. Babies are never easy, not even for women who grew up tough, molded by the grit and grind of the 1940s and '50s, working from sunup to sundown on a farm. But this pregnancy; this one; had been a real trial, filled with unexpected challenges and no shortage of worry.

At least she wasn't facing it alone. Chance's Daddy was right there beside her, his notebook in hand, furiously scribbling down every silly, nonsensical thing she muttered while under the influence of the sodium pentothal they'd given her. Labor is no picnic, in case anyone needs reminding. Back then, sodium pentothal was the answer to managing pain, though it came with the side effect of loosening tongues in the most unfiltered way. They called it "truth serum," and Mama, bless her, was proving the nickname right every step of the way.

Man alive, was she ever layin' on some humdingers.

Dad swore he'd never open that journal again or share the ridiculous, unfiltered ramblings Mama had spouted under the haze of sodium pentothal. It was a vow made out of love and maybe a bit of self-preservation, as if sealing away those raw, chaotic moments could somehow soften the memory of what they had just endured.

The delivery wasn't just tough; it was brutal. Despite Mama's explicit instructions, the doctor reached for the forceps. With cold, unyielding steel, he pulled Chance from the safety and warmth of her womb into the frigid, sterile air of the delivery room. The damage was immediate and obvious. Mama was too groggy to fully comprehend what had happened at first, but when they refused to let her hold her baby, panic set in.

Tiny. So tiny. Her baby boy, born almost six weeks early, bruised and battered by the ordeal. The bruising on the back of his little head, a deep gash stretching across his face from cheek to cheek, and his tiny, delicate nose broken under the unforgiving pressure of those instruments; all of it was too much to bear. Hours passed before they finally placed him in her trembling arms. Tears rolled down her cheeks, mixing with the lingering pain of labor and the overwhelming love she felt for the fragile little soul in front of her.

"Hello, little man," she whispered, her voice breaking as she kissed his forehead.

As if he understood the depth of her love, her baby boy reached up with his tiny hand, brushing the edge of her chin, catching a tear as it slid down her cheek. She had thought she'd love him, but in that moment, there was no room for thought; only an all-consuming bond that swept away everything else in the world.

As she cradled him, her hands gently explored his tiny, perfect form. But then, something caught her attention. Rolling him over, she noticed an oddity on his back; something that didn't look right. The doctors had mentioned something briefly, almost dismissively. *Spina bifida,* she thought she'd heard. But they never explained it, never brought it up again.

"No," she thought fiercely, her mind refusing to entertain the possibility. "Not my baby boy. God wouldn't do this to him, to me, to us."

Her prayers started then, and they didn't stop. Hour after hour, she begged and bargained, pleading for her baby's survival. There was so much stacked against him; measles, smallpox, the looming shadow of polio. It was a dangerous world for such a fragile child, born into a time when vaccinations were still new and uncertain.

"By God, he'll make it," she resolved, her determination hardening into steel. "We'll make it."

Her love and faith anchored her in that moment, as life hung in the balance. If God would only let him survive this night, she would dedicate her every breath to ensuring he had the best, fullest life she could give him.

And she named him *Chance.*

He Never Cried

Those first months were nothing short of relentless. Chance was sick more often than not, a constant cycle of illnesses that had Mama shuttling back and forth between the doctor and the hospital. Each trip felt heavier than the last, both emotionally and financially. But she didn't waver. Somehow, she always found a way to get the medicines he needed, sacrificing things she never thought twice about because her baby came first.

The doctors said Chance might need braces for his little legs and feet; bent and weak, not because they were deformed, but because his muscles weren't developing properly. They just weren't strong enough yet, almost as if his body hadn't caught up to his spirit. It was some form of spina bifida, they'd said, a condition that many children in those days didn't survive. But by the Grace of God, this little fighter pushed through. Without even knowing it, Chance poured every ounce of his willpower into his mother's heart, keeping her going when the days felt unbearably long.

Mama didn't just sit back and wait for him to get better. She worked tirelessly. She'd rock him gently, her hands rubbing his bald little head, moving his tiny legs up and down, in and out, encouraging blood flow and keeping the skin soft and alive. She'd press and massage his feet, determined to give his fragile muscles a chance to grow.

And through it all, Chance never cried.

Instead, he'd look up at her, his wide, solemn eyes fixed on hers, tears brimming as if they both knew they were fighting this battle together. Every now and then, he'd squeeze her hand with all the strength his little body could muster and flash her the kind of smile that could light up the darkest room. Words weren't necessary between them. Their connection ran deeper than any conversation, an unspoken understanding that passed between their hearts.

That sweet, familiar scent of a newborn filled the air around them. That milky, powdery aroma that only a baby can carry; a balm for a mother's soul. Love, pure and boundless, seemed to pass between them without touch, a meeting of souls long before words or gestures could express it.

And then, as if by some miracle, Chance began to grow stronger. His toothless grin gave way to a full mouth of teeth. His legs, once frail and uncertain, began to straighten and hold weight with the help of those braces Mama had so carefully fought for. The surgical scars began to fade, and the fevers that had haunted him so mercilessly started to become fewer and farther apart. By the time he was a little over two years old, things were finally looking brighter.

One sweltering afternoon, in that humid, sticky southern heat, life took another unexpected turn. A tall, lanky young preacher strolled right up to their front porch, his crew cut sharp, his pencil-thin black tie straight as an arrow. He carried an air of conviction, the kind you couldn't ignore. It was as if he belonged there, like he'd walked straight out of some divine plan.

And that wasn't all. That same day, Chance's Daddy made an announcement that would change their lives forever. With a quiet pride, he revealed that he'd been setting aside a bit of money on the sly and had finally done it; he'd bought them a house.

A house in Savannah.

The news hit like a cool breeze on a scorching day, and just like that, their world began to shift, opening up to a future full of promise and possibility.

Foundations

Southeast Georgia in the summer was a beast all its own; hot, humid, and so oppressive it felt like the air itself was trying to pin you down. If you were lucky enough to live in the city during the early 1960s, you might have had one of those newfangled contraptions called an air conditioner. It was a lifesaver for cutting through the sweltering heat radiating off the asphalt. But for those out in the country, relief came from little more than an open window and a prayer for a breeze. An electric fan, if you were lucky enough to own one, was a prized possession.

South of Augusta, heading toward the coast and just west of the Savannah River, lay a patchwork of farming communities. These weren't towns filled with suits and ties but hard-working folks who spent their days tending fields of cotton, peanuts, tobacco, and corn. Their livelihoods were earned by the sweat of their brow and the resilience of their spirit. They hunted and fished for extra food, grew tomatoes as big as your hand, and ate meals that spoke to their roots; fried chicken, grits, butter beans, and those towering, golden biscuits that practically melted in your mouth.

Saturday nights were for the Grand Ole Opry on the radio. For those lucky enough to have a phonograph, records spun the tunes of the Beatles, Frank Sinatra, and The Supremes. Music filled the air, from living rooms to front porches, where the occasional dance might break out. On rare, cherished nights, Mama might shed her apron and dance barefoot in the kitchen, pulling one of the kids into an impromptu spin while Daddy was out feeding the dogs.

Television, a marvel of its time, arrived for many households in the 1950s. Though the picture was black and white, it felt like magic to children and adults alike. By the early 1960s, when Chance and his brother were old enough to appreciate Saturday morning cartoons, "living color" was the buzzword, and every new show seemed like a window into a different world.

Of course, back then, changing the channel wasn't the click of a button; it meant getting up, crossing the room, and physically turning a knob. With only two, maybe three channels, choices were slim, and poor weather could reduce even those options. On a lucky night, usually late, they might pick up a station from Savannah or Augusta and catch something like *Boris Karloff's Shock Theater*. Chance had a thing for spooky, hair-raising movies, the kind that left a thrill in his chest and a nervous glance over his shoulder.

In the late '50s, most stations signed off at sunset, leaving the screen blank and the room quiet. By the early '60s, however, programming stretched until midnight. That's when the nightly ritual began. The station would close with a short film of a jet soaring through the clouds, paired with the solemn recitation of *High Flight*. Images of a serene America followed, then the National Anthem played. Finally, the screen gave way to a test pattern, and for the rest of the night, there was nothing but static; just a field of "snow" and the signal was cut off from the transmitter.

Sorry. I digress.

Into all of this came the union of two well-intentioned, reasonably well-behaved young adults from the same county. They shared similar backgrounds, customs, and a deep sense of faith. In rural southeast Georgia in 1956, they began their lives together, building a small family with quiet determination and unwavering commitment.

This simple beginning became the foundation for a life and story that would unfold in ways they could never predict. This is Chance's family, the starting point of it all.

***

Chapter Two

—◦✦◦—

Family Ties

Mama's People – The Jensons

Growing up on a farm in rural Southeast Georgia during the 1940s, life was tough, especially before television made its way into homes. Entertainment came from a tube radio that barely picked up any stations. Occasionally, we'd catch a broadcast from Augusta late in the evening. On rare occasions, if the conditions were just right, a distant station like Charlotte's WBT might come through, playing the smooth melodies of Frank Sinatra or Nat King Cole.

The real treat, though, was on those cold, clear nights when the wind seemed to work in your favor. That's when you might hear the unmistakable sounds of banjos, fiddles, and Roy Acuff's voice drifting through the static. The music from Nashville's Grand Ole Opry on WSM would skip across the airwaves, fading in and out like an old friend dropping by for a visit. Those moments made the isolation of farm life feel a little less lonely, bringing a touch of the wider world to our small corner of Georgia..

Now - just lean back, and think about that for a minute.
Let it really sink in. Okay, we can move on.

Her name was Annette, though everyone just called her Anne. She led a remarkably simple life, yet there was something about her that made people take notice. She was a pretty little thing, with naturally curly, raven-black hair that seemed to shine in the sunlight. Anne had an effortless charm, whether she was wearing rolled-up jeans and a linen shirt or turning heads in a pink poodle skirt and buckskins at the Saturday night sock-hop. She was the picture of teenage grace, a boy's dream, and she knew how to carry herself without pretense.

At school, Anne was the kind of girl who seemed to have it all. She was at the top of her class and always had a couple of suitors vying for her attention. But beyond the looks and the grades, there was a down-to-earth quality about her that made people feel at ease.

Chance, however, had an unusual quirk that set him apart. From as far back as he could remember, he was obsessed with the name Robert. It started in grade school when his best friend was named Robert, and Chance thought it was the coolest name in the world. Time and again, through childhood and into his teens, he would bring it up with his mother, asking why she hadn't named him Robert. She would always smile but never gave him a straight answer.

It wasn't until decades later that his mother finally revealed the odd coincidence behind his fascination with the name. The truth, when it came out, was as surprising to her as it was to Chance, leaving him to wonder if some things in life are simply meant to be.

Anne and Chance's Daddy, Bernie, dated through junior and senior years in high school. Bernie had some competition to keep his lady's charms; among the heaviest hitters was Robert Sinclair, a tall, handsome ball player from Louisville. She could have married into money, his Dad was an attorney, and they were loaded. But she chose Chance's Dad instead and never looked back, except for a moment now and then when the boy brought it up. He never brought it up again once he learned how weird this was.

Chance called his grandmother Granny. She was a woman of strong American Indian heritage, with distinctive facial features, soft, understanding eyes, and strong hands that seemed made for the life of a farmer's wife. She came from a small Georgia town where, incredibly, slavery was once openly celebrated at an actual marketplace in the heart of the only settlement for miles. Hard to imagine, isn't it? And yet, that sleepy village was once the capital of Georgia. Speaks volumes, doesn't it?

Despite the times and her surroundings, Granny raised her children with unwavering moral character and a deep faith in the one true God; the Father, Son, and Holy Ghost.

This gentle soul had a magic touch in the kitchen. Her biscuits, made from scratch in a large wooden bowl with lard, flour, and buttermilk, were unforgettable. They'd come out perfect every time; fluffy, tall, flaky, and so delicious the memory alone could make your mouth water. They'd rise so high you could poke your finger into the middle knuckle, creating the perfect "bo-hole" to fill with fresh, sweet cane syrup.

Alec was a simple, God-fearing country farmer, a man who kept mostly to himself. To Chance, he was simply Papa. Hard work ran through the old man's veins. Besides raising a family of four, he was a rancher, a farmer, and the foreman of a sprawling hog and cattle operation owned by a wealthy banker in Screven.

For as long as Chance could remember, Papa drove the same old Chevy pickup, its cab steeped in the smell of Camel cigarettes and Prince Albert tobacco, the tins and loose strands forever baking in the sun on the dashboard. That truck seemed like an extension of him, a constant presence on the dirt roads and fields.

When Chance was a boy, his Papa managed a farrowing barn; a vast metal building that housed hundreds of sows and their piglets at any given time. The air around it carried the sharp, unrelenting odor of animal waste, afterbirth, and sweat. The smell clung to everything, lingering in the humid Georgia air for what felt like miles.

"It's the smell of money," Papa would say with a half-smile, as if to remind himself that the stench was just part of the life they lived.

That smell only got worse in the thick, oppressive heat of summer, when the days stretched long and the nights turned damp with humidity. Those evenings could be rough; flies buzzing in swarms, mosquitoes biting at every patch of exposed skin, and lightning bugs flickering faintly against the dark; but that was life in southeast Georgia. And like everything else, you just got used to it.

Papa wasn't an alcoholic, but he did enjoy his whiskey. A mix of Wesco, Etowah, and Creek Indian, his heritage ran deep and showed in every part of him; his appearance, his character, and his quiet but commanding demeanor. He was a big man, with ruggedly sculpted features: high cheekbones, jet-black hair, a ruddy brow, and heavy, gentle brown eyes that seemed to hold both wisdom and weariness. His hands were massive, etched with deep furrows and tough as alligator hide, hardened by years of working the arid yet fertile Georgia soil.

Papa was a simple man, a father to two daughters and two strong sons. He had an uncanny ability to move silently through the woods, even in the dead of winter, his footsteps never betraying him as he tread across the heavy, leaf-covered forest floor. Not a single sound would give him away.

Whiskey, though, had its way of changing him. It could make him mean, a little too proud, and quick to anger. But in other moments, it softened him, like when he'd laugh quietly while sitting in the back of a wooden Jon boat, fishing. You'd know only by the gentle wiggle of the seat that he was enjoying himself.

Papa farmed corn, cotton, tobacco, and peanuts for a wealthy banker who practically owned half the county. But for his family, he worked a small acre of sandy Georgia soil, coaxing fresh peas, beans, sweet corn, turnips, and tomatoes so big and juicy you'd swear they weren't real. Granny would take those tomatoes, peel the tough skin away with practiced care, and slice them just right; so tender you could cut through the sweet, juicy flesh with a fork. Paired with a little salt, fresh cucumber, fried chicken, butter beans and rice, and her famous hot biscuits, a meal with Granny and Papa was nothing short of heaven on earth.

The old house in Midville, where Chance's mother Anne, her sister, and two brothers were raised, was a magical place to Chance and his brother Alden. The yard was a wonderland of towering, mature Rose of Sharon bushes that bloomed in vivid shades of purple, pale pink, and white from spring through late fall. Their fragrance mingled with the scent of overgrown lantana, bursting with a mixture of colors near the front porch.

Behind the house, near the old barn, Papa kept several pens for his coon dogs, deerhounds, and a bird dog or two. The smell of Jim Dandy Field Chow would float on the evening breeze, drifting into the kitchen as Papa "fed up" the dogs. Interestingly, the dogs seemed to get his attention whenever something on TV didn't suit his taste; like that tenor on the *Lawrence Welk Show*. Somehow, Papa had a knack for timing it perfectly, heading out to "check on the dogs" just as the segment started and returning to his easy chair as the song ended and the commercial break wrapped up. Cool as could be.

Down the road from the old house were the workers' shanties, including one where his foreman, Sam, lived with his wife and their eight kids. One day, Chance wandered down to the shanties and stumbled upon a sight he'd never forget. Sam's wife stood on the porch, surrounded by her brood. She was a well-built woman who looked much older than her likely 30 years, and she was completely naked from the waist up, standing there in all her glory. One baby was perched on her hip, happily sucking a tit, while her other bare breast hung free for the unassuming eyes of her kids; and to Chance's absolute horror.

A big ole blowfly buzzed around, lazily licking the sweet, milky nectar dripping from her still-warm nipple.

Now, that's a sight a young, fairly sheltered white boy just never forgets.

Anne had a crazy, annoying sister we'll just call Julia. She had a big mouth; one of those highly opinionated types who simply couldn't stop forcing her ideas, thoughts, idealism, and rhetoric on anyone and everyone. And, of course, she was always right.

That trait didn't soften with age.

She never caused any real problems for Chance; until one day, much later in life, when she insulted his Mama, dismissing her by saying she was "too stupid to drive a Cadillac." That didn't sit well with Chance. To prove Julia wrong, he bought his Mama a Cadillac for Christmas. When the ole bitty found out, she was beside herself. Anne, on the other hand, loved that car; a slick, new Cadillac DeVille sedan. She cried when he handed her the keys, and those tears made the moment unforgettable for Chance. It was the only gift he'd ever given her that meant so much it moved her to tears, and he kept that day in an incredibly special place in his heart.

As for Julia, life took a sad turn after she lost her husband. She spiraled into madness, becoming a hermit and eventually dying alone in her little shell of a home. She probably drove herself insane, spending her days compulsively drawing circles over and over on the kitchen floor. Did I mention she was crazy?

Anne's two brothers took very different paths. Both joined the Navy in the 1960s and served in Vietnam, but the war shaped them in opposite ways. One came back a bitter, angry alcoholic with the disposition of a badger. They called him Bud, but we'll just call him Dan. He was the kind of man who spoke first with his fists and asked questions later, a habit that got him into trouble; constantly. While he fit the stereotypical image of a sailor, the lifestyle and attitude didn't stick for long. His career didn't amount to much, and he washed out of the Navy and straight into a bottle.

The other brother, Stone, chose a different path. He made a career of the Navy, supporting his family and marrying a beauty he met while serving in the South Pacific. Her name was Sadie, and she was from the Philippines. Like his dad and his hot-headed brother, Stone was a strong-willed man. But he also had a gentle soul and could be remarkably compassionate. This was a man who understood the value of family, faithfulness, honor, and respect for others. Maybe he picked it up from his military service, or maybe it was just in his nature, but either way, he stood apart. He wasn't terribly religious, but he was fiercely proud of his family and his country.

After retiring, Stone returned to Georgia and bought what was left of the old homestead. It was his way of preserving the family's legacy, keeping alive the memories of their early years and the home that had meant so much to them all.

Remind me to tell you about the naked man and the chainsaw. Hilarious.

The rest of Anne's family lived in Augusta. She had an uncle who was an optometrist, another who owned a shop, and an aunt who worked in the garment business. Her grandmother was a tiny little woman whom the entire family; children, grandchildren, and great-grandchildren; affectionately called "Rice Krispy Granny."

She earned that nickname for her knack of making Rice Krispy marshmallow treats long before they became a commercial sensation. Crispy, ooey-gooey, and irresistibly sweet–dee–licious, they were a family favorite. We could always count on her to show up with a pan full during holidays or special occasions. Back in the early 1960s, making those treats was something special; not everyone knew how to whip them up, but Rice Krispy Granny had it down to an art. And she was so good at it.

Dad's Clan – The Brogdons

In a certain area we'll come to know well, State Route 24 crosses State Highway 21 between Newington and Midville.

Route 24 is an old blacktop road, its thin layer of asphalt peppered with millions of tiny, round pebbles that stick to tire treads and make a rhythmic "tick, tick, tick" sound as you drive along. Back then, the asphalt was poured directly over clay roads, and those little rocks were meant to give tires some extra grip, keeping cars from sliding into the ditches during rainstorms. Cars in those days were bigger, heavier, and harder on the roads, so they had to repave them about every other year.

One of Chance's fondest memories was the smell of rain hitting that hot asphalt on a sweltering summer afternoon. Cold raindrops would pool on the dry road, coaxing the rocks embedded in the pavement to squeeze out the petroleum below. That slick oil would rise to the surface, releasing a unique, almost earthy scent that blended with the rain; a smell as vivid in his memory as the road itself.

That's why you need to slow down when it first starts raining.

A heavy, putrid chemical odor of black oil and softened tar mingled with the sharp, earthy smell that only wet, red Georgia clay can produce. From somewhere in the distance, the sweet fragrance of wet corn or freshly plowed peanuts wafted in from a nearby field, cutting through the thickness of the air. That scent filled Chance's nostrils and awakened his senses, etching itself into his memory as one of many vivid experiences he would cherish from visits with kinfolk during those wonder years.

Route 24 stretches about 30 miles, connecting the town of Statesboro to the South Carolina line. As it winds from southwest to northeast, it passes through a little town called Newington. Nothing more than a filling station, a post office, and a handful of houses, this quiet spot was where Chance's Mama and Daddy made their first home and began their life together.

I have to say, as country stories go, this one checks all the boxes: near-kin relations, deep family roots, and tales woven through generations. Chance's Mama and Daddy both hailed from the same county, went to the same high school, and grew up just 15 miles apart; one family from around Newington and the other near the county line.

Just saying.

Chance's Daddy, his two sisters, his Mama and Daddy, their siblings, their cousins, and their siblings; all of them lived within a five-mile radius of one another. Family ties were so strong that they even built their own church.

It made sense, considering his Mama's brothers were all in construction. One was a plumber, another a carpenter, one an electrician, and one a peanut farmer. And, well, one was just an all-around asshole.

Sorry. One sibling just didn't sync with everyone else,
and he moved to the other end of the county away from everybody.

Anyway, between the brothers, they built most of the houses and a substantial portion of the county seat over the years. They brought the first pre-manufactured Adrian homes into the county. And they farmed; peanuts, corn, cotton, and grain.

Grandpa was a mechanic. They say he could hold a set of spark plug wires in his hand with the motor running, checking the engine timing by the rate and intensity of the electric shock in his palm. A single wire would shock the pee-turkey out of anyone else. Who can do that? He could.

Chance never really knew the man he called "Gan-gah" because he died of a heart attack sitting on the toilet at age 40. Chance was only about three or four at the time. They say he loved that grand-baby like there was no tomorrow. Mama said he used to sneak into the house on payday when he knew she was in the kitchen or hang-ing clothes on the line, grab all the unpaid bills off the counter, and run down the road to pay them. It made Mama so angry for him to do that, and Chance heard her say so on many occasions.

One day, Gan-gah came into the house, picked up the envelopes on the counter, and started out the door. Chance spoke up and said, "Gan-gah, where ya going with them?"

"Mama and Daddy need ev'y one of they li'l bills," he replied.

The old man got so tickled he sat them back down and seemingly forgot what he'd even come for that afternoon, spending the rest of the day enjoying his grandson's company.

Chance was the first grandchild on this side of the family, and he called his grandma Mammie. She raised Chance's Daddy and his two sisters and later became the family's matriarch. At one point, her brother gave her about five acres down the road from his place, and her siblings all joined in to build her a house. That house even-tually became the home for nearly all her grandchildren; except Chance and his brother, Alden.

Mammie was a small-framed, feisty little woman who always wore her hair the same way. Always. Remarkably similar to the

Egyptian queen Nefertiti; swept way back on the sides, forming a large triangle or angled bowl. Never saw it any other way. Ever. She always wore wire-framed, horn-rimmed glasses, culottes, and tennis shoes. I think they were Keds. She had a huge straw hat she wore only when she was going fishing. The lady loved; absolutely loved; to fish. She'd sit on the banks of the Savannah River at Poor Robin Landing for hours with a single cane pole and a basket of crickets or worms, right by herself. The payoff was often a long afternoon of fruitful, solitary time with the Lord, rewarded by a modest haul of colorful red-breasted bream or bluegills. Usually three or four, just enough for a gratifying meal.

As delightful and filling as they were, the sweet taste from the flesh of those little fishes was never as fulfilling as whatever she and the Lord talked about during those times.

Her favorite perfume was White Shoulders. She used Tide detergent, Dial soap, and Jergen's lotion, and her house always smelled clean. She kept a bowl of butterscotch candies on the coffee table in the living room of her single-wide mobile home. Sometimes, usually around the holidays, she'd change those out to strawberry hard candies with a soft, chewy liquid center; Chance's favorite.

Nothing was ever out of place. You didn't sit a glass with ice down anywhere without a coaster. She could cook like there was no tomorrow, and she made these little biscuits called "cat-heads." Small, thin, they didn't rise; sometimes, she'd put shredded cheddar cheese on top. Man! And her lemon-pineapple layer cake; now that was something else. She'd make the layers so thin, usually at least four, and fill between each with a wonderfully tart lemon-pineapple filling. You had to be careful when you took a bite, though. Mammie held the layers together with toothpicks. On more than one occasion, Chance remembered getting stuck in the roof of his mouth when he forgot to check for that little piece of toothpick.

During his childhood, Mammie lived at the Bethesda Boys Home down Ferguson Avenue in Savannah, where she was house mother to abandoned boys who were either wards of the state or simply waiting to be adopted. She loved that work, and those boys loved her back. Founded in 1740 by Rev. George Whitfield, Bethesda was one of the nation's first and oldest orphanages for boys. Oh, the tales and adventures those twisted old oaks near the banks of the Skidaway River could tell of the 12,000-plus souls it gave refuge to, served, and nurtured over its three centuries of love and care. How fitting it was for such a good-natured, Christian woman to spend her middle years there.

In early grade school, Chance remembered when Mammie moved outside of Newington to look after the other grandchildren living there. Her house was on a hill about five miles from the river, ten miles from town, and just two miles down the road from where her brothers would construct a church the whole community of Blue Springs would come to know and love as home.

Everyone in the county and the family referred to Mammie's new homestead as "Brogdon Hill" because several siblings and cousins came to occupy lots and homes within shouting distance of hers.

What an appropriate way of putting that. "Shouting distance." There sure was enough of that over the decades. Those people fought like cats and dogs.

Mammie also cared for the church, cleaned it regularly, kept up the cemetery, and ensured fresh flowers were in the sanctuary before Sunday school every week. It's hard for me to describe it, but you sure could tell when that lady hadn't been to the church. There was a fragrance that just exuded from the very walls and floors and pews inside that hallowed enclosure – a mixture of fresh linen and Windex; of bookbinding glue and worn leather bibles and hymnals; of diluted Pine-Sol, sweet sage sachets, and the faint wisps of White Shoulders perfume. It was the pure essence of a woman beloved by the entire community as much as by her family.

Undo Favoritism

Chance and his brother, Mom, and Dad only made the trip to see Mammie about once a month. The drive from Savannah was just over an hour; close enough to be convenient, but far enough to feel like a chore. Sometimes, Mammie would make the trip instead, usually arriving on a Friday night, ready to take Chance downtown for some shopping the next day.

In those days, Broughton Street was the heart of shopping in Savannah; a vibrant hub of fashion and commerce. There were no malls. Instead, Lerner's, Levy's, JC Penney, and the massive S.S. Kresge Five-and-Dime dominated the scene. Cobblers, dressmakers, Army/Navy surplus stores, and men's clothiers lined the sidewalks, mingling with walk-in sandwich shops, soda fountains, and bustling lunch counters. For a young, impressionable boy in the 1960s, it was nothing short of magical.

As I mentioned, Chance was Mammie's first grandchild, and she clearly favored him in those early years. Why? No one really knew, but she did.

On those Saturdays; often the first of the month when she got her check; Mammie would take Chance shopping. Her favorite stop was Asher's, where she'd buy him new shoes, pants, or a shirt, ensuring the boy never went without plenty of clothes. They'd always pop into Kresge 5 & 10 for hot buttered popcorn or freshly roasted peanuts. The air was alive with the mingling aromas of popcorn, grilling hamburgers, and orange soda; a sensory experience that seemed to envelop Chance's very soul.

The pair would stroll leisurely through Savannah's historic squares, pausing among the statues of fallen heroes and monuments to the Old South, shaded by the moss-draped oaks and fragrant magnolias. More often than not, their walk ended in Forsythe Park, where they'd spend hours near the grand fountain. In those days, an old man wandered the park's sidewalks with a cart of freshly roasted green peanuts. For ten cents, you could buy a bag of joy, feeding the squirrels that would hop right onto your knee or shoulder for a tasty morsel. To Chance, it was pure magic, and Mammie's joy mirrored his own.

Occasionally, they'd duck into the Krystal restaurant off Broughton and Drayton for a five-cent burger and a small Coke. Those little square hamburgers, fried with tiny, chopped onions and steamed in the bun, practically melted in your mouth. Other times, they'd stop at Tanner's Sandwich Shop for a quick egg or tuna salad sandwich and a glass of freshly squeezed orange juice. With no seating, Tanner's had only stand-up counters meant for busy shoppers and office workers. The place buzzed with activity from morning to late afternoon.

At Lerner's Department Store, on the corner of Abercorn and Broughton, there was a confection counter that sold freshly made candies, peanuts, popcorn, and sodas. The moment you walked through the doors, the scent of hot caramel, popcorn, and maple nougat candies would fill your nostrils, a heavenly aroma that lingered in Chance's memory long after.

Oddly enough, Mammie never brought Chance's brother, Alden, downtown. Why? Chance had no idea. It wasn't as if there was anything wrong with Alden. Yet Mammie's favoritism toward Chance persisted well into their adult lives, to the point of near indifference toward his brother. It was baffling.

As her favorite, Chance benefited from Mammie's generosity. She even gave him his first car; a 1943 Ford Mainline. It was massive, with a straight-six engine and three on the column. Compared to other cars in the early 1970s, it was like driving a Sherman tank. All it needed to run was a glass Holley carburetor bowl. They found one in a salvage yard in West Savannah, installed it, and the car fired right up, purring like a sewing machine.

The car had originally belonged to Mammie's brother, Pat, who had given it to her for fishing trips. It had sat in a field for years until Pat restored it; cleaning, repainting, reupholstering, and putting new tires on it. The pewter airplane hood ornament gave it a distinctive flair. Though the AM radio was its only luxury, the car looked great and ran like a dream. Chance drove it to high school, and while every girl wanted a ride, for some reason, they still wouldn't date him. Damnit.

Mammie held a special place in Chance's heart for decades, her love and memories intertwined with his happiest times. He always looked forward to visiting her on that little family hill in the country. But as Chance grew into a young man, the family hit hard times, not unlike many during the late 1980s and 1990s. One day, Chance found himself at a crossroads, forced to choose between defending the honor of his mother and holding on to the love and memories of his father's entire family.

Little Brother - Alden

Probably more than an opportune time to introduce Chance's little brother, his only sibling, to the fray.

They named him Alden Braxton Brogdon.

Now that's a name!

This little guy came into the world on a hot, dry summer morning in Savannah, Georgia; the Hostess City of the South, no less. He was punctual, arriving right on time after a full-term pregnancy. The doctor had predicted the delivery date almost perfectly. A great start, right? Well, not exactly.

Alden was sickly during the first couple of years of his life. He suffered from relentless, chronic diarrhea that persisted for months. The family worried it might be dysentery from the city water. Maybe it was a bug he picked up at the hospital. Or perhaps there was something wrong with the absorption of water and proteins in his gut lining. The diagnosis was never entirely clear. Mama couldn't recall much about what the doctors said; her days and nights were consumed with worry, prayer, and sleeplessness.

To make matters worse, the large, bald, and rather sassy doctor they had been assigned didn't inspire much confidence. His bedside manner was abrupt, and his decisions often felt more experimental than sure. All Mama could remember clearly was that Alden was dangerously sick for months on end.

He became frail and malnourished, his eyes sunken deep into dark sockets. It wasn't for lack of effort on Mama's part; Lord knows she tried everything. But Alden's little body refused to retain food or water long enough to sustain his growing, desperate tissues. He looked like a walking skeleton, too weak to lift his head.

Chance was just over three years old when Alden was born that warm July morning in 1961. Being so young himself, he didn't remember much about the earliest days of his brother's life; only that Alden was terribly ill. But one day stood out vividly in his mind. It was the day Mama rushed Alden to the doctor, so sick that he couldn't lift his tiny head off the pillow.

That morning, their usual doctor wasn't available. Instead, a young, new physician was on duty, and Alden was rushed into the nearest exam room. By the Grace of God, that doctor likely saved his life.

Dr. Brennan acted swiftly, inserting two needles into each of Alden's fragile, emaciated thighs. Over the course of an hour, he administered half a liter of fluids directly into the muscles, stabilizing Alden right there in the office.

Chance recalled thinking, at the time, that the needles looked like pencils to his little eyes. They were so big. Remember, Chance was

4.

His little cheeks pinked up, his eyes opened fully, and for the first time in what felt like forever, he smiled. Within minutes of receiving the last drops of life-giving fluids, Alden even began to be a little playful. Mama used to recount that moment with tears in her eyes, her voice breaking as she remembered how close they had come to losing him.

On the way home that morning, as they passed the Krystal restaurant on the corner of Victory Drive and Bee Road, Alden pointed a tiny, trembling finger at it.

"Hm, bugga," he muttered in his hoarse, shaky voice.

"Well, sure," Daddy replied. "Why the hell not?"

Although Alden couldn't eat much of it, Daddy bought him a single Krystal burger for a nickel, right then and there. Mama made sure he ate as much as he wanted and even let him wash it down with a couple of sips of Coca-Cola, adding a little extra Coke syrup to help settle his stomach.

With a course of antibiotics over the next few weeks and several more visits to *this* doctor, Alden made a remarkable recovery. Within a few months, the frail, skeletal little boy transformed into a healthier, more robust child.

Oddly enough, despite their bond as brothers, Chance had few clear memories of special moments involving Alden over the years. Though they grew up together, they were never particularly close and rarely played together. When they did, it usually ended in a fight. Things could get physical quickly.

Chance, being much bigger; even at 7 or 8 years old; had a size advantage over Alden, who remained small for his age. Alden's fiery temper would flare up, and he'd grab whatever he could find to chase after his big brother. Chance, amused by the spectacle, would push Alden to the floor and pin his arms down until the veins popped up in the little guy's forehead.

"Damn, that boy could get mad," Chance would later recall with a laugh. Often, Alden's rage meant Chance had to escape the house and stay away for a while, giving his little brother time to cool off.

"I Got A Gun..."

One time, when Mama was working across town for a furniture distributor and the boys were home from school, they got into a heated fight that quickly turned nasty. Chance was about 12, and Alden would have been around 8. The argument was over something trivial; a toy or the TV selector, most likely. Tempers flared, and before long, they were slapping at each other, wrestling, and knocking over furniture. A nice lamp got smashed in the chaos.

Chance, being older and stronger, pinned Alden down until his little face turned beet red. When Chance finally let him go, Alden sprang up, furious, and ran to the hall where Dad's guns were kept. Sensing trouble, Chance bolted outside, with Alden hot on his heels. Once they were both outside, Chance circled back into the house and locked all the doors, leaving Alden stuck outside; angry as hell and now armed with Dad's .30-30 rifle.

Mrs. Franks, the neighbor across the street, heard the commotion and looked outside to see little Alden pacing the yard with the rifle. Alarmed, she promptly called the police. Meanwhile, Alden stormed around to the back porch, smashed the window above the washing machine, and crawled into the house, gun in hand.

Within moments, he grabbed the kitchen phone hanging on the wall and dialed Mama's office.

"Mama... Chance is pickin' on me, and I'm gonna get him!" he shouted, his voice echoing through the office for everyone to hear.

Mama tried to calm him, but Alden kept yelling, his words tumbling out between sobs. "I am so mad! He locked me out of the house, he made me break a window to get in, and I got a gun... and I'm gonna kill him!" Then he slammed the phone down.

Mama froze for a moment, horrified, before grabbing her pocketbook and keys. "Oh no, this is not gonna work," she muttered, heading out the door. Turning to her boss, she said, "I gotta go home and take care of a little business."

By the time Mama got home, a police car was parked at the curb, and the officer was chatting with Mrs. Franks. She approached them calmly, excused herself to the officer, and assured him she'd handle things. The officer gave her a knowing grin, tipped his hat, and drove away, leaving Mama to restore order in her house.

Back then, parents were allowed to take care of problems like this themselves – and expected to. No social services needed. Mama could handle this quite nicely, thank you. And if she couldn't... Dad would be home in a couple of hours.

Mama walked into the house, closed the door firmly behind her, and blistered two little butts good. That was the last time Chance teased Alden so badly. Later that evening, with some added "encouragement" from Dad, both boys got the message loud and clear: their behavior needed to change, especially when they were home alone after school.

From that point on, Chance and Alden mostly kept their distance. Chance had his group of friends and confidants; Alden had his. Despite sharing a roof, they seemed generations apart, even as adults living in the same house. Years later, they would come to realize a hard truth: they were never really even friends.

What Chance didn't find in his relationship with his brother, he did find in his faith. His bond with his Savior filled that void. Chance often felt he walked with Jesus and, at times, talked with Him directly; like a friend would talk to a friend, the way brothers *should* have talked to each other. That relationship with Jesus became a cornerstone of Chance's life, continuing unwaveringly through the years.

Next to Jesus, his Mama was his best friend. She was always there for him, and he for her. If there was one regret Chance carried, it was that he never developed a closer bond with his little brother. He wished it had been different, but that connection just never happened.

Don't Forget the Little Guys

When the boys were growing up, his Dad ensured there was always some kind of pet around the house for entertainment and companionship.

There was a squirrel named "Nutty," once somebody stole him off the back porch on Halloween night.

Siamese cats, goldfish...

They "thought" they were goldfish. Came from a lady with a bait shop in Screven advertised as 'goldfish.' They were actually wild, hybrid, endangered carp this lady was breeding to sell as bait.

The game warden was not amused. Georgia Department of Fish & Game didn't think well of that, either, and they impounded all of our stuff.

There were parrots and fish of all kinds (tropical and saltwater); that hobby cost his Dad a lot of money in other ways as well. One night, in the heat of passion, anger, or stupidity, he threw a shoe right through the 50-gallon aquarium during an argument with Mom. What a mess. Then, in the 70s, they had iguanas...

Yep, I said I-GUA-NAs; big damned lime-green lizards.....

...in a hole built into the living room wall next to the television! Those damned things ate lettuce and small insects, and that cage smelled like hell. But despite the rotating menagerie of animals over the years, the family's favorites were always the dogs. They brightened their lives and brought endless humor to the household.

One of the most memorable was a dachshund the boys named Schultz, after the character on *Hogan's Heroes*. The squatty little guy loved to sit in the recliner with the boys, perched on his butt like a human, watching TV. They nearly lost him one winter when Daddy decorated the Christmas tree with pink, silver, and blue aluminum icicles. Schultz, being the ding-a-ling he was, ate every single icicle he could reach on the lower half of the tree. The vet was astonished. He had no idea how those icicles didn't kill the dog, wrap around his intestines, and strangle him from the inside out. Instead, the backyard was covered in little blue, silver, and pink-striped piles of poop for months.

Over the years, the family had a collection of ankle-biters (chihuahuas), a couple of terriers, and two or three German shepherds.

Among them, the one most beloved was a little black-and-tan shepherd named Rex.

Rex absolutely adored Alden, as if the boy were his entire world. Obedient and fiercely protective, he watched over Alden with unwavering devotion. At the time, Alden was just a toddler, probably two or three years old.

One day, little Alden managed to slip out the backdoor and toddled across the yard to the garbage cans by the back gate. Somehow, he climbed onto the wooden frame surrounding the cans and perched himself right on top of one. There, he found a hammer Daddy must have left behind and decided to have some fun.

BAM – BAM – BAM – BAM.

The sound must have startled Rex. Realizing something wasn't right and noticing Alden was missing, Rex bolted out the backdoor. The shepherd spotted the baby on top of the cans, hammer in hand, and instantly sprang into action. Without hesitation, Rex ran to Alden, grabbed him gently by the diaper, and started carrying him back toward the house.

Of course, Alden screamed bloody murder.

Mama, hearing the commotion, rushed to the backdoor. She arrived just in time to see Rex prancing proudly across the yard, baby in his teeth, while Alden, still clutching the hammer, repeatedly bopped the dog over the head with it.

Rex didn't let go. He marched right up to the doorstep and delivered that baby safely into the house before finally releasing his grip.

Good dog, indeed.

Dearly Departing

It must have been the summer of 1968 because Chance was in the 5th grade. That summer started with a particularly ugly incident between his Mom and Dad, sparked by a woman the ole man had been seeing on the side while working as a police officer at the port. One evening, they were watching the *Porter Wagoner Show* when Dad made the mistake of comparing this woman; whom we'll call Jean; to Dolly Parton.

Mama didn't let it slide. She looked him square in the eye and asked, "Who the hell is Jean?"

They were sitting at the kitchen table having supper at the time. The way Mama said "Jean" must have struck a nerve because Dad cursed at her and threw a fork in her direction. Mama retaliated with a glass of iced tea; and her entire plate of food.

At the time, Dad was wearing a freshly starched, white cotton uniform shirt, ready to head to work right after dinner. The sweet tea left a massive stain on the pristine fabric, while crowder peas, rice, and shredded coleslaw dripped from his silver police bag and brass name tag. The sight was almost comical; almost.

Dad stared down at his ruined shirt, at the chaos on the table, then back at Mama. His face twisted in rage, and he let out a blood-curdling, "Son-of-a-Bitch!" The yell must have carried halfway across town.

And then it escalated. He slapped her. She slapped him back.

Back and forth they went, the fight spilling out of the kitchen, down the hall, and into the bedroom. Chance saw his dad hit Mama hard; at least twice. Then he saw him grab her and bang her head against the bedpost. Twice.

Terrified, Chance bolted out into the street, yelling, "Help, help! Daddy's on Mama! Help!"

But no one came. The lady across the street peeked out her door and quickly slammed it shut. Mr. Hendrix next door was in his yard. He glanced over but turned back to his house without a word. No one wanted to get involved.

That night in late March 1968, Mama packed up the boys, and they ended up at Granny and Papa's house. They stayed there for the entire summer. The boys were enrolled in school for the remainder of the year, riding the bus; a new experience for them; back and forth some 30 miles into town.

That summer was a rough one. Both boys came down with red and German measles. Chance got the mumps. One day, Alden got stung by a hornet in the kitchen, and the force of it knocked him clear across the room.

Around mid-summer, when the cotton was ready for harvest and the combines were cutting bolls to bale, both boys caught chicken-pox. The heat in the old house in Midville was bad enough, but the suffocating humidity made the blisters between their fingers and toes itch unbearably. Mama painted them with calamine lotion and dusted them with cornstarch to ease the irritation, but nothing could take away the misery. For the rest of his life, the smell of rain on a cotton field brought Chance back to that summer, to that house, and to how incredibly miserable they'd been.

Through it all, Rex was there. That loyal shepherd stayed by the boys' sides as they played outside in the brutal heat for hours. They climbed into the big barn filled with hay, rolling around in the dusty, dank environment despite the risk of encountering a corn snake; or worse. Sometimes, they'd jump into the big bin of dried field corn, unaware of the dangers. The dust could cause severe lung infections, and the boys could have sunk into the corn and suffocated before anyone even realized they were missing.

But none of that mattered to them. They were boys playing in the country; rough and wild, as kids were back then.

Kids nowadays? They'd never survive this kind of play.

Funny how your memory can recall events so vividly at times that your senses can recycle odors, sounds, the feel or texture of an object, the ambiance of a place, the softness and moisture of a kiss. Even decades later.

The smell of that hot white sand on *that* farm on *that* particular day was one of those times for Chance. It was a very 'unique,' downright peculiar odor. An acrid, acidic scent that burns your nose and your eyes. In fact, it was very much like the vapors released from an anthill when you stepped on a bed of piss-ants. Maybe that was something only country folk knew; it was intense.

That afternoon, the boys were out at the edge of the road in front of the old house near the entrance to the barn, digging in the sand with old spoons, just being boys. The day was particularly hot, and the smell from the freshly disturbed sand was especially pungent. Occasionally, Chance would dig up a huge piece of quartz out of that sandy drive and chunk it in the grass.

There is literally no telling what those crystals would be worth these days but I bet they are still there, and more, right now.

Rex was fiddling around, chasing after Papa's feral cats, just bein a dog.

Up on the porch, Granny and some woman from the church were sitting, shelling peas or shucking corn or something. Papa wasn't around right that moment; maybe he was out back feeding his coon dogs or across the road feeding up the hogs. Anyway, everything was great and peaceful on that hot, humid summer's day.

Daddy had come up to visit the boys and brought a huge cardboard box with an amazing assortment of candies of all kinds to say how much he missed them at the house in Savannah. Then they watched him cry and plead with Mama to return home and forgive him for being so stupid.

She absolutely would not budge. Stubborn? No, determined and resolute.

At first, the boys didn't hear anything. They were playing, yelling at each other. Rex was barking at the cats. Maybe a tractor was running across the road; I don't remember.

That road was especially dusty on that, by now, extremely hot, and very dry in the late afternoon. Even traveling slowly on the powdery road, a car could kick up quite a cloud with the road in this condition. It took a turn beyond where the boys could see anyway, and the heavy woods in that direction deferred sound until the last minute.

One of them, I don't know which, threw one of those crystal chunks over his shoulder, and it hit one of those tabby cats smack in the head. The kitten cried out and ran toward the road, with Rex in hot pursuit.

Old Sam, Papa's colored side man, had gone to town that morning to buy groceries and have a nip.

Shouldn't have had anything to drink, but to think that you would not know Sam. And he was on the way home.

Like I said, they didn't hear the car – until that last minute.

Suddenly, there was an awful *BOOM* of a heavy vehicle hitting the bumps in the road, then a loud *WHOOSH* as it raced by within just feet of where the boys were playing: within just a couple of *feet*!

Sam didn't see those boys. He certainly didn't see that cat run across the road, Rex in hot pursuit. That dog yelled out when that heavy old Chevrolet wagon hit him with a yelp that would pop your ear drums. And he lay there as the car continued at break-neck speed down the road and pulled into the old cabin where Sam and his family lived about a mile away.

Rex lay there on the side of the road, his pelvis crushed, leg bent abnormally out and up, pointing in the wrong direction, whimpering softly. Papa, not Daddy, came out from behind the work shed, picked up the gravely injured pup, and took him to see Doc Hogzit. The doctor would set the leg, but if he were to live, Rex would need someplace to mend the rest of his life. He sure couldn't go back to the city.

Dad found a retired woman at an old fish camp on the Ogeechee River outside Meldrum to make Rex a new home. He lived there for several years with the lady and her family, looking after the vast property and his new companions.

Dad took them out in their teens to visit their old friend one weekend, and Rex did not meet them at the gate. Several weeks before, a big black bear had wandered up on the property near the house while his lady was out in her garden. Rex ran between the two, diving at the beast, and died in the crushing arms of that bear in service to his master. She placed a metal statue of a shepherd dog overlooking the river he loved in honor of his memory.

I've already alluded to so many of the wonderful, if not magical, moments Chance experienced during his childhood when he would get out of the hustle and bustle that was city life and venture into the simple, unhurried existence that is country living.

He liked spending time with his Dad's mom, Mammie. Still, there was far too much friction, argument, and hectic interaction always present between his aunts and uncles, cousins, and a mixed mess of assorted near-cartoon characters in and around Brogdon Hill all the time.

Although he didn't realize it until years later, his most memorable times were spent on the farm with his Mama's folks, his Granny and Papa. Of those times, his absolute favorite moments were down by or in Briar

Creek. Those cold, cypress-tainted, caramel-colored yet crystal clear waters provided a waiting canvas for Chance to escape and paint life-long memories of his times in the swamps of Screven County.

Among the water moccasins, gators, yellow perch, and bluegills were an assortment of ducks, deer, beaver, and turkey. Papa had always warned that he had seen black bears and an occasional panther, but Chance never even saw tracks for these critters. He'd also heard about packs of wild dogs roaming the swamps with groups of feral pigs; these animals were vicious, dangerous, and could be quite deadly if encountered alone or unarmed.

And there had been reports, on at least one occasion anyway, of *unusual* encounters along the banks of the usually serene and majestic Savannah River delta.

A Briar Creek Encounter

Although not about or involving Chance, human interest tales and experiences play such a huge role in character development for us all. Chance's family was so full, really over-flowing with already-developed characters. Stone, Mama's older brother, was unique, humorous, and such a wonderful part of his life that I was compelled to provide this delightful novella of Chance's favorite uncle.

During his later years, after Stone settled down on the property, he went to work for himself doing odd jobs throughout the county. Not a bad-looking man, he was called upon by some of Screven's more influential and prominent spinsters who frequently required the services of a 'handyman.'

By this time, he was 73, but Stone was still in very good physical shape. Just him and his bride, he built a couple of porches, a storage shed, a wheelchair ramp, and a big pergola in the back by himself. He was quite the handyman. His wife, Sadie, was sickly and wheelchair-bound and couldn't help at all. His nearest neighbor was about a mile in either direction. No problem, no hurry for anything. Retirement is nice like that. In addition to his community services, he loved spending time right by himself in the woods. Not hunting especially, although he'd bag a deer or a feral pig to put meat in the freezer once in a while, he just liked walking through the forest — alone. Papa was a lot like that, too, and I am certain that was exactly where he got it. Stone's property was located just a mile or less from a pretty big creek, Briar.

Creek, that ran the length of the county and emptied into the Savannah River to the south about 10 miles. He'd grown up swimming and fishing in that ole creek and loved that clear, icy water that literally ran through his veins and his soul.

Chance's Mom and Dad used to tell tales of wading through the creek shallows when they were dating in high school, shooting moccasins, and water snakes, off the limbs with a .22 caliber rifle. Papa would fuss when they got back, admonishing them to, *"Leave my damned snakes alone. If they ain't fishin' you ain't catchin'."*

Years ago, Stone had decided to take it upon himself to be something of a caretaker for that run of the creek. Got him out of the house and into nature, extremely relaxing, peaceful. Besides, the country club bordering parts of the run agreed to let him do whatever he wanted to. He was their handyman as well.

So, he'd put in on the main highway and float downstream, cutting downed trees and limbs from the main run along the way. Then he'd usually stop, sleep by the edge of the water overnight, get up and paddle further until he got to Brannen's Bridges, take the boat out, and call his wife to have someone come pick him up.

On one particular weekend, not unlike most any of the others, he put his hand-made wooden boat in the creek at US 301 to begin his usual trek. Stone purchased a new, bright yellow McCullough chainsaw the day before, a little red gasoline tank, a pint of machine oil, and a new mini cooler that he'd filled with 2 or 3 Diet Cokes. Before he left the house that morning, he'd also made himself a bacon and egg sandwich and thrown it in the cooler.

With just the clothes on his back, he pushed off the bank and started downstream. About three miles down, there was a pretty good-sized sweetgum the wind had blown over recently. A big limb was stretched out across his path: easy fix. He fired up that chainsaw, sliced right through that fresh, softwood-like warm butter in a couple of seconds, chunked the pieces to the bank, and was off again. This sequence continued, as usual, for the next three miles or so, stopping occasionally to clear the main channel.

61

It was a warm day in early autumn. The sky was clear, a beautiful blue, with just a few *"decorative* clouds" here and there. By midmorning, he'd already seen a beaver, a small doe drinking at the edge of the current, several big egrets, and the fresh tracks of a pretty good-sized gator in one deep, muddy turn of the creek. Then, as he came around a particularly tricky bend, the creek opened out to an amazing sight.

The bank slowly rose on either side to make a sharply sloping, natural berm, heavily dressed with freshly fallen leaves of yellow and orange. That tract suddenly straightened out, creating a long, narrow bowl in the expanse. Out of nowhere, he was startled by a sound to his left, and he snapped his head in that direction just in time to see a pair of wood ducks skim across the water and fly off into the trees.

What a sight! Amazingly clear today, he could clearly see the stream's bottom: bream swimming along and an occasional big cat here and there in the icy water under his draft. A breathtaking tea color, this ole soul of the river was deeply shaded and dyed from the tannin of oak, sweetgum, cedar, and cypress, tainting the cold waters over decades – or maybe centuries, who knew? The canopy of the extraordinarily tall cedars filtered the midmorning sun in intriguing beams of light that gently danced through and across the surfaces of this majestic place.

Mother nature was certainly showing off her brightly-colored flowers, ferns, and twisted, moss-covered gems on the floor of the swamp this morning.

"What a great day God has given to me," he thought to himself.

In the distance, he couldn't tell which direction; he could faintly hear the sounds of people. Maybe it was a family having a weekend picnic. Maybe just a couple of teenage lovers, playing, teasing each other. He kind of grinned to himself, shrugged his shoulder, and paddled on.

Sometime after noon, he stopped, pulled his boat up on the bank, got out, and ate that sandwich. How much better do simple things like that simple bread and meat combination taste in a setting like that? Delicious. Diet Coke wasn't bad, either. Then he thought he heard the water gurgling, rushing unusually loud up around the next turn. Instead of returning to the boat, he just decided to wade along the muddy bank to check it out. So, he removed his sandals and left them on the bank near the boat.

Up ahead, the sound he heard was a very large cedar, down, laying across the breadth of the waters, preventing any further passage by boat beyond that point. The wind had blown this ancient master so hard it uprooted the entire plant, its huge root ball still attached intact on one bank, crown on the other.

"What a job this'll be," he thought. *"Oh well, what I'm here for. Might as well get started, I guess."*

After surveying the situation for several minutes, he resigned himself to the fact that he would simply have to straddle this thing and just separate it from the root base first. Once he did that, he thought, he could then cut the remaining trunk into sections and float them across to the bank to clear the run. Cool. Got a plan.

So, he proceeded to mount that cedar trunk – all of 18 to 20 inches in diameter - with that bright yellow, brand-new chain saw in hand. Felt like straddling a Brahma bull. Fired that new saw right up with a single pull. *VROOM! A WHAKAKAKA*! Beautiful instrument and tool. Positioned himself on that massive phallic monster and began cutting in the dense flesh from the topside, crossways as he sat on top of that thing. About halfway through, things were going really well; he suddenly realized what a huge mistake he had made.

Just about then...

... crack.... whine .... crack...POW!

With a huge explosion of noise and splinters, that damned tree trunk suddenly, violently, viciously separated! That root ball, still attached to the bank behind him, provided a fulcrum against the release of the pressure applied from the expanse of that heavy, downed behemoth. As that blade separated the grain and that immense tensile strength was released, the earth reclaimed her property, and she stood that base up promptly and proudly.

Stone flew about 20 feet in the air in one direction. That bright yellow chain saw - still running – went in the opposite.

SPLASH! Right in the deepest part of the current. The chain-saw *and* Stone!

"What in the hell was I thinking? Son-of-a-gun!"

A few scratches here in there, mostly on his legs, and a fairly large but superficial laceration on his right cheek, but everything seemed to be intact. His pride hurt more than anything else. Right below where he landed, he could see the saw, and he reached down to pluck it from the water's grip.

"Damn, soaking wet to the crack of my butt," he said, realizing there was no one to hear him at all.

"Bet this damned new saw won't work now".

He sat that tool down across a stump he'd cut there several weeks ago in hopes it would dry in the sun enough to start again. Water ran out, rather, it *poured* out, and he left it on its side as he turned his attention to other matters.

Stone didn't have another stitch of clothing anywhere, and it was too far back up the creek to his truck.

No problem, nobody around anyway. So, he stripped: took off every stitch of clothing, including his skivvies. Wide open and fully exposed to God and all creatures, great and small, Stone was laid out there on that bank, drying himself and his clothes in the plentiful sunlight. And he fell asleep.

He had no idea how long he'd been lying there when he was startled by something. He looked around, didn't see or hear anything for several moments, and shrugged it off. Then he got up, walked over to that stump, picked up that chainsaw, and sat down again. He primed the saw with a couple of pumps on the little rubber plunger, and pulled that cord. *VRRROOOOOM!! WHAK-A-KAK-KAK.*

"Well, I'll just be damned!! Look a-here. Just like new."

There was that sound again, closer. Sounds like …. voices. *Women?!*

Coming fast around the bend where he'd left his boat, a new aluminum flat-bottom was rounding the corner with two middle-aged women in wide-brimmed sunhats, shorts, sunglasses, and their mouths flung wide open – staring at Stone. Imagine that sight. A fully-grown older man with a pretty great physique, sitting on the creek bank, on a stump, holding an outstretched and running chainsaw, buck-assed naked. And now, grinning like a mule eating briars.

Mortified would not begin to describe what the ladies were feeling, They screamed, he screamed, and they screamed again, trying desperately to paddle against the current. What a tale they would take back to town this day.

Well, Stone covered himself, then explained himself and apologized for their shock and awe. They regained their composure and went on their way. He continued his exploits for several more years then his health ended his trips and adventures. But those ladies never forgot the day they encountered to *"naked chainsaw slinger"* of Briar Creek Swamp.

****

Chapter Three

Bernie (Daddy) – Miss You

Chance's dad was a man who was often misunderstood, underrated, over-criticized, and unfairly denigrated for so much of his life. Despite this, he left an indelible mark on Chance; both as a figure to respect and, for much of his childhood, someone to fear.

This man, so important to Chance's life, had a sharp sense of humor and an exceptional talent with his hands. He could draw anything he put his mind to; whether it was detailed floor plans for a house, intricate diagrams for building cabinets, cartoon characters, or even risqué girlie pictures. His creativity seemed boundless.

For years, one of his most impressive creations adorned the family's living room. A mural covered an entire wall, depicting a white-tailed deer bounding through an open southern field, complete with pine saplings and thick underbrush. It was remarkably well-done and received countless compliments from visitors. The kids in the neighborhood were particularly fond of it, often stopping by just to marvel at its lifelike detail.

We'll get into the "girlie pics" thing a little later.

Tall and lean, he had a larger-than-life nose with a prominent hump right in the middle; a true schnoz. It wasn't the result of any trauma; he was just born that way and grew up with it. That nose became an unmistakable part of who he was. His Daddy had one too, though not quite as pronounced.

Between his prominent nose and his distinctive haircut, his profile looked like it belonged on a granite carving; striking and unforgettable. Whether by dumb luck or the hand of fate, that incident with the forceps at birth left Chance with the same unmistakable facial profile.

May also have been a little of the guardian angel Chance would come to know, marking him with a little humility for later in life.

Bernie had big hands and feet, he could swim like a fish, and he had a smile you could see from a mile away. The ole man had a habit of reaching up, slapping the top of his flattop haircut whenever he got excited or happy about something. He'd do that same thing whenever he'd see some long, lost, or unexpected friend pull into the drive - or the arrival of a son he maybe hadn't seen in far too long.

Daddy forever sported a crew cut that only one man in all of Savannah was entrusted to cut for him. It had to be cut regularly, almost like clockwork, uptight and just right. If you've never seen one, a crew cut is a very short, very specific men's haircut of the 1950s. He grew up with his hair like this and couldn't stand to let it get more than a week and a month old. How 'specific?' Ok, check it out.

The barber would cut upward from the lower hairline, against the grain, on both sides and the back, right next to the skin, tapering about a half inch from the top of the scalp. Then the hair on the top had to be combed straight back, straight up for the next phase. Very carefully, strategically, purposely, and with great concentration, he would then cut that hair on top – leaving it all an inch long – no more, ever – making certain that top was FLAT!

When I say "flat" I mean like the deck of a danged aircraft carrier.

***

Faith of a Man

Chance's Daddy always lit up whenever he got a fresh haircut. It brightened his whole day, transforming his mood; at least for that afternoon. He had a quirky way of showing it off, too. He'd balance a crisp piece of copy paper on his head, bragging that he could keep it there all day without it falling off. Swear to God.

Speaking of God, Daddy had a unique way of expressing his devotion to the Almighty. For much of Chance's early life, his father seemed to be a devout Christian. He and Alden were raised in the church; Methodist at first, then Baptist, and eventually Southern Baptist (and yes, there is a difference, a *big* difference).

Daddy was even preaching when he and Mama got married, continuing for a while into Chance's early years. He knew the Bible inside and out, and Chance often watched in awe as his father grew so emotional while testifying his love for Jesus and the Holy Word. Tears would well up in Daddy's eyes, and he'd cry openly during those heartfelt moments of worship.

But as the years went on, things changed. The family's devotion to church waned, and Daddy's commitment fell out of favor. Tough times came knocking, and with them, a change in Daddy's relationship with faith. Chance saw Bernie, his father, far too often blaming God for his misfortunes and far too rarely giving thanks for his many blessings.

Daddy's attitude shifted drastically during those years. He couldn't seem to hold down a good-paying job, and the family's financial situation became precarious. He mortgaged, re-mortgaged, and re-mortgaged the house again, buying things they didn't need but he thought they wanted. There were whispered stories of extramarital affairs, and the family went through multiple separations. Inside the house, tempers flared, and things got broken; a lot.

As Daddy's health began to falter, his accident-prone tendencies only worsened. The falls became more frequent, the injuries more severe. He fell from the attic stairs for no discernible reason, his foot catching in the steps as he tumbled backward. The result? A snapped foot, ankle, and lower leg. Another time, he fell from the roof while installing a tall CB antenna tower, breaking several bones. Accidents with saws, sharp tools in the woodshop, and power tools in the yard piled up over the years.

One night, during a particularly fierce thunderstorm, Chance witnessed something he'd never forget. His father, the man he had once admired for his unwavering faith, stood in the middle of their modest living room, cursing at God. He wasn't praying for strength or acceptance of God's will; he was shaking his fist toward the ceiling, addressing God directly, and unleashing a torrent of profanity and rage.

Chance could hardly believe his ears. This man, who had once been so soulful, talented, and witty, was now screaming some of the most vile, ferocious, and hellacious language Chance had ever heard; or ever wanted to hear again.

And then, as if in direct response, lightning struck. It hit the pine tree in the backyard, traveled up the powerline, and surged straight into the house. The force of it blew out both the TV and the CB radios in the den.

Maybe it wasn't a "thunderstorm," after all.

Of course, things only got worse for several years. Sure, there were moments that were better than others, but it seemed clear that God had heard the ole man calling Him out. While I don't believe God seeks vengeance in any sense of the word, it's possible He allows events to unfold, by human hands, without intervening; perhaps to test how much we love Him and trust in His mercy.

Chance prayed for his Daddy; often and deeply. But as the saying goes, God works in mysterious ways. It's an old adage, but it's painfully true.

Anne and Bernie's marriage continued to crumble; slowly disintegrating, deteriorating, and dissolving. Odd, inexplicable things began to happen. Animals died for no apparent reason. Trees in the yard were struck by lightning repeatedly, often resulting in costly damage to the home and its electrical appliances. Both boys, Chance and Alden, struggled in school and eventually fell out of favor with teachers and peers. Neither graduated in the traditional sense; both earned high school equivalency diplomas in alternative ways. Both enlisted in the U.S. Coast Guard, and both washed out in boot camp.

Their personal lives fared no better. Both boys married young, only to divorce within short periods. Chance eventually remarried and moved out to build a new life, while Alden stayed in the family home for several more years. Alden later married into a wealthy but deeply dysfunctional family; a group riddled with alcoholism. His wife bore him one daughter, but their marriage was perpetually contentious, offering no stability for their child during her formative years.

Chance's second marriage was no better; perhaps worse in some ways. Twenty years spent with the same woman, building a home through blood, sweat, and tears, raising two boys, and enduring constant struggles. All of it, it seemed, traced back to a single night of defiance and disobedience against Almighty God, in that tiny living room in Avondale, East Savannah, in 1973.

Prophetic? Perhaps.

Predictable? Not necessarily.

Avoidable? Maybe.

Troubles are meant to be brought to God in prayer. Faith and patience are essential to sustain one's understanding of the complexities and blessings of the Lord. His love is so precious, but it's a two-way street. In the simple, timeless words of Christ: *"Ask, and ye shall receive."* It's not just a promise; it's guaranteed.

Yet arrogance and pride have a way of clouding that truth, leading to results that are often more disastrous than anticipated. The power of prayer doesn't reside in the mind but in the heart; not in standing tall, but in kneeling humbly. Over the years, Chance's knees would grow bruised and calloused as he wrestled with the

Devil and sought refuge in prayer. The trials weren't over. Not by a long shot.

House Work

An authoritarian when it came to the discipline of the boys, he demanded they show respect to their elders, adults, and anyone they didn't know. He did not spare the rod, and his favorite correction instrument was whatever leather belt he was wearing at that moment. The boys always begged Mama to do the spanking when they needed it – Daddy just hit too hard, and it hurt a lot more. And, for God's sake, you absolutely did NOT run from the ole man when he was trying to get you to administer family justice.

Later in life, "junior" Alden, also learned that you didn't call the ole man OUT, either.

He worked as a mechanic and was pretty darn good at it. Over the years, he drove trucks hauling everything from black oil in the Smokies to steel beams on flatbed trailers. At one point, he even bought an old Peterbilt cab-over that he nicknamed "Granny" (not a jab at Mama's mom, I'm sure). That project didn't last long, though; the IRS came and took it.

He had a stint as a city policeman, then worked for the county for a while, even riding a motorcycle. Unfortunately, he managed to break nearly every bone in his body at least once; he wasn't exactly a skilled rider.

But his true, ongoing project was the house. When they bought it in 1959, the little place was just 800 square feet. By the time Chance was grown, it had nearly doubled in size to 1,600 square feet. Between the four of them, they added two bedrooms, a den, a second bathroom, re-roofed the entire house, remodeled the kitchen and living room, added a pantry and washroom, built a workshop, constructed kitchen cabinets, installed new siding, and bricked up the exterior walls waist-high all around. Whew!

Originally, Mom and Dad's bedroom was in the front of the house, with the boys sharing the other bedroom, complete with bunk beds. That arrangement wouldn't have worked once the boys hit high school, so the expansion plans were drawn up early. Alden got the enlarged front bedroom, while Chance's old room was transformed into a small study-bedroom combo with cabinets lining the back wall. Mama got the biggest upgrade; a spacious new bedroom with an adjoining bathroom, a shower, and a private dressing area she adored.

Window AC units cooled the house during those sweltering Georgia summers, but the place was still heated by an old kerosene floor furnace until the mid-70s. That floor furnace was something else. In the middle of a chilly night or first thing in the morning, standing over that exposed metal grate to warm your cold butt was one of life's little comforts. But stepping on that searing hot grate with a bare foot? That was a mistake you'd only make once. Daddy eventually replaced the furnace with electric wall heaters through-out the house.

Home improvement was a true family affair. Everyone pitched in. The boys mixed mortar and carried bricks. They climbed rafters, balanced joists, and held boards while Daddy nailed them in place. And if a board shifted even a fraction of an inch, you'd better duck fast; because chances were a hammer or that same board was about to come swinging back at you.

There was no shortage of calamities. Someone was always fall-ing, dodging tools, or narrowly avoiding a flying piece of lumber. In-evitably, all three would end up on the ground, doubled over laugh-ing; well, everyone except Daddy. He'd jump down to chase after one or both of the boys, only to land square on a board with a nail stick-ing straight up. That nail would go right through the bottom of his foot.

And what did the boys do? They'd get tickled and laugh, which only made things worse. It was humiliating.

Damn, that would make him so- angry.

This guy could cuss foul enough to embarrass a sailor. And he was loud enough so that everyone within a quarter mile could hear every word – stuff I wouldn't even begin to repeat. Chance was sure, over the years, that everyone learned at least a couple of new curse words they never knew even existed — a few he had no idea what meant, just blurted right out.

Mama would get so embarrassed.

Whistling Terror

Speaking of things everyone could hear, Daddy had a unique way of calling the boys when it was suppertime or when he needed their help. He wouldn't shout or holler; it just wasn't in him to do that. Instead, he had a special weapon, a tool, a talent so distinctive it became legendary in the neighborhood.

Daddy had a whistle. Not just any whistle, but a sound like nothing you've ever heard before; or since. Somehow, he could curl the tip of his tongue against the inside of his tightly pursed lower lip, place his thumb and middle finger on the sides of his mouth, take a deep breath, and blow. The result was a piercing, unmistakable whistle that could carry for miles. Forget cell phones, CB radios, or walkie-talkies; Daddy's whistle was all he needed.

Chance could be all the way across the neighborhood, maybe at a friend's house, when out of nowhere around four or five o'clock, the friend's mom would pause and say, "Do you hear that whistle? Somebody way off is whistlin'."

"Geez, sorry, gotta go. That's my Dad," Chance would explain as he bolted out the door, hoping to make it home before the second whistle. Because that second whistle? That was always bad.

By the time Chance was in his teens, the whole neighborhood knew the drill. Other kids would come running up to wherever he was, laughing as they delivered the news.

"Hey, man; your Dad's whistlin' for ya."

Chance would groan, drop whatever he was doing, and head home. Daddy's whistle wasn't just a call; it was a command, one you couldn't ignore.

Right down humiliating is what it was, sometimes.

I said earlier that Chance feared his father. Not all the time, but enough. His dad had a temper, and it showed often. More often than not, the target of his rage was Chance's mom.

He couldn't seem to hold a job. Something someone said or did would set him off, he'd curse out the boss, and that was the end of it. Every time he lost another job, Mama would remind him of these episodes, and every time, it would escalate into a fight.

Chance's dad also struggled with keeping his privates where they belonged. It just so happened he was well-endowed as those things go, and one morning, Chance accidentally caught sight of him stepping out of the shower. In that brief moment, he thought, *"What the hell happened when I was born?"*

There were several "affairs" over the years. Mama didn't seem to get particularly jealous; or at least she didn't show it much; but her feelings were obviously and deeply hurt. Every time, she confronted him. And every time, they fought.

His father hit her. He hurt her frequently, both emotionally and physically. Sometimes, he went way too far.

Many of these fights played out in front of Chance. By the time he was old enough to understand what was happening, he knew she needed help, and more often than not, he was the only one around when it got bad. Usually, it was slaps; he'd slap her, she'd slap him back; but sometimes it was worse. Chance saw him punch her, knocking her down. He saw him choke her once. One time, he even beat her head against the top of the bed. That was the worst of all.

And yet, there were moments that felt normal, even happy. Once in a while, they'd have a peaceful dinner together. They'd seem almost affectionate, maybe even lovey-dovey, and everyone would go to bed thinking things were fine. Chance's room was on the other side of the wall from theirs, and he could hear them talking or cuddling; or whatever it was couples do.

But then, out of nowhere, the mood would shift. He'd hear a slap. Then shouting. Something would crash to the floor. The bedroom door would fly open, and the fight would spill out into the hallway or the living room.

Oh, man, that would scare the hell out of Chance.
He never remembered seeing Alden get upset, or even get up those
nights.

Whenever she'd load the boys up in the car, they'd haul butt to a friend's home or run up to Granny, and Papa's some sixty-five miles out of town. They'd stay apart for the weekend, or a week, once they separated for a whole summer when Chance was about 11 – a particularly rough summer. That'll come later.

Maybe it was a fluke, poetic justice, or *his* guardian angel getting even for his foul mouth and hot temper, but the ole boy was terribly accident-prone. It was terrible, funny at times, usually painfully so.

***

Didn't See That Coming

To say that Chance's Daddy was a walking accident would be an understatement, and frankly, a mistake. Highly intelligent, a bit of a "hot-head" (another understatement), and a jack of all trades but master of none, Bernie Brogdon was more like a mishap waiting for an opportunity; or a victim.

Take any given day in the yard, for example. Bernie could be trimming an overhanging limb on an azalea bush with a sharp pair of bypass loppers. Snip, snip, snip; everything going fine. Then suddenly, **PING**; a tiny shard of wood snaps off the next limb and flies straight into his eye.

Did he stop? Did he drop what he was doing, flush the eye, and take a short break to minimize the injury before getting back to work?

Nah.

Rub it – yeah, that'll work.

Nope, "shit," that makes it worse.

Nothing like a good ole home remedy in a time like this. He would go inside and find that little blue plastic eye cup and fill it with cold tap water and a couple of drops of white vinegar.

Mammie always said that'd take care of everything. Yeah, that'll do it.

"Jesus Christ! That frickin' burns like hell!"

The situation had gone from bad to worse. His eye hurt; badly; and his vision was noticeably impaired. Time to head to the ER or, better yet, to the ophthalmologist he'd seen a couple of times before for minor injuries and check-ups.

You guessed it. That little shard of wood had entered his eye at breakneck speed, penetrating the outer coating of the cornea. But Bernie didn't stop there. No, his instinct to rub the injured eye had made things exponentially worse, scraping the already-damaged corneal tissue. And then, as if that wasn't enough, he added insult to injury by trying a homemade vinegar solution, which caused an alkali burn to the damaged organ.

The cornea responded as corneas do in the face of such trauma: the lens muscles spasmed, the pupil contracted painfully, and his vision blurred further. Sensitivity to light skyrocketed, and his brain essentially said, *"The hell with this crap, shut it down."*

The ophthalmologist patched the eye, prescribed drops to prevent infection and pills to manage the pain, and gave him strict orders: "Take it easy for a few days."

A few days. Right. Not Bernie Brogdon.

The very next day, he was back outside. Eye patch firmly in place, pain meds kicking in; good as new, right?

"Damn patch," he muttered to himself. "Aggravating thing."

Every time he blinked his good eye, the injured one blinked in unison. It's called "sympathetic reflex," and it drove him absolutely insane.

I don't see anything "sympathetic" about that at all. Not a lot of help, actually.

He should've just quit for the day and, as the doctor told him, take it easy and rest the eye.

Nope. Not THIS guy!

"Take this damned thing off, pain in the ass anyway," he said to himself.

He took the patch off, picked up the shears, and back at it again. No problem at all.

"Yeah, that feels better."

And it did – for about 10 minutes.

"Son of a bitch!" he exclaims.

Sharp, stinging pain enveloped the eye, and tears began to roll down his cheek.

"I know, I got this," said this rogue scholar of Brogdon lore. Mister bad-ass.

Bernie threw down the clippers and went into his workshop. Rummaging through the saw-dust-covered recesses of the old musky building, he searched for his cleanest roll of tape.

"Duct tape? Nope. Too sticky. Probably hurt like hell coming off," he thought.

"Here we go," he spied a small roll of 3MScotch brand, clear adhesive tape.

Now, this well-educated middle-aged man with plenty of common sense took a length of tape, about 2 inches or so, and secured the upper and lower lids of his eye to his cheek and forehead.

Wide-ass open!!

"There. Now blink, bitch!"

And with that brilliant declaration, Bernie proceeded to work for the next three hours under the relentless glare of the South Georgia sun. His injured eye, fully exposed to the elements and unable to lubricate itself with tears, took the brunt of the abuse. You can imagine the result.

The next morning, there he was; back in the doctor's office. This time, the prognosis was worse. The damage was so severe that the doctor patched **both** eyes. No more debate, no argument, no alternatives. He was out of commission for a week. Bernie had managed to sunburn the cornea and surrounding tissue of his eye.

Who the heck sunburns their eye? Accident-prone Pop; Bernie Brogdon, of course.

***

The ole man wasn't just a walking disaster; he was also a builder with a knack for leaving his mark on projects that most people never think about but certainly take for granted.

He laid the bricks lining the interior facade of the manholes along River Street during the construction of Rousakis Plaza in Savannah. His craftsmanship in carpentry could be seen in the exterior charm and intricate detail of the now-famous *Gingerbread House* on the corner of 36th and Bull Streets in Savannah.

But Bernie didn't stop there. He built and remodeled numerous homes in Sea Pines and Hilton Head Plantation in South Carolina, leaving behind a legacy of sturdy structures and thoughtful design. He also hauled black oil; the liquid portion of asphalt; up perilous, winding roads to the peaks of some of the steepest mountains in North Georgia, western North Carolina, and southeastern Tennessee.

His work contributed to the construction and refinishing of the Blue Ridge Parkway, the upgrading of US-441 through the Great Smoky Mountains National Park, and the paving of the treacherous roads leading to and from Clingman's Dome.

Bernie Brogdon wasn't just accident-prone; he was a force to be reckoned with, for better or worse.

One Fell *"Swoop"*

Chance's Dad was actually a pretty decent brick mason. Completely self-taught, he mastered the trade the same way he had most of his talents; by sheer determination and a lot of trial and error.

In many ways, Bernie set an example for Chance simply by deciding he wanted to do something; and then doing it. They didn't have the money to hire professionals for things like adding rooms to the house, building fences, fixing cars, repairing broken pipes, or updating cabinetry. There was no YouTube or Google to offer guidance back then. If something needed to be done, you figured it out yourself. And that's exactly what Bernie did.

The guy was actually pretty cool to have around; not just as a dad but as a person. Over the years, he taught himself just about everything. He became whatever the situation demanded: a carpenter, a brick mason, an electrician, a plumber, an auto mechanic, a cabinet maker. Whatever needed fixing, building, or creating, Bernie figured out how to do it.

His adaptability didn't stop at home projects. Bernie re-invented himself professionally more times than most people could count. He worked as an insurance salesman, a cop, a preacher, a car salesman, a truck driver; whatever it took to pay the bills or satisfy a whim. He'd dive headfirst into a new trade or vocation, learning as he went, often surprising everyone with just how well he pulled it off.

And that knack for re-invention? It wasn't limited to jobs. Oh, no. That last part about fantasies? That applied to women, too. But that, as they say, is another story altogether.

Back to the point.

There was an Ace Hardware in the Victory Drive Shopping Center where Chance's Dad shopped all the time. The manager, Mr. Ketchum, was a soft-spoken, easy-going guy who knew Bernie well from his frequent visits to the store for supplies. Over time, Mr. Ketchum learned that Bernie was skilled at laying brick. So, when he needed a nice brick fence built around his home in Mayfair, he asked Bernie to take the job.

Bernie delivered. He built a beautiful row of brick pillars with inlaid red-stained cedar, creating an expensive-looking fence that elevated the property's curb appeal. Mr. Ketchum was so impressed with the craftsmanship that he referred Bernie to a prominent Savannah attorney who needed work done on his roof.

Now, back in those days; through the 1960s and well into the 70s; it was common for craftsmen to hire laborers for day work. Downtown Savannah had several spots where groups of Black men gathered early every morning, waiting to be picked up by construction crews. This wasn't about discrimination or profiling; it was simply how work was found in the impoverished parts of town.

These men weren't interested in food stamps or government handouts; they wanted a hard day's work and fair pay.

Chance's Dad had two laborers he worked with regularly: Sammy and Joseph. Sammy, in his forties, was older and more seasoned, while Joseph, in his twenties, was just starting out in life. Both men bore the marks of hard times and harder work; calloused hands, deep furrows in their brows, and an unyielding determination to earn their keep. They were dependable and always on the corner at the crack of dawn, ready for a full day's work.

When Bernie accepted the roofing job for the attorney, he set a fair price and a reasonable timetable for completion. Sammy and Joseph, of course, would be right there by his side, helping to get the job done.

We'll call the attorney Mr. Price for one particular reason. Chance thought the guy looked a lot like country singer Ray Price.

Mr. Price wanted a new roof to put on his den and asked for an additional overhang to be constructed during the project.

No problem, Bernie knew how to do that.

Construction began, and everything went great for a couple of weeks. At one point, I think we mentioned it earlier, Dad injured his eye and had to take a few days off to recover.

You can't very well measure accurately or use a skill saw if you can't focus your vision. Besides, throws off your equilibrium. And that ain't good when you're balancing yourself on a roof!

As I mentioned, this guy was a prominent attorney. His house was located in a genuinely nice residential area; Ardsley Park, I think; and his neighbors kept a watchful eye on anything happening in his yard during the day. Mr. Price, the attorney, had a couple of grown sons who would occasionally drop by to let the dogs out, check the mail, and handle small tasks like that. His wife, however, was rarely around; Chance vaguely remembered something about her spending most of her time at another house on St. Simons Island.

One quiet afternoon, just after lunch, Bernie was up on the roof working on the overhang while Sam cleaned up around the worksite. The neighborhood was peaceful, with most folks either inside watching *All My Children* or *As the World Turns* or lying out by their pools, soaking up the sun.

To construct a proper overhang, the plywood roofing had to extend at least a foot (12 inches) beyond the side of the building. The plywood needed to be supported by an extension of the existing rafters (the 2x4 wooden framing for the roof) to bear the weight of the new roofing. It was a straightforward enough process: measure the width of the plywood, fit it in place, and nail it down securely with 10d (ten-penny) sinkers. These nails, oil-coated to prevent rusting, were ideal for roofing because they "sank" into the wood with the last hammer strike, ensuring they stayed in place over time. Regular nails, prone to rising over time, wouldn't cut it for a job like this.

But as anyone who knew Bernie Brogdon could tell you, he never did things quite the way he was supposed to.

On this particular day, Bernie needed a piece of plywood cut to a specific width. Since he couldn't get down from the roof to cut it himself, he scanned the area for a solution. Sam, having just finished his lunch break, was at the truck, cooling off with a cup of water from the cooler. Bernie's eyes landed on a piece of plywood nearby that was close to the right length, though just a hair wider than needed.

No problem. He'd just nail the piece of plywood in place and trim away the excess to fit. Done that dozens of times before; worked like a charm.

Like a well-oiled machine or a potter delicately molding his vase, Dad moved the lumber into position right where it needed to go. Nail after nail, he secured the lightweight material to the rafters as if made to order - *except* for the "little" 6 to 8 inches sticking out just a "little" further than it should.

"Can't step out on that overhang to cut that off," he thought.

About that time, right on cue actually, Sammy came around the corner.

"Hey, man, how 'bout coming up and steady me while I cut this off?"

"Yessu, boss," he shouted.

Sammy climbed the ladder, then that already slick, bare roof, until he was right beside Bernie on the perch.

"I just need you to hold my shirt and belt while I lean out to cut off the excess edge. I've already pulled the chalk line so the measurement is just right," said Bernie.

"I gotcha, boss," replied Sammy.

Bernie leaned out to cut, but a new problem presented itself. He needed to lean much further out than he had anticipated for the saw to cut with the wood grain. This is an important concept to prevent bucking against the grain, increasing the danger of injury to the user. Imagine something like that – *smart ass.*

As a solution to the problem, and against his better judgment, he chose to turn the saw around and cut from the bottom of the overhang toward himself. You can guess what happened next.

With Sammy holding onto his shirttail and belt with all his might, Dad held to the piece of overhanging plywood and started the cut at the very bottom edge of the roof. Within what seemed no time at all, that saw just ran sharply up the board, releasing the extra material to the ground in one fell swoop – and running right over the top of his left hand.

Well, Sammy saw the whole grizzly thing and started jumping up and down on that roof, shouting at the top of his lungs.

"Missah Bernie, oh my sweet Jesus. Yawl done cut yo hand clean off! Cut it CLEAN off!"

As he turned around in shock, Bernie moved his arm and injured hand so suddenly that he flung bright red blood all over the surface of the slick, bare roof right under the feet of this frantic right-hand man.

"Oh, lawd, missa Bernie.....yo's bleedin' to def. Oh, my God!" Sammy exclaimed in anguish.

"I gots to get yu help right now."

Right about that moment, just as Sammy was moving to take that first step toward the edge of the ladder against the roof to get help, and stepped in that warm, bright red blood, and his feet came right out from underneath him.

"Oh shit!" And down he went. Fell right onto the flat of his back, down the angle of that roof, and right off the edge. This guy fell something like 12 feet onto the hot, dry, un-cushioned dirt lot.

BAM!

Damn, that must've hurt.

Knocked the air out of his lungs for a moment for sure.

After what seemed like several minutes, but actually only a few moments, Sam regained his composure, got up, and looked back up: dazed, a little confused.

What kind of man does that? Guy fell 12 feet, knocked the air out of his lungs, and saw stars and little birdies, what's the first thing he asked as soon as he came around?

"You still alright, Missa Bernie?"

"Yeah, Sam, damnit, I'm OK. Bleeding like a stuck pig, but OK," he declared.

Blood was now heavy enough, and Chance's Dad had bled enough to start dripping off the roof's edge and onto the ground.

Sammy got up, brushed himself off, and headed for the sliding glass doors to the den underneath the calamity. Thank God, they were unlocked. Threw both doors wide open and rushed into the dark, pleasantly cool comfort of the attorney's plush, exquisitely decorated interior, desperately looking for a telephone.

Um, I think I mentioned earlier, in passing, that the boys came to be occasionally to, "let the dogs out."

Into the abyss of the house, Sam bolted, lunging for the first phone he could find, which sat atop Mr. Price's desk in the dimly lit den. Just as he reached for it, two very well-groomed, very handsome, and very large adult Doberman Pinschers made their grand entrance; and their acquaintance with Sam.

Running silent, stalking, the pair had been watching him since he entered. From their perch on a small two-step rise in the labyrinthine darkness of the room, they had waited, vigilant sentinels of patience, ready to pounce on anyone who dared intrude on their lair; uninvited and unwelcome.

The first Doberman latched onto Sam's lower left ankle, its teeth sinking in with precision. The second went for the seat of his pants, clamping down firmly. All Sam could think about in that moment of sheer panic was his six little kids at home and his newly pregnant wife.

"To hell with that stupid white man!" he screamed. "Help! HELP!"

"Oh my God, these dogs gonna kill me!" he shouted, voice trembling with fear and desperation. The dogs bit, snarled, barked, and pulled him in every direction, refusing to let go. One had his leg, the other an arm, and they were relentless.

"Help! Help me, somebody. Oh, my Gawd!"

One of the neighbors, noticing the commotion from early on, had already called the cops. Within moments; though it felt like an eternity to Sam; the Savannah Police and EMS arrived. Alongside them came Mr. Price, who rushed to pull the dogs off Sam and secured them in their respective spaces.

Bernie, meanwhile, needed more than 30 stitches to repair the damage to his hand. Thankfully, he recovered full functionality; just enough to keep doing more foolish things that would inevitably injure himself again.

The experience was too much for Sam, though. That afternoon, he quit working for Bernie and never returned to the day laborer site. He was done.

As for Mr. Price, he hired someone else to finish the roof. But to his credit, he paid for Bernie's hospital bills and honored the full contract amount for the job. It was the least he could do after all the chaos.

And, well, it made for one hell of a story; and a good laugh afterward.

Be Fretful – and Prosper?

Everybody knew the ole boy was always just one step away from his next injury. He couldn't even take an innocent stroll without managing to stick something in a live wire or his foot in something it didn't belong. One Saturday afternoon, he and Anne went out into the woods behind Mammie's place on Brogdon Hill, looking for wild plums. They didn't find a single one, but next thing you know, they're running back up the hill, and Bernie's bleeding like a stuck hog.

Turns out, he'd pulled down a big, sturdy limb on a wild apple tree so Anne could pick some of those bitter, green fruits. Right as she was about to grab a particularly good-looking one, a bumblebee landed on Bernie's hand. Startled, he let go of the limb.

Unfortunately, he was bent over just far enough that when the limb snapped back, it popped up and smacked him square in the nose. Hard. The hit was so strong it broke off a piece of the limb; about three inches long; which somehow lodged itself right up inside his right nostril. Apparently, the stick was just the perfect size and shape to slide right in there and make itself at home.

The stick wasn't coming out easily. It was angled just right, catching on the upper part of his inner nose. Daddy pulled, twisted, cursed. Mama pushed, twisted, and probably cursed right back. Blood poured everywhere. Finally, after a lot of effort (and probably some yelling), they worked that thing out.

Of course, they still had to go to the hospital to make sure nothing else was stuck up there and to get some antibiotics.

Mammie, by then, had seen him injured so many times that she didn't even seem surprised anymore; no matter how bad it was or how ridiculous the story behind it. She just rolled with it.

One day, she was sitting at the dining room table in their home, sewing something by hand like she always did. She loved sewing and would hum little tunes to herself while she worked. Chance and Alden were doing something in the living room, and Mom was in the kitchen. Meanwhile, Daddy was up on the roof, right above the dining room, replacing part of the overhang that had been damaged by a hurricane that year; Betsy or Debbie, I think.

Seemed like every year, right before hurricane season he would get out and do something to the roof that never ended well.

So, right out of nowhere, *"Oh, shit!"*

BAM...BAM-A-LAM-BAM

There was a plate glass window right behind where the old lady was sitting at the kitchen table, peacefully, pointedly stitching her garment, ever mindful of the presence of her son on that roof right above her head. If you had been a fly on the wall that day, you would have seen the next chain of events better than anyone else possibly could have – except maybe the ole man.

She sat right there – needle in, out the other side, pull it tight, needle in, out the other side – completely oblivious to the mishap.

First came that skill saw, blade still turning, winding down.

.... then the entire length of the cord, plus the extension.

.... then that piece of plywood overhang,

.... then the ole man.

.... then the ladder he should have been standing on, fell over; right on top of him.

Without even looking up, she softly, gingerly said, *"Anne, Bernie just sawed himself off the roof again."* The old girl didn't miss a lick - no sirree - kept right on stitching.

Mama dropped what she was doing and ran outside to check on him. Thankfully, he was alright; he didn't break anything this time. Hurt his pride more than anything.

Mammie sat right there till she was finished with what she was sewing. She got up, excused herself, went to the back of the house to her room, and took a nap.

***

Chapter Four

Early Years

In Savannah in the early 1960s, life was something else compared to country living. Most streets in the "Hostess City of the South" weren't paved with gold, but they might as well have been with all the great prospects for a better way of life than you'd find in any other city within 100 miles. Her sister city, Charleston, was nearly a carbon copy, but even Charleston couldn't quite match what Savannah had to offer back then.

Situated right on the Savannah River, the city had been meticulously laid out by Gen. James Oglethorpe in the 1700s. The grid design featured straight streets running east and west, avenues running north and south, and perfectly proportioned squares scattered throughout downtown for community meetings and public gatherings. Savannah was literally built for people to congregate.

Originally, the city was settled by a boatload of English debtors. These settlers; mostly white; had been given a choice: prison for their unpaid taxes or a chance to colonize an English settlement in the New World on behalf of King George.

Well, twist my arm. I know a party when I hear one!

When Chance's new family arrived, River Street was still in ruins. Factor's Walk was one of the best places to get your throat cut. The city was strategically and politically divided along tight racial lines throughout several areas of the city proper.

White people simply did not venture downtown between East Broad and Wheaton, from President Street down to just below Gwinnett; west of Jefferson was essentially off-limits to whites, stretching out as far as the traffic circle near Garden City on Bay Street.

A former Army base off East President Street called "Debt-ford Homes" had been recently converted into affordable housing. Later renamed Savannah Gardens, this quaint development sprouted dozens of little parent-plus-two, middle-class, mostly white, two-bedroom, asbestos-sided homes. And with that, the birth of Savannah's suburbs began. The list seems endless: Avondale, Gordonston, Victory Heights, Sylvan Terrace, and Ardsley Park.

As I said earlier, Broughton Street was the hub of shopping for most Savannahians. The mall concept had not yet been introduced, but it was in the preliminary stages of development. Forsythe Park and Grayson Stadium were two of the largest entertainment centers. Motion picture theaters were a huge hit at the time. Admission was low, refreshments were plentiful, and the locations were lavishly decorated, fancy, and comfortable. In the downtown area alone, there were more than a dozen walk-in movie venues (the Weis, the

Avon, the Regal, the Lucas Theater, the Savannah Theater, the Pal). The suburbs had something altogether different for the well-intended, lazy families of the day; the 'drive-in' theater. What great fun! Victory, Hwy 80, Montgomery, Westside Drive-ins. One price for a car full (and all you could pack in the sedan's huge trunk), pull up to a stall, roll down the window, mount the speaker, and enjoy the show. Got a pick-up truck? No problem, back it in and set up the lounge chairs. Plenty of great snacks, hamburgers, a new fad called 'pizzas,' candy, and sodas right there in the convenient concession stands.

Chance and Alden loved it when Dad came home and announced they were headed to the drive-in. That was where young Chance fell in love with the ever-witty Wile E. Coyote and his quick-footed nemesis, the Roadrunner; Elmer Fudd and that wascully wabbit, Bugs Bunny; Yosemite Sam and Daffy Duck. Where else could you learn the catalog of all the Acme products available to bop your brother on the head or fling a boulder across a chasm? After all, nobody really got hurt and never needed to go to an Emergency Room from those injuries. Right?

These family-friendly entertainment mega domes would lose appeal and popularity by the mid-1970s when they were inadvertently transformed into dens of perversion and frequent, unintended sexual assault. "R-" and "X-rated" films were displayed to young, eager eyes within easy viewing distances of surrounding neighborhoods. About that same time, adult bookstores began to pop up here and there throughout the city in previously safe, heavily Christian-based suburbs, tainting both morals and property values.

Bowling alleys, skating rinks, tennis courts, a Super Slide in the K-mart parking lot on Victory Drive, drive-in restaurants with car-hops on skates, soft-serve ice cream shacks on nearly every corner; the burbs were the bomb! On Skidaway Road, blocks in either direction from its intersection with Victory Drive, you could smell the aroma of cheese and tomato sauce tickling your senses from Mr. Pizza. Further down the street, you could watch Krispy Kreme donuts get punched out, rise, flipped over into hot grease, rolled onto conveyors, sprayed with a thick, sugary glaze, and boxed right in front of your eyes. Yup, big glass window outside where you could get out and watch the whole cotton-picking process. Amazing.

McDonald's opened Savannah's first store on Skidaway Road and burgers were .15 cents. A cup of ice cream at Dairy Queen with your favorite topping was a quarter; a milkshake was about half a buck.

If the boys were really lucky, Dad would take them up to the parking lot of Tom's Restaurant in the Crossroads Shopping Center on a Friday or Saturday night just to see if they could catch even a glimpse of Mel Mixon spinning the hits 'live' on top of that burger joint. There was a huge studio window where fans could easily watch the activity and showmanship of WBYZ radio. The building is still there to this day, but the only 'hit' you'll get now is an extra shot of caffeine from the Starbucks coffee shop downstairs.

Don't know why there's no historical marker there, cause it sure was a special place in the day.

Tybee Island was always a great option for those hot, humid days in Savannah. Originally, Tybee Road ran parallel to the old railroad tracks connecting downtown to Fort Pulaski to Savannah during the Civil War. US Highway 80 was still very narrow then, not much wider than the tracks themselves, and travel was risky at best. Accidents were very common, many of them deadly. Bull River Bridge was especially scary for the boys because vehicles would be so close to each other on the expanse that car mirrors would nearly hit as they passed within just inches of each other. So many accidents on that road, and most of the time, Dad just took the family as far as the bridge to eat at Williams Seafood Restaurant.

The boardwalk at Tybee was still open and operating in the early 1960s with the original rides and concessions still operating at full tilt. The Tybee Pavilion was still open and operating until Chance was in grade school. Nighttime on the Strand back then was really something to see.

Chance and his family preferred going to the island's north end, Fort Screven, where they could surf fish and crab. Back then, the original jetties were still present, and huge iron breakers stood 10-12 feet above the sand extending out from the lighthouse. Even at high tide, you could wade for what seemed like forever out into the ocean; there was no rip tide. At low tide, the base of those panels and around the jetties left good-sized tidal pools trapping small fish and crustaceans; crabbing was simply a matter of skill with a dip net. On average, the family could leave the beach with a good bushel of large blue crabs. Mama would take them home and boil them in a blend of spices for several hours. Then she'd break the cooked crabs open, clean the bodies from the shells, and separate the claws; then she put everything back in a creole sauce for a couple of hours longer. There is nothing like eating seafood that fresh.

**

That Day in '63

Daddy was working as a mechanic for Bill Kehoe Tire on Drayton Street back then, while Mama spent most of her days at home; cooking, cleaning, and, always, ironing. It seemed like the ironing board was a permanent fixture in the living room.

A black-and-white console TV stood against the wall, serving as the boys' entertainment hub during the day. On Saturday mornings, it played cartoons while Mama set up her ironing board nearby. During the week, it was all about soap operas. In the evenings, when Daddy got home, Mama would have supper ready, and the family would sit down together at the kitchen table: Dad across from Mom, Chance across from Alden.

It was a picture of domestic normalcy; until it wasn't. Inevitably, someone would annoy someone else during dinner, and what began as casual conversation often ended with cross words, a chair slammed to the floor, or a glass of tea tossed across the table. You get the picture.

Saturday nights, though, were special. If there was a good movie on *Saturday Night at the Movies* or a thrilling episode of *The Outer Limits*, Dad would pull out the metal folding TV trays, and Mama would heat up some good old-fashioned TV dinners. Those evenings felt like a treat.

Chance's favorite was the meatloaf dinner, while Alden and Dad both loved the Salisbury steak with mashed potatoes. Of course, this shared preference sparked occasional battles as the boys grew older. By the time Alden hit high school, he'd started raiding the freezer for those Salisbury steak dinners as after-school snacks, much to Dad's annoyance.

Swanson was the preferred brand; hands down; but Mama would sometimes pick up Banquet dinners if they were on sale. She could snag six for just $3 at the M&M, a deal too good to pass up.

On the morning of November 22, 1963, Chance and his little brother were playing on the floor in the living room. Mama was ironing Daddy's shirts, the TV was on, and they were watching something; probably *Father Knows Best* or *Truth or Consequences*, who remembers? The front door was open, with the screen door latched, so she could keep an eye on the weather. It was a Friday morning, and Chance must have been out of school for the Thanksgiving holidays.

Suddenly, the TV program was interrupted.

"This is a CBS News Special Report. And now, here's Walter Cronkite."

Cronkite's familiar, steady voice filled the room, but his words sent a chill down the spine.

"It's been one hour since that electrifying flash came over the wires that bullet shots had been heard to ring out in the Kennedy motorcade. There is the report, in Dallas, that the President is dead, but that has not been confirmed by any other source," Cronkite said.

Mama froze. The iron slipped from her hand and hit the floor with a thud. She gasped, a sharp intake of air that conveyed absolute disbelief. Her face turned pale as she processed the unimaginable news: the President of the United States; *her* President; had been shot.

How had she missed this? She couldn't remember hearing anything before now. Maybe she'd stepped out of the room for a moment, to use the bathroom or refill her coffee. Perhaps Chance had changed the channel briefly. She couldn't recall. None of it mattered now.

Cronkite continued.

"As late as 15 minutes ago, it was reported by aides in the corridor of the hospital that he was still alive. The extent of his injuries is not known either."

Ten agonizing minutes later, Walter Cronkite returned, his voice heavier, more deliberate. Through tear-filled eyes and a visible struggle to keep his composure, he delivered the nation's darkest news.

"From Dallas, Texas; the flash; apparently official. President Kennedy; died; at 1:00 p.m. Central Standard Time. Two o'clock Eastern Standard Time; some, 38 minutes ago."

There was a pause. Cronkite hesitated, clearing his throat, his voice breaking slightly as he pushed forward.

"Vice President Lyndon Johnson," he continued, "has left the hospital..." He faltered again, then cut away to another correspondent.

By now, Chance's Mama was sobbing uncontrollably.

The iron lay forgotten on the floor, its heat scorching the tongue-and-groove oak hardwood, leaving an indelible black mark. The acrid smell of burning wood and faint smoke began to fill the room. Mama lowered the screen on the metal storm door to vent the air, but her focus remained on the tragedy unfolding on the screen.

The gravity of the moment overwhelmed Chance, and he began to cry softly, not fully understanding the scope of what had happened but deeply affected by his mother's despair. Alden, now about 18 months old, lay in the bassinet nearby, blissfully unaware, his innocent contentment a stark contrast to the anguish surrounding him.

Boy, would that ever become a prophetic (or pathetic) omen of his future life?

Chance recalled how, in her shock, Mama quickly made her way to the kitchen. She grabbed the receiver of the white princess phone hanging on the wall and dialed the number for Kehoe Tire. After a few rings, someone in the Service Department picked up, and she asked to speak to Chance's Dad.

"Did you hear the news...Oh, my God...Someone has shot the President...Yes, in Dallas...He's dead!"

For a moment, there was silence on the other end of the line. Then, as if snapping out of a daze, his father responded with an expletive; typical of the ole man. But what he said next left her aghast:

"Well, they've finally killed the son-of-a-bitch! I hope he rots in hell."

Mama stood there in stunned disbelief. It took her several minutes to regain her composure. Pacing back and forth across the kitchen floor, the long 10-foot cord from the phone stretched taut as she moved. When she finally hung up, her thoughts were clear.

"What an ass," she muttered to herself. *"They killed the President."*

***

In the aftermath of this earth-shaking event; the assassination of John F. Kennedy; life changed. For Mama, for little Alden and Chance, for the world, everything shifted that day.

For their family, changes came quickly. Chance's Daddy switched jobs, leaving Kehoe Tire to work at Backus Cadillac, where he earned over $100 a month; enough to provide some financial breathing room with a house payment of $49. Mama finally got her own car, a 1957 Ford Fairlane. No longer would she have to catch a bus or rely on Mammie for groceries and errands.

With newfound independence, she established a routine. The Bargain Corner on Bay Street downtown became her go-to for dry goods and sundries, Shore's was the spot for quality meats, and the State Farmer's Market in Garden City was her source for fresh produce.

As life carried on, the boys started school at Charles Herty Elementary. First Chance, then Alden, enrolled and spent six years there, enjoying primary education and the early socialization that would shape their childhood.

Well, almost. That comes later.

For Savannah, the winds of change were blowing strong. J. Curtis Lewis became Mayor, twelve black students transferred to the previously all-white Savannah High School, and the city underwent a remarkable transformation from the racial tensions that had defined the early 1960s. During a speech in January 1964, Dr. Martin Luther King Jr. referred to Savannah as "the most desegregated city south of the Mason-Dixon line." It was a monumental acknowledgment of progress in a deeply divided region.

For the nation, however, the mid-1960s marked a particularly turbulent chapter in American history. The passage of the Civil Rights Act in 1964 and the Voting Rights Act a year later effectively ended Jim Crow laws; not just in the South, but across the country. These legal triumphs signaled the beginning of a new era, though the road forward was anything but smooth.

Cultural revolutions swept across the United States. First, the Beatles arrived, followed closely by the Rolling Stones, bridging the Atlantic to ignite a musical movement that would redefine generations. At the same time, darker currents of resistance and unrest surfaced. The Ku Klux Klan experienced a brief resurgence, while black counter-culture movements like Stokely Carmichael's Black Power, Malcolm X's advocacy for militant self-defense, and Huey Newton's Black Panther Party emerged to confront the systemic injustices head-on.

The decade closed with an extraordinary high note: the Apollo 11 mission's moon landing in July 1969. For a brief moment, the nation united in awe as Neil Armstrong's first step on the lunar surface symbolized the boundless potential of human achievement.

But before the moon landing, 1968 delivered a devastating double blow that shook the country to its core. On April 4, the nation witnessed, through the magic and horror of live television, the assassination of Dr. Martin Luther King Jr., the civil rights movement's most charismatic leader and moral compass. His death on the balcony of the Lorraine Motel in Memphis, Tennessee, was a brutal and gut-wrenching loss.

Just two months later, on June 6, tragedy struck again. Senator Robert F. Kennedy, a leading Democratic presidential candidate and beacon of hope for a fractured nation, was assassinated at the Ambassador Hotel in Los Angeles. These two visionary leaders; cut down in the prime of their lives; had stood as unwavering advocates for justice, equality, and unity. Their deaths underscored how violently a society could resist the very progress it so desperately needed.

These were the times that shaped Chance's young life. They were moments of upheaval and resilience that today's generations can only read about; though, sadly, many likely never will.

***

Growing Up Avondale

For all his growing and formative years, through adolescence and into early adulthood, Chance knew only one place he called and thought of as "home." It was a modest 800-square-foot house on a corner lot in the suburbs of east-side Savannah, nestled in a middle-class neighborhood called Avondale.

The front yard was a lush carpet of thick St. Augustine grass, soft and inviting. In spring, wild clover would spring up, creating a fragrant, velvety bed where Chance and Alden loved to tumble and play. But nature sometimes reminded them it wasn't just for their amusement; a honeybee or two would deliver a painful lesson when they forgot it was feeding its family, not theirs. A narrow concrete sidewalk divided the yard into neat segments, with two stately palm trees flanking the walkway like sentinels.

When they first moved in, a graceful willow tree dominated the backyard, its long, sweeping branches swaying gently in the Savannah breeze. The willow held its own until the boys reached middle school. By then, its days were numbered, as it had become the source of too many "good behavior reminders" in the form of Mama's switches. One day, mysteriously, the tree "died," much to the boys' quiet relief.

In its place, a massive cottonwood tree stood proudly against the backyard fence. This tree became the centerpiece of Chance's childhood adventures. When Chance was in middle school, he and Dad built a treehouse high up in its branches; a sturdy hideaway that felt like a world all his own. Poor Alden, allergic to the sap, couldn't join in the fun, leaving the fort exclusively to Chance. It became a retreat where he could dream, hide, and later in his teens, sneak peeks at pretty little Nicky next door. It also served another purpose during puberty; a private spot where Chance could explore a stack of his Dad's hidden girlie magazines, gaining what he generously referred to as "personal education."

Avondale was more than just a neighborhood to Chance. It was layers of history; a landfill once, later part of a dairy farm, and even a cow pasture before becoming a quiet suburban enclave. For the first two decades of his life, Avondale was his Mayberry, a 20-something block stretch bordered by Pennsylvania Avenue, East Gwinnett Street, and Robard's Dairy. This place, tucked just off Bonaventure Avenue near Thunderbolt, was his sanctuary and his world.

Chance's Dad had signed the contract for the house after tiring of the long commute between Newington and Savannah; a grueling 60 miles each way. To him, the drive was worse than the backbreaking work he did in the city. Mama, however, hadn't been fully informed about the property's history. On their first weekend in the new house, she awoke to the sound of a rooster crowing, followed by cows mooing. Disoriented, she sat up and thought, "I thought we moved to the city!" It wasn't until later that she discovered the house sat on land that had once been part of that very dairy.

****

Chance's Haircuts — The Dance

Down at the end of the block, around the corner on Georgia Avenue, there was a small convenience store and a barber shop. That barber, George, was where Chance got his very first haircut and learned some of his earliest lessons in social interaction. It was also where he began to acquire what some might call the art of thoughtful persuasion and determined negotiation.

Haircuts with George weren't just routine; they were a ritual, a cherished event that Chance looked forward to every time.

First, George would pump up the big, shiny, ornate brass chair with its thick burgundy leather seat, raising it to a level where he could reach Chance without stooping too much. Then came the sheet. With a quick "pop," George would lower it over Chance's chest, wrap it snugly around his neck, and pin it securely behind his head.

Chance loved that part. It made him feel important; like a big boy.

Then the haircut began.

Clip, clip, brush. Better.

Snip, brush, snip. A little more off the side.

"OK. All done."

Well, not quite.

This was where the magic happened. George would reach for his barber's mug from the shelf, which always had a small piece of high-lather soap in the bottom. Adding a bit of water, he'd whip up a thick, creamy foam using a soft horsehair brush. To Chance, that dollop of fluffy lather looked just like whipped cream.

This was *it*. The part he loved the most, the part that thrilled him beyond words. It wasn't just a haircut anymore; it was a whole production; a special, private exchange between him and George. Mama, oh my goodness, would get such a kick out of watching the two of them go through this little ritual.

Chance would throw his little head back against the cool leather headrest, just like a grown-up, brimming with eager anticipation for his favorite part of the experience. George, grinning from ear to ear, would grab a warm towel from the heater. Draping it over Chance's face and around his neck, he'd cinch it snugly in the back and secure it with a giant safety pin.

Then came the theatrics. George would pull the leather strap from the side of the chair and start slapping and popping it rhyth-mically, making the sound of sharpening a straight razor. The rhythmic pops were like music to Chance, adding an air of drama to the scene.

After a few moments, George would gently remove the warm towel from Chance's face. Chance, with a sparkle in his eye, would glance around to make sure his audience; Mama, of course; was paying attention. Satisfied with her delighted smile, he'd lay his head back again, ready for the next act.

George would then dip the horsehair brush into the warm, fragrant lather and gingerly apply it to Chance's face. The soft bristles tickled just enough to make Chance giggle, and the clean, soapy scent filled the little barber shop.

Did I say it was made of "horsehair"? OK, thought so. Chance thought that was so cool. Giggled when he heard that word.

And then, George would carefully paint Chance's face, starting at his nose and working down under his chin, spreading the lather from ear to ear. Somewhere on or under the counter, George kept a fake, plastic straight edge reserved exclusively for this very moment. With great ceremony, he'd slowly and gently 'shave' that innocent yet manly, baby-soft face, leaving just a tiny smidgen of cream right under Chance's nose.

"Be really, really still now, fella," George would say, leaning in with mock seriousness. *"Don't want a boo-boo, might cut that nose clean off."*

Sometimes they'd have to stop for several minutes right there cause Chance would get so tickled; George would laugh out loud. Mama would just grin and shake her head, turn the page of her magazine.

George would take the towel and gently wipe off any remaining soap, patting the little man's face dry with care. Then came the final flourish: a dab of something green from a tall glass bottle sitting on the counter. It smelled fresh and clean, like something a real gentleman would wear.

Splash, splash; George rubbed the fragrant liquid onto Chance's face, finishing with a playful slap on each cheek. Next, he reached for a bigger horsehair brush dusted with powder and briskly applied it to the back of Chance's neck and shoulders, leaving a faint, clean scent in its wake.

"All done," George would declare with a satisfied grin.

And then, with a tap of the button at the bottom of the chair; *WHOOSH*; down it would glide. Chance loved that dramatic descent almost as much as the haircut itself.

It tickled his tally. Sorry. But it really did.
Least, that's how it described it to Dad.

Take the drop cloth off, pop it back (Chance liked that sound, too), kick the fancy footrest out of the way, and off he'd jump. Mama would hand him a dollar, he'd hand it to George, get a "Thank you, my friend" from George, an exchange of handshakes, and the deed was done. Almost.

Sometimes, George would make him wait a couple of agonizing moments that seemed like forever in the tiny man's continuum for it; then, George would place a shiny penny in the center of his now outstretched, expectant palm.

"Thank you, Mr. George," Chance would whisper, and out the door and around the corner he'd run.

Mama could barely keep up sometimes. Inside the little store, he'd run over to the counter full of penny candy and grab that piece of chewy purple nectar in the bin; a piece of his now most favorite-ist thing in his world at that time: grape bubblegum. Yum.

This was always and forever one of Chance's greatest memories from his childhood and this time in his life.

Oh, this "dance" continued unabated every couple of weeks or so for several months that year until, as they say, "someone got poked in the eye," figuratively, of course. About six months later, Mama was ironing (of course) and suddenly realized in the middle of the afternoon that she hadn't seen Chance in a little while.

"Where the heck can that boy be now?" she thought.

The little terrier they had was asleep under the TV. She turned off the iron and feverishly began searching his common places to "ecs-cape" (sp purposely). Not in the bathtub, under the table, in the utility closet, under the bed, behind the sofa; where the hell was that boy?

At that moment, after frantically imagining all the worst possibilities, it struck her.

"He better not be."

She slid on her slippers, poofed her hair a bit, buttoned up her sundress, threw open that screen door, and swiftly descended the stairs to the street.

"George... if that boy..." she kept muttering.

She rounded the corner at Georgia Avenue in a flash and, within moments, was in sight of the shop. A concrete wall about five feet tall lined the front yard of the corner house at Texas and Georgia. She stopped at the corner and peered into the picture window of George's Barber Shop.

"There you are, little bugger."

George was sitting in the barber's chair, feet propped up on the fancy footrest. Chance was calmly sitting in his lap, cheeks full and puffed out, chewing for all he was worth, a Double Bubble grape wrapper clutched in his tiny hand.

She couldn't help herself and started snickering.

Chance's head shot straight up. His eyes went wide as saucers, and he suddenly stopped chewing, his mouth flying open in shock. Mama lost all her reserve and burst into a full-on belly laugh.

What do you do with that?

Apparently, Chance had gotten bored sitting and playing by himself while she ironed, as always. So, he'd found his way out the door, down the street, around the corner, and into George's shop. Seems that George had forgotten to give him that penny last week after his cut, and Chance was there to collect. He was, of course, wrong, but George couldn't resist the directness with which his buddy approached him. Besides, George was laughing too hard to do anything other than reach into his pocket and accommodate the little shark.

***

"For I know the plans I have for you, declares the Lord, plans for your welfare and not for evil, to give you a future and a hope."

Jeremiah 29:11

Chapter Five

Wonder Years

Like I said before, Avondale was a peaceful place to live and grow up in Savannah during the late 1960s and '70s. Life moved at a steady pace, filled with the kind of simplicity and charm that only those years could offer. Even though we were busy soaking in the experiences, learning from every twist and turn, and loving the beauty of just being young, we carried with us the greatest expectations for adulthood. These were the wonder years of the Class of '75; a golden era of innocence, mischief, and dreams as vast as the Savannah skies.

The main streets in the neighborhood were paved, forming the backbone of Avondale, but the cross streets were unpaved stretches of dirt. Those 50-foot expanses of gritty, loose sand might not seem significant to an outsider, but for the local boys, they were nothing short of an adventure waiting to happen. By 1973, most of the boys had hit their 16th birthdays and inherited their freedom in the form of hand-me-down cars; fifties-model Chevys, Fords, and Oldsmobiles, each with its own personality. Those cross-street stretches became testing grounds for bravery and skill.

The boys quickly mastered the art of hitting those sandy patches at just the right speed, letting their tires spin, and punching the gas at just the right moment to send their rear wheels fishtailing in controlled chaos. They weren't just driving; they were performing, each fishtail a declaration of youthful defiance and joy. Of course, such antics weren't without consequence. Chance vividly recalled the rare but unforgettable times when the cops; summoned by concerned neighbors; rolled into the neighborhood. The arrival of a police car was both a buzzkill and a badge of honor, adding just the right amount of edge to their adventures.

Avondale wasn't just about youthful recklessness; it had all the hallmarks of a real-life Mayberry. At the heart of the community was Andersen's Grocery, the cornerstone of daily life. It wasn't just a place to buy local meats, milk, bread, and fresh vegetables; it was a gathering spot where neighbors exchanged news, laughter, and a sense of belonging. Every Wednesday, like clockwork, the Byrd Cookie Company brought magic to the store. They filled a large glass canister with warm, fresh-baked, fruit-filled oatmeal cookies.

The aroma was irresistible, wafting down the block like an unspoken invitation. Chance could never resist its pull. Every Wednesday morning, his mom would give him a dime for extra milk at school, but by the afternoon, that dime had a new destiny. On his way home, he'd stop at Andersen's, trading that coin for a small paper sack of those heavenly cookies. The warm, soft sweetness didn't stand a chance of making it home. By the time Chance had walked the two city blocks to his house, every last crumb was gone, leaving only the memory of the indulgence; and maybe a few sticky fingers.

Avondale was more than just a neighborhood; it was a world-sized kingdom spanning twenty blocks. It was a place alive with characters who seemed larger than life and as colorful as a kaleidoscope. Each person Chance encountered brought something unique; a quirk, a story, a lesson. Over time, he absorbed bits and pieces of them all, unknowingly piecing together the essence of his own character.

These weren't just people; they were the tapestry of Chance's world, each one adding a distinct flavor to the recipe of his life. Whether it was the wise advice of an elder, the laughter shared with a friend, or the silent but powerful influence of a neighbor, every encounter left a mark. In hindsight, Avondale wasn't just a place to grow up; it was a place that shaped who Chance was and who he would become.

Meet the Gang

Behind the house, two doors down and over the back fence, there was Mickey Greensman. For all the world, Mickey was the living, breathing image of Shaggy from *Scooby-Doo*. Tall and lanky, with unkempt shaggy hair and those skinny, hairy legs that seemed to go on forever, Mickey's appearance was only matched by his easygoing nature. He had a huge Adam's apple that bobbed comically when he laughed, which he did often. Mickey wasn't just Chance's best friend;

he was his partner-in-crime and near-constant companion from grade school all the way into junior high.

Every weekend, the two boys roamed the neighborhood on their Schwinn bikes, complete with banana seats and colorful streamers on the handlebars. They had a knack for spotting treasures where others saw trash. In those days, families discarded old bikes on the curb when upgrading to the latest models for their kids. Chance and Mickey saw opportunity in every rusty frame and bent wheel. They would haul these abandoned bikes back to Mickey's backyard, which served as their makeshift workshop, and spend hours piecing together functioning rides.

Once they'd finished assembling a bike, they often found kids in the neighborhood who didn't have one and dropped it off as a surprise gift; no strings attached. To them, it wasn't about being heroes or making a difference. It was just something they did, a quiet tradition that reflected the unspoken kindness of those times.

Mickey's family, however, was a unique bunch. Chance never fully understood what Mickey's dad did for a living, but he figured he must have been a mechanic because the man could fix *anything*. Seriously, *anything*. Mickey's mom, on the other hand, always seemed to be in a bad mood, barking at the boys whenever they got too rowdy. Mickey's older brother, Ed, was tall and brooding, with jet-black hair like their mom. For some reason, Ed had a habit of smacking Mickey on the back of the head every time he walked past him. Odd, indeed. Adding to the quirks, Ed seemed to have *Abraxas* by Santana on an eternal loop, playing it so often that by junior high, the record had developed a skip right in the middle of *Black Magic Woman.*

As they grew older, Chance and Mickey traded their coaster brake bikes for gas-powered dirt bikes. With engines roaring, they tore across fields and cow pastures, testing the limits of speed, daring, and maybe even fate. Their adventures reached a climax one fateful afternoon. The two boys were racing across a densely grassed field, throttles wide open, laughter trailing in the wind. Suddenly, Mickey's bike vanished from Chance's sight. One moment he was there; the next, he was gone.

Panicked, Chance turned back and found Mickey sprawled at the bottom of a massive hole; 20 feet across and six feet deep; where a storm had uprooted a giant live oak. Mickey was hurt badly, with several broken ribs and a neck injury that could have been much worse. He spent weeks in the hospital recovering. After that day, the boys gave away their dirt bikes, leaving behind their high-speed escapades for good.

Right across the street lived Jay Amaran, Chance's "best-est" buddy through grade school. Jay's mom was a Broadway composer who had moved to Savannah in the 1950s to produce the Little Theater. While Chance never met Jay's two sisters, he and Jay shared a love for climbing trees. They spent countless afternoons perched high in the branches, surveying their tiny world from above. Jay also introduced Chance to figs, thanks to the massive tree in his yard that seemed to bear fruit all year round. But with those sweet fruits came trouble; brown wasps built nests in the sticky branches, and black widow spiders spun webs in the neighboring live oaks. Jay once got bitten by a black widow and nearly died before reaching the hospital, a close call that left both boys far more cautious.

A block over lived Bobby Borchers, and around the corner was Johnny Plunkett, whose dad drove a city bus. While Chance wasn't particularly close to either, they were always good for a game of stickball.

Down at the corner of Bonaventure lived Eddy Harper, affectionately known as "Dirty Eddy." With a perpetual cloud of dust trailing him, he was the group's very own "Pig Pen" from *Charlie Brown*. Eddy's disheveled appearance belied a heart of gold, though no one could quite figure out how he managed to stay so, well, dusty.

Around the alley near Mickey's house lived Charlie Peppers, the kid who introduced Chance to basketball. Though Charlie wasn't much taller than the ball itself, he played with a scrappy determination that left an impression. When denied the ball, he'd resort to smacking other players on the knees, earning both laughs and grudging respect. In junior high, Charlie and Chance bagged groceries at Winn Dixie, and Charlie eventually became the produce manager there after high school.

And then there was Lynn Lucus, the prettiest girl in the neighborhood. By high school, she had a crush on Darwin Jesup, Chance's best friend. Lynn's house was the neighborhood hotspot for sock hops and weekend get-togethers. With Smokey Robinson, The Supremes, and Three Dog Night blasting from her mama's stereo, her home buzzed with life and laughter. Her mom, Ms. Diane, was the life of the party, teaching the kids dance moves and joining in the fun.

Chance, however, had a secret crush; not on Lynn, but on Ms. Diane. She was his first "older woman" fantasy, a fact he never shared with anyone but carried as a warm memory of those carefree days.

Maybe that's a little harsh or brash, but you get the idea.

Anyway, he thought she was probably the prettiest woman alive and reminded him of a lot of the country heart-throb, Tammy Wynette. In her mid-30s, Diane was tall, her blonde hair always short or pulled back into a ponytail; she was always happy, with a real open, bubbly disposition. She had the prettiest, perfectly shaped legs and frequently wore these little cotton shorts. At one point, he found himself thinking that she could have been a model in one of those magazines that Dad kept in his bottom dresser drawer.

It was a one-time, one "flash" thought. He sure didn't think of Ms. Diane like that at all. That would have just been really weird.

Ms. Diane and Lynn's Dad played guitar; he played rhythm and she played lead on a 12-string. They had matching red Univox guitars and a really nice amplifier that they bought through mail-order. Fingerhut, yep, that's the mail-order catalog a lot of stuff came out of those days.

Before there was Amazon – waaay before Amazon – there was "mail-order." JCPenney, Belks, Spiegel, Montgomery Ward. Sears had a huge Christmas "Wish Book" every year full of toys.

The family would have these lively sing-alongs where everyone joined in, including Lynn's two brothers, belting out tunes with unabashed enthusiasm. The warm, inviting atmosphere made their house the place to be, especially on weekends. The air was always filled with laughter, music, and the aroma of something delicious wafting from the kitchen. Chance didn't need much convincing to head over there; any excuse would do. Whether it was a casual gathering or one of Lynn's impromptu events, Chance was there, wide-eyed and ready to soak it all in.

His motivations, of course, weren't entirely wholesome. He was completely smitten with Lynn's mom, Ms. Diane, who seemed to float through the house with an effortless grace. Whenever she wore those little white shorts, Chance's adolescent heart skipped a beat. This pimple-faced, awkward bundle of teenage hormones lived for the fleeting moments when she smiled his way or teased him about his fumbling attempts to act cool.

When Lynn casually mentioned that her mom had offered to teach him how to play the guitar, Chance jumped at the chance. He didn't hesitate for a second. You betcha! With dreams of strumming heartfelt tunes and maybe earning a smile of approval from Ms. Diane, he threw himself into those lessons with more focus than he'd ever shown in school.

Four blocks up and one block over lived Darwin Jesup, another fixture in Chance's life. Darwin's dad was a plumber, a steady man who passed down his work ethic to his son. Darwin spent most of his days raking leaves, mowing the lawn, and helping his mom with household chores. He was the kind of kid who always seemed busy, but when he finally had free time, he and Chance started to connect.

Their friendship truly took root when Darwin turned 15, and the two discovered they shared a mutual crush on Lynn. She was the sun around which their teenage world revolved, and each boy vied for her attention in his own way. Darwin, however, had a secret weapon; a thoughtful, romantic gesture that would tip the scales in his favor.

For Lynn's 16th birthday, Darwin presented her with a copy of Bread's 45 rpm vinyl, *Baby, I'm-A Want You.* It was the perfect gift;

sentimental, sweet, and timed just right. Lynn was over the moon, and with that one simple act, Darwin managed to edge out Chance in the quiet competition for her affections.

Chance, though disappointed, couldn't help but admire Darwin's bold move.

Rats!
Then she gave him a copy of Bread's song, 'Diary' for his 16th birthday. True puppy-love. How cute.
Well, just - damn.

What can I say? This was the early 1970s, and the music was pure magic. Every night, as the world settled down, radios across the neighborhood were tuned to WSGA, the local rock station. The soft glow of the radio dial and the steady stream of hits created the soundtrack of our lives. Three Dog Night, Chicago, Paul Davis, Gordon Lightfoot, the Moody Blues, Santana, Eric Clapton, the Beatles, the Hollies, Simon and Garfunkel; the list was endless.

Some songs seemed to play on repeat, sinking deep into our subconscious. I'm sure I could have recited *Precious and Few* or *Joy to the World* in my sleep from how often they filled the airwaves. Back then, it felt like the music was simply part of the moment, something that brought comfort and connection. We didn't fully grasp how timeless it would become or how it would shape memories for decades to come.

We couldn't have imagined then how the world would change; how music, once shared through scratchy AM radios and vinyl records, would become something you could carry in your pocket or stream from anywhere. At the time, it wasn't about convenience; it was about feeling, and every note mattered.

If you didn't buy the individual singles right away, you could always wait
until K-tel came out with a compilation LP "for $5.99 at Woolworth, K-mart or Eckerd Drugs."

Sometimes, when Darwin could manage to slip away from chores, he and Chance would head out for a bit of fun. Whether it was bowling, catching a movie, or hanging out with the Boy Scout troop down the street, they were always looking for something to do. Both loved camping and spending time in the woods with the troop. Darwin had a knack for practical jokes, and Chance often found himself as the unwitting scapegoat. Still, it was all part of the fun.

Most evenings, the real excitement came from tearing through the neighborhood in their classic cars. Darwin had been gifted a light-blue-over-dark-blue 1957 Ford Ranchero for his 15th birthday by his dad, Mr. Jesup. Chance, on the other hand, would borrow his mom's '57 Fairlane, a pale yellow-and-white beauty that seemed to collect dirt as if by design. They'd race down the streets, fishtailing through the sandy stretches and kicking up clouds of dust that inevitably landed in someone's garden. Their antics usually ended with a call to the cops, at which point the boys would hightail it home, park the cars, and pretend nothing had happened. It was the kind of reckless fun that only teenagers could dream up.

In junior high, Mickey started dating Beth, a sandy-haired girl from a nearby neighborhood. She was sweet and unassuming, but Mickey didn't treat her well. It wasn't long before Chance stepped in, gradually building a relationship with Beth that lasted, on and off, through high school and into their early adult years. Beth was kind and loyal, and Chance's mom adored her, always hoping they'd make it work. But Chance could never fully commit.

Over the years, Beth would reappear at pivotal moments in Chance's life, often when he was at his lowest. They'd reconnect briefly, sharing good times before drifting apart again. Eventually, Beth had a child; a little girl with developmental challenges. The news hit Chance in a way he couldn't quite explain, and it marked the end of their on-again, off-again connection.

Even so, memories of Beth lingered, tied to the soundtrack of their youth. Gayle Garnett's *We'll Sing in the Sunshine* became their unofficial anthem, a bittersweet reminder of what could have been. But like the lyrics of the song, they never did.

***

Formidable Year — the Force of Change

High school should forever be a special time for any adolescent as they ascend into early adulthood. It's supposed to be a time for learning to socialize, to build interpersonal relations, some of which will last for years, if not all, of their adult lives. First dates, first kisses, and first loves evolve during these years. Sometimes these firsts are so intense that they overshadow the rest of what is so important during these same years — education. These three to four years are so important to build on the basics learned in grade school and junior high. The skills and lessons learned over the first eight years of school, public or private, are the backbone for areas of higher learning. Skills like these are important in developing habits, insights, plans, and ideas for everything from business to career choices. Chance's time in the earlier years of junior high school had been grossly displaced and disrupted by unfortunate times and events far beyond his control. The last joyful experience in his junior high years was 7th grade while attending Shuman Junior High. After that, things went straight to hell for school and his attitude about almost everything. Avondale was a planned neighborhood with an elementary school, Charles Herty, within easy walking distance of every child in the neighborhood. Except for the 5th grade when his Mom and Dad separated, and he was moved out of town. Chance enjoyed walking to school and home every day for the whole six years in grade school. What a wonderful experience. A little Mayberry right there in east Savannah.

He'd ride his lime green Schwinn bike with the white banana seat back and forth to school every day, rain or shine. Down the block, round by the park, up New York Avenue, stop for the crossing guard on Pennsylvania Avenue, up through Gordonston by the house George C. Scott owned, around the Boy Scout Park, across Gwinnett Street to school – so peaceful. It seemed as if something was always blooming somewhere; some smell was always in the air along the way. Sweet, comfortable, heartwarming times in those years, riding those streets without fear of harm or danger.

Toward the outer perimeter of several neighborhoods bordered by President Street, Skidaway Road, Victory Drive, and the old Deptford Homes tract was a single middle school planned to house all students of those ages from the area. That school was Shuman Junior High. It, like Charles Herty, was a 'neighborhood school.' Every neighborhood in the entire city, in fact, the entire country in those times, was enhanced and reinforced by the freedom to choose one's friends, one's neighbors, where one's children went to school, where to vote, shop, socialize, or worship. All that changed dramatically in 1970.

That year, under pressure and lawsuits by the American Civil Liberties Union (ACLU) federal Judge Anthony Garcia ordered that all schools in the city of Savannah and Chatham County would, by decree, conform and adhere to the dissolution of 'neighborhood schools' and would formulate a plan to bus students from an affluent area of the county to impoverished school zones, and in-kind impoverished to affluent, to satisfy equality of opportunity in education for all. This removed all freedom of choice for all communities uniformly.

Black people were shipped from their crime-ridden communities in east and west urban Savannah into affluent, overwhelmingly white neighborhoods. These well-maintained, clean, and orderly schools in Gordonston, Savannah Gardens, Ardsley Park, and east Savannah suburbia were quite the sight for the city's poorest children. In turn, affluent white children from these relatively crime-free areas of the city and the unincorporated county were forcibly bused into the poorest, undisciplined, largely ignored communities bordered by East and West Broad, Bay Street, and Victory Drive. The schools in these neighborhoods were unimproved, poorly maintained, and lacking the discipline of order or rule, and the children were extremely overwhelmed and apprehensive.

For Chance, the line in the sand for his new school was right down the middle of Texas Avenue. Everyone east of that line would continue to enjoy the comfort and convenience of Shuman. All the kids west of that line, including Chance and about twenty more blocks west to Victory Drive, would have to go, or be bused to, Sol C. Johnson High School in Thunderbolt. An entirely black community surrounded this school, and the kids in Chance's neighborhood were scared shitless.

Savannah was a powder keg in absolute upheaval over the ruling. Chance's Dad actually helped form and led a group of several thousand Savannahians to oppose future rulings by the courts. At that time, the county's most affluent areas were unaffected by the busing issue because the ruling only affected the incorporated area. Those communities constantly teased and touted those affected by busing as 'unappreciative,' 'prejudiced,' 'non-conformist,' and 'white supremacists.' He was pulled from public school and thrust into a private conclave of poorly prepared, under-supplied, and over-whelmed parents with no idea how to proceed or educate these children in mass.

In 1971, the judge extended the moratorium to include the un-incorporated area of Chatham County. Spoiled and entitled lily-white kids from Windsor Forrest, Isle of Hope, Wilmington Island, Rio Vista, Whitmarsh, and Tybee Islands were now thrust into their worst fears. With the extension of the territory, the lines of enforcement changed again. This time, ALL the kids he had gone to school with all of his life would be sent to a middle school in the heart of one of the most heinous areas for crime in east Savannah – east Gwinnett Street and Hubert Junior High. Chance's brother, Alden, was bused to Spraque Elementary, just a few blocks away, and he spent every day that first year in constant fear.

Chance had his problems with black boys; most were between the ages of 16 and 18 years old and had been cycled over and over through the same 8th and 9th-grade classes. They were not motivated to better themselves. These kids resented the forced acceptance of white kids into their community, and they spent most of every day bullying the smaller white boys, threatening them for their lunch money, and accosting the pretty little white girls. This was two full school years of pure Hell for Chance.

By 1972, many white Savannah residents who could afford to do so made a mass exodus from the public school system to enroll their kids in expensive, private schools. At the same time, preliminary developments were springing up in previously undesired areas completely out of Chatham and into both Bryan and Effingham counties. Chance and his classmates had only one choice for senior high – Savannah High School.

As a result of all this mayhem, undue stress, and fear of uncertainty and their safety in school, the magic and the romance of senior high school were, by and large, gone for both boys.

By the 11th grade, Chance was already working to pay for a car: a 1966 Mustang Pony. Dang, that was a great ride. He was slinging pies for Pizza Hut on school nights, skipping class at times the next day after spending too much time cleaning equipment the night before. Two teenage boys, now quickly approaching manhood with corresponding appetites, were costing much more than ever. Alden was not quite old enough to help pull any weight, so Chance sucked it up to help mom provide food and utilities.

Dad became progressively more unhinged. He had checked himself into Clark Pavilion for psychiatric evaluation of suicidal ideation several times in recent months. There were several extramarital affairs. He'd get angry seemingly for nothing, throw things, break up furniture, discharge firearms – one time firing a .22 rifle into a lamp in the living room that wound up across the street into the neighbor's living room. He liked to keep all of his weapons (several high-powered rifles) loaded, and once in a while, he'd just walk by the display, pull the trigger, and laugh when the gun went off.

Did I say 'unhinged?' How about, just frickin' CRAZY!

Those years held too many dark episodes, moments Chance would rather forget. He had to endure the pain of watching his father lash out at his mother in fits of anger, episodes that often came dangerously close to leaving her seriously injured. The violence at home cast a heavy shadow over his once-bright dreams.

Chance had always envisioned himself finishing high school, going to college, and maybe even becoming a doctor. Medicine fascinated him, and he saw it as a path far removed from the aimless job-hopping that defined his father's life. But by the time he turned 17, the weight of everything had ground him down. His outlook on school had soured so badly that he faced the humiliating possibility of not graduating with his peers. The only way to avoid being held back was to enroll in summer school; a blow to his pride but, unbeknownst to him, a turning point he would later treasure.

It was the sweltering summer of 1974 when he met her. Kathy Smits, with her gentle smile and doe-like eyes, walked into his life during that unremarkable summer school session and turned his world upside down. From that moment on, nothing was the same.

***

Sweet Mama....and Jesus

Let's get one thing clear right away: Chance Brogdon was blessed with one of the greatest moms the world has ever known. Anne Brogdon was the backbone of their family, a woman of remarkable strength and enduring love who endured more than her fair share from Chance, his brother, and their father, Bernie.

Anne wore countless hats; she was the cook, housekeeper, laundry attendant, banker, bookkeeper, teacher, counselor, entertainment director, gardener, stock clerk, cashier, and accountant. She was also Chance's unwavering rock, his first and truest soulmate. Whenever he fell, she was there to pick him up, often with tough love and words of wisdom that gave him the courage to face life's next challenge. But beyond her earthly support, she reminded him not to forget the eternal love of the One who loved him first and always; our Lord and Savior, Jesus Christ.

Anne's resilience was extraordinary. She put up with Bernie for 40 years, enduring his faults and failings for one reason; actually, two: her boys. Her sons were her everything, her highest priority.

No matter how hard times got, whether there was just enough to scrape by or not nearly enough to make ends meet, she poured her heart into giving them a sense of security and love. Together, they found ways to laugh through the tears and make the best of what they had, regardless of whether Bernie was around.

Anne's devotion extended to teaching Chance life skills, one of the most cherished being how to drive. She started him young, letting him sit on her lap in her beloved gray and white '57 Ford Fairlane, easing down quiet country roads. That Fairlane, with its power steering, automatic transmission, and front disc brakes, was her pride and joy. Little Chance, at just 9 or 10, learned to keep the car steady between the ditches.

By the time Chance was 13 or 14, Anne had upgraded to a 1966 Chevy Impala; a car he remembered fondly despite its troublesome, slipping gearshift. Weekend drives between Newton and Rincon became their tradition, with Anne guiding him through the nuances of country driving. One of Chance's favorite routes was along Highway 24 between their home in Midville and Newington. The roads were smooth, the scenery beautiful, and the drive itself a mix of fun and learning.

Chance became quite the problem solver, too, when it came to that temperamental Impala. Whenever the gearshift jammed, he'd pull over, pop the hood, and realign the shifter rods with a practiced flick of his wrist. Problem solved, they'd get back on the road, laughing and enjoying their journey until the next little hiccup came along.

Anne's teachings extended far beyond driving lessons. Through her steadfast love, her faith, and her tireless efforts, she instilled in Chance the values of perseverance, gratitude, and the importance of family. She was, and always would be, the heart and soul of his world.

Don't know who taught Alden to drive — ain't about him no way.

Anne Brogdon was more than just a devoted mother; she was an intelligent and resourceful woman who knew how to make things work. Throughout her life, she held several key positions in accounting and comptrolling at various prominent companies in the city. Builderama, Kings Appliance, W.J. Bremer Concrete, Union Bag Paper Company, and Dixie Crystal Sugar were just a few of the places where she worked, demonstrating both her skill and versatility in the business world.

But beyond her professional success, Anne had a knack for slipping beneath the radar when she wanted to. She could be clever and shrewd, always managing to handle difficult situations with grace.

One of her favorite pastimes, especially in the evenings, was playing the game *Password* with her husband Bernie and another couple, Joe and Teresa. Joe was a tall, freckled man with flaming red hair, always impeccably dressed. He and Bernie shared a love of scuba diving, often going on salvage dives together in the local area. They even amassed an impressive collection of scuba equipment and wetsuits in an array of colors; black, yellow, white, and red; that could rival the crew of the *Seaview* from the TV show *Voyage to the Bottom of the Sea.*

Joe's wife, Teresa, on the other hand, was a completely different character. The less said about her, the better, as her actions were hard to ignore. Teresa had two small children, babies really, whom she neglected to the point of recklessness. She didn't even bother to put diapers on them. In many ways, she was an unfortunate presence in their lives, someone whose behavior left much to be desired.

Despite the drama surrounding Teresa, the game nights were a bright spot for Anne and Bernie. It was one of those simple pleasures they enjoyed as a couple, a reminder that even in the midst of everyday chaos, there were moments of fun and lightheartedness to be had.

Sorry, did I say ever?

I meant, NEVER!

Teresa's neglect of her children was appalling. She allowed them to roam the house, a young boy and a baby girl, completely naked, with no concern for cleanliness or their well-being. The floors, furniture, and even the children themselves were often covered in filth, as they pooped and peed without restraint. The poor children's skin was constantly irritated and raw, scalded by their own waste. It was heartbreaking to witness how they suffered in this environment, with no one stepping in to care for their basic needs.

The chaos extended beyond the children, as two puppies shared the space, competing for areas to relieve themselves. The house, once a brand-new property in the desirable Halcyon Bluff neighborhood, had become a den of filth. Its once-pristine condition was now tarnished by the stench and mess that filled every corner. The neighbors, though they may have tried to avoid confronting the issue, surely knew what was going on behind those doors; the overpowering smell of decay could not have been ignored.

In stark contrast stood Chance's own home, where cleanliness, order, and care were of the utmost importance. His mother, Anne, was the epitome of tidiness. She took pride in maintaining a spotless home and attending to her children's every need, often changing diapers at the mere thought of their discomfort. Her home was a sanctuary, filled with warmth and fresh scents, where her children could thrive.

Chance couldn't comprehend how Teresa, with her filthy living conditions and indifferent attitude toward her children's care, could have been allowed into anyone's home. It was a vivid and lasting memory for him, one that highlighted the vast difference between the love and care he experienced and the neglect that others endured. The disparity was not lost on him, and he would never forget how dirty and neglected those children were.

I digress...again.

Anyway, Joe and his stinky wife, Teresa, would come over, usually without their kids (thank goodness). After Mama helped them get a little more 'presentable,' the fun would start. Chance was early school age, but he loved watching this show go down when the four nuts got together. They didn't drink alcohol, just iced tea or coffee, but you'd think they were smoking something when they got going. As smart as Mama was, and Daddy could be, you'd think neither had enough sense to pour water out of a pail. I don't think the other couple was acting, at least not 'stinky.'

Now, to play the game, you had to take a card of words from a stack and place it in this blue plastic sleeve showing only one word at a time through this little red, see-through, transparent plastic slit. Your opponent had the same card and the same word. The object of the game was to give your partner a one-word clue, one turn at a time, trying to get them to guess the word you were holding in your hand.

Easy, right? Nope.

His Dad would take a good minute to come up with just the right clue he thought would surely prompt the right, or at least the best, response, if not the answer itself. She'd think for a moment, teasing him mercilessly at times, then blurt out a ridiculous word that had little or nothing to do with the clue. He'd slap the top of his crew cut, mutter something in disgust, or just burst out laughing. Somebody would spill something or accidentally pee themselves from laughing at least once or twice during the evening; often, it was Daddy or Joe. As for Teresa, she was just Teresa when it came to lack of bladder or bowel control. Chance would say to his Mama, "She jus' nas'y, Mama."

*****

Anne taught her boys respect for their Daddy, their elders, strangers, and each other. They knew how to dress themselves from the time they were very young and how to look neat, clean, and later fashionable. She bought them clothes that were popular from Belk. JC Penney and Sears, even when she couldn't afford them for herself. They ate well, never went hungry, and never wanted much of anything they needed or really wanted. Her boys were numero-uno.

On the other hand, Dad never got the memo that said everything earned by the two should go into the same pot for the family's best interest. He was quite clear in his interpretation of wages. He may have worked hard for what *he* made and ought to have whatever *he* wanted. He bought cars he didn't need, tools he didn't use, guns he forgot to unload, CB equipment, junk. He re-mortgaged their home so many times they paid for it at least five times in 30 years. Thank God, Mama had control over the bank account, at least the checkbook, most of the time. That was why Mama went to work, and wouldn't stop, even though he tried many times to get her to stay home.

She taught the boys how to show their love for Jesus and that they had to pray every night before bedtime. Chance never forgot that, and he developed such a close, very personal relationship with the Lord that saw him through so many trials and tribulations. Because of his faith, despite everything the world through his way, the Lord blessed him in more ways than he came to appreciate fully. It was his Mama who instilled the devotion to his Savior and gave this man his bearing and his being.

Yeah, his Mama was there all the time. When he was in high school and then as a young adult, they enjoyed just sitting down in the morning at the kitchen table over a cup of instant Maxwell House coffee, flipping through the separate pages of the morning paper. She'd take the front national section; he'd take the local news; they'd split the funny papers. Dad wasn't around a lot in those days; I think he was driving a truck. Alden was always either still in bed or already off and out someplace; too much going on in his world for such foolishness.

Dad worked as a salesman at Singer sewing machine company for a few months when Chance was eight or so and Alden was around four. One time he brought home something that looked for the world to Chance like an old briefcase, just carrying on about how special this thing was. Then he put it on the table, snapped open clips on either end, and pulled two speakers off. Cool. Next, he opened the top to that thing, and there, to Chance's amazement and his Mom's, was this round metal plate with a rubber disk sitting on top right in the middle. It had a little chrome rod sticking up through the middle of the plate and an arm-looking thing off to one side, switches and knobs everywhere. *"What the heck was this thing?"* he thought. It was a record player, and Dad brought home a vinyl disk he called 'a record,' put it down on that plate, turned a knob that made it turn by itself, moved that little arm over, and gently sat it down on the edge of that 'record.' He brought home the LP of greatest hits by *The Ventures,* and the song he chose to introduce his family to the miracle of stereo sound was 'Telstar.'

A slow rumble began to build from the speakers, low at first, then the sound of a jet taking off crossed from one speaker to the next. Chance's little eye got the size of saucers. Music was everywhere, all at once, filling that living room with pure magic to everyone's amazement.

From this time and for months to come, only on nights when Dad was away working or whatever, Chance, Alden, and Mama would turn off the TV and turn on that player. Chance listened so often and intently that he eventually knew most of the words and could carry a tune well enough to lip-sync for Mama. They didn't know squat about karaoke; they were just having fun.

He got pretty darned good at playing that air guitar to pick and grin at almost anything they played: Johnny Cash, Eddy Arnold, the Beatles, Hank Snow, Pattie Page, and Patsy Cline to name just a few. Mama's favorite was Eddy Arnold's song, 'Folk Singer.' Chance's was Johnny Cash's 'Ring of Fire' and 'Bonanza.' Sometimes Dad would invite people over from church, mostly young couples, some woman named Becky who looked like she could be Chance's older sister that he noticed Dad liked to dance with a lot. And they danced to those records. Somebody would play Marty Robbins's RFD album and the song, 'Change That Dial' would come on, Mama would start to cry, and that would pretty much end the evening.

A time or two, he'd catch Dad playing music – something really rare – he'd put on something by Jim Reeves like 'Welcome to My World' or Eddy Arnold's 'Molly,' and tears would fill *his* eyes. He'd have to get up and close it down. Then, at that time in his life, Chance never knew why people got so upset from listening to music. He sure found out later what that emotion was all about starting in his teens with his first crush and continuing through the rest of his life.

She was there when Rex got hit by that car to comfort his heart and wipe his tears as they found a new home for him to recover. She was there to wipe away the dirt, asphalt, and little rocks most every time he fell off his bike, skates, or that damned mini bike she hated.

Mama was there through countless episodes of tonsillitis, and strep throat, and when they got their tonsils removed. Through mumps and measles, chicken pox, and when each of the boys contracted whooping cough. To doctor them through colds and cold sores, bumped heads, and bruised egos. When he finally got his nose repaired after being broken at birth, blocking his ability to breathe for 18 years, she was there: the sudden rush of unobstructed air flooded his newly opened nasal passages, nearly causing him to choke. What an emotional day *that* was.

She was there when Susan Futrell gave him his first broken heart in the first grade. And when that scary guy from Olan Miles came through the neighborhood, sat both boys on the back of that fuzzy black and white pony, and took their pictures dressed in those ridiculous cowboy outfits. She was there to dry their tears and kick him to the curb for scaring her two little rangers.

She was there to console and comfort him the first time someone, his first young wife, walked in by surprise and caught him pleasing himself with a stack of open adult magazines. They were both so young and sex was so new. She was fooling around on him with a guy at work, a black coworker, and he was not touching her at all. Kathy couldn't understand his behavior at all because she'd never known anybody who did that kind of thing. She left him over it. They were only married for about a year.

150

She was there as a friend on so many occasions, not just when he needed someone to talk with but when *she* needed someone to share *her* feelings with. He sat up with her so many nights when the ole man had physically hurt her, or the tension of something he'd done with their money stressed her so badly she was about to go bonkers. They were not only mother and son – they were true friends.

Mama was there for him as she always had been, years later, when he lost the one thing he loved most in life and had devoted so much of his time and energy toward – when he truly thought his whole world had ended. She gave him the encouragement and strength to take his troubles to the Lord and surrender *everything* to Him.

Then, after he thought nothing could happen worse in his life, with all the chips down and he found himself constantly kissing concrete, his guardian angel turned away for a moment – just a fleeting moment – and he lost something even more precious than life itself from his world. It took everything she had inside her to bring out everything he had left in him, all his remaining love, faith, and devotion for his Lord, to bring his world back from the brink of an unbelievable loss.

The only saving grace for Chance truly was his sweet Mama and his faith in Jesus.

***

Guardian Angel

Chance felt an unusual connection to the Word of God from a very early age. Strange way to put it, maybe, but he genuinely felt the warmth deep inside; an undeniable presence of the Holy Spirit every time he heard, read, or talked about Jesus. It wasn't just a fleeting sensation; it was like being suddenly immersed in a pool of wonderfully warm water, enveloping both his body and soul.

His Mama devoted much of her time teaching Chance and his brother about God's love and the virtues of living a Christian life. She often talked to them about how they could talk to Jesus, share their troubles, calm their fears, and express their gratitude for His blessings and God's grace through prayer; not just at bedtime, but anytime. She taught them all the important prayers that little boys should say before sleep, but her lessons went far beyond that.

Chance always felt like he had a guardian angel watching over him, someone who was there when he needed guidance or comfort. There were countless moments throughout his childhood when he would speak with Jesus or his "special angel," just like any other friend: sitting alone in the yard, walking through the woods, or lying in bed at night. Occasionally, the Lord would answer him, not in a voice he could hear, but in a way he understood deeply; a sense of peace, a lifting of his spirit, the fading of illness, a moment of relief when despair seemed endless.

When Chance was born, the doctor had crushed his little face with surgical instruments, but his angel was there, ensuring his face was made whole again. At age 10, when he nearly drowned in swimming class, his angel pulled him to safety just as he was slipping from consciousness, his last breath escaping. When he was a toddler, and the passenger door of Mama's '57 Fairlane popped open while she was turning, before there were car seats or seat belts, his angel reached down, cupped him in His hand, and protected him from injury.

Now, the name "Earl" might not have seemed like the best fit for an eternal guardian, but then again, maybe his name was something grander; Elias, Leviticus, or Aliisha. Something Greek, Roman, or Thessalonian. Who knew? One doesn't really get to know unless a sign comes along, or something hits you square in the face, making the identity of your guardian crystal clear. For most of Chance's life, he never had a name for this presence that walked with him. He just felt it, sometimes right beside him, guiding him and offering protection when needed.

I'm getting ahead of myself when I say that not until his midlife renaissance did Chance finally uncover the probable identity of his guardian; at least, a name he could call him when they talked.

It was on the eve of his 60th birthday, preparing for a motorcycle ride with friends in the mountains, heading for the Blue Ridge Parkway. Chance was sitting on his custom Harley Softail, waiting for the others. One of the guys, who had heard Chance talk about his guardian angel before, teased him once again, "Hey, man, that angel of yours ridin' with us today?"

"Sure is," Chance replied.

The guy, curious, pressed on, "What do you call him, anyway? Still haven't named him yet, huh?"

Chance laughed. "Nah, man, you don't name an angel. Who cares, as long as he's here."

"Hey, no prob, just asking. I think he needs a name," the rider insisted.

At that moment, as Chance fired up his bike and turned on his stereo, the XM radio chimed in with the last words of a Dixie Chicks song: "Let's go for a ride, Earl, hey, hey, oh hey."

"Well, I'll be damned." Chance burst out laughing. "I guess his name is Earl." He shook his head, still chuckling. "Hey, y'all, IT'S FRICKIN' EARL! The Chicks just told me!"

And from that point on, the name stuck.

Chance may have been a simple man, but his life was anything but. Full of absurdities, revelations, and moments that defied explanation, the story of Chance and Earl, his guardian angel, would unfold in ways that brought him closer to the Almighty and to a deeper, more precious walk with Jesus. Just wait and see how incredibly fitting that name truly was.

Chapter Six

Loves...Learning Years

Despite the summer school session of 1974, Chance didn't let too many distractions cloud his vision for the future. He pushed aside the chaos, though he had forgotten the mantra his dad had always drilled into him and his brother whenever they lost sight of their goals: "Never sacrifice the alternate for the immediate."

It didn't take long into the new school year, late in 1974, for Chance to realize that this last year of high school would be different. He'd already met the girl he thought he might marry during summer school, and his work at the pizza place consumed most of his attention. His appearances in Mrs. Adam's English Lit class were so rare that, on the few occasions he showed up, the entire room would stand and clap. Mr. Kent, having watched him skip class time and time again, eventually stopped scheduling him for detention. He simply wished Chance a good day as he walked out of the classroom before lunch; at least twice a week.

By Christmas of 1974, Chance had pretty much checked out. He took the high school equivalency exam, passed it, got his diploma, and immediately enlisted in the Coast Guard. He caught pneumonia during boot camp, failed the swim test, and a week later, they put him on a bus back to Savannah.

Meanwhile, his younger brother, Alden, now about 15, was getting into everything his parents forbade, as adolescent boys often do. A tall, good-looking guy with long blonde hair, the girls loved him. There was never a shortage of young people at the house, lounging around, eating Mama's groceries.

Mom told Chance he could stay at home, but there was a catch: he needed to find a job, fast, and start paying room and board to help out. He couldn't return to Pizza House, and he didn't know what else to do. Working with Dad was out of the question; Dad was barely keeping things together as it was. He floated between odd jobs, from brick masonry to auto mechanics to driving trucks.

Then, as if by fate, a series of events; or perhaps a string of co-incidences; fell into Chance's lap, setting him on a new path he hadn't seen coming.

***

No One Counted; Kathy Did

Maybe meeting Kathy in summer school had something to do with Chance's transformation. He was from a working-class community on the east side, and she came from a well-off family on the south side of Windsor Forest. His dad was a jack-of-all-trades but a master of none; hers was a celebrated structural engineer with the Corps of Engineers. While Chance's dad was lucky if he could keep a job driving a semi-truck or selling cars for more than six months, Kathy's dad had worked with NASA during the Apollo missions, helping develop everything from the latches and hinges on the spacecraft to the zippers and pressure seals on the space suits for astronauts like Buzz Aldrin and Neil Armstrong.

Where Chance's dad was worrying about whether his mom would come home and catch him with another woman, Kathy's dad was stressing over the astronauts approaching the moon in June 1969. The contrast between their families couldn't have been more pronounced.

Chance couldn't help but laugh every time the big guy got a little tipsy and reminisced about the day the Eagle landed on the moon. He'd talk about how nervous everyone was when Armstrong stepped out onto the lunar surface, stepping into the vacuum of space as though it was just another Tuesday. The stories made him laugh, but they also made him think about just how different life had been for Kathy and himself.

Apparently, Jim and Jack had a lot to do with the design and fabrications.

Her mom was a tall, wiry-haired, loud-mouthed alcoholic who treated her dad like an afterthought, more a nuisance than a husband or father. She belittled him at every opportunity, whether in private or out in public, and he cowered in response, beaten down by years of habit. When she got drunk, she'd throw knives at him, hurling curses his way for not being the man she thought he should have been. Most men would have walked away, but Dessy stayed, sticking it out for the sake of their two boys and Kathy.

In stark contrast, Anne was the steady foundation for Chance's family, the unwavering support that held everything together. She was there for her sons no matter how unreliable or unpredictable his dad was. Anne was the rock, the inspiration, the guiding force that shaped Chance's adolescence and gave him a sense of purpose when everything else seemed uncertain.

But then there was Kathy, and Chance couldn't help but be completely captivated. He was utterly obsessed with this auburn-haired beauty from the other side of the tracks. At times, it seemed Kathy might share his feelings, but then she'd throw him into emotional turmoil by flirting with another boy down the street. This tug-of-war of affection, combined with the chaos at home and the pressure of after-school jobs, distracted Chance to the point that his grades slipped. He found himself failing the 12th grade. Missing what should have been the night of his life; senior prom; he made the decision to leave behind the shame of graduating outside of his peer group. With just enough credits to get a diploma, he took the exit and moved on.

His next attempt at a new life was enlisting in the Coast Guard, hoping to carve out a future for himself and Kathy. But that, too, was short-lived. Six weeks into boot camp in Cape May, New Jersey, Chance was struck by pneumonia, and his dream of military life came crashing down. The dismal weather and the isolation only added to his sense of loneliness and longing. And to make matters worse, the damn cook in the mess hall kept playing Bobby Bare's "500 Miles Away From Home" on the jukebox in the rec room, reminding Chance of everything he was missing. The squab served on Sundays was the same, too; he finally realized that it was only available after the big Coast Guard choppers had made their routine maneuvers. The seagull population around the airfield seemed to thin out for a couple of weeks at a time, an eerie reminder of the strange, disconnected life he was living.

Hey, tasted like chicken!

Chance found himself right back in Savannah.

Doesn't take long for a washed-out shallow-water sailor without a job to find something to do with himself – especially if he wants to rekindle his flame across town before the other guy moves in and makes a commitment.

Chance had been intrigued with medicine, anatomy, the disease process, and human physiology all his young life. At one point, early on, he imagined she might find a way to graduate, go to college, and wind up in medical school. In junior high, he was even invited to a program with Savannah State to explore medicine and a career in the health sciences. He was hooked. But college would not be possible for Chance. His parents had nowhere near the income, there was no such thing as a HOPE grant in those days, and his grade average in high school was a joke.

On television in the last half of the 70s decade were shows about cops like Police Story and Adam-12. Hawaii Five-O was huge. What really sparked his attention and enthusiasm, though, was a program called "EMERGENCY" - the series about a team of Los Angeles County Paramedics responding to medical rescues and accidents, home emergencies and disasters with medical kits in one hand and portable equipment they called "telemetry" in the other. These medics assessed the situation and delivered pre-hospital medical care and drugs in the house or the backseat of a car. The show was hugely popular, the concept was real, and Chance believed he might have found his calling.

About that time, mama told him about a cousin in charge of a group of medics with an ambulance service in Screven; maybe there was an option for him there. Within a couple of months, Chance was enrolled in and taking night classes to get his license as an Emergency Medical Technician driving back and forth to classes in Statesboro three times a week. His dad even knew the owner of a longtime Savannah ambulance service who was looking for attendants at that time, and he got the job working shifts while attending school.

Mr. Gelding did everything in his power to convince Chance he really didn't need the licensing to work for his service, but the boy stuck with it anyway. To Mr. Gelding, his attendants needed only a clean towel to wipe their hands and a clean sheet to change the stretcher. They didn't wait to be called.

A police scanner in the ready bay provided the catalyst these 2-man crews needed to set the streets on fire, and they would "jump" the call for ambulance assistance by several minutes over any other service.

Within days of landing this position with Gelding, fate delivered a clear message to Chance.

On May 26, 1976, 20th Century-Fox released a movie that Chance accepted as his swan song, an omen from his guardian angel that he had made a wise choice. The movie, *Mother, Jugs & Speed*, starring Bill Cosby and Rachel Welch and an all-star cast was the hilarious story of a newly graduated EMT and the competition for a city contract between two competing ambulance services in LA county. The storyline, comparing the absurd feuding between

F&B Ambulance and Unity with the battle for superiority between Gelding Ambulance and Chatham County EMS was simply uncanny.

Gelding's Ambulance Service was largely a collection of previous funeral home hearses converted to ambulances by adding an oxygen tank, a red light, and an old siren from a retired fire engine. But his boys knew how to drive those rigs – *fast!* That was the main requirement for his crews to keep their jobs and him in business. Get to that accident, shooting or cutting; get there *first*; load up those patients and haul ass to the closest hospital at breakneck speed. There were <u>NO</u> enforceable rules at that time for ambulance safety or public regard.

Gelding had two of the fastest rigs around: a converted '69 Ford Fairlane wagon with a 351 Cleveland and a '72 Oldsmobile 98 440 Hi-top with all the latest bells and whistles, fire engine red with a fancy electric wah-wah siren. These guys made a mess of an intersection when they'd blow through on the way to a call with very little regard for traffic.

Chatham County put together the first-of-its-kind Emergency Medical Service in SE Georgia one year earlier. Many of the county service's resources, management, and staff were drawn from an existing contract with Savannah Ambulance Service run by Mary Ginn. The county had also recruited, hired, and trained a couple of dozen former military medics to premier the first pre-hospital medical service to the taxpayers in the greater Savannah area. Their training came through cooperation with US Army Rangers and the 101st Infantry Medics from Fort Stewart. These guys were sharp, and the county invested in the newest ambulance technology they called "cracker boxes" to reach persons who might not have access to care via the existing cash-and-carry conveyance.

Similar to military mobile field surgical vehicles, these "units" were full of all the latest gizmos and gadgets:

- Portable defibrillators.

- Compact, hand-held radios capable of transmitting EKGs to waiting physicians in local emergency rooms.

- Full intravenous fluid capability.

- Life-saving medications and surgical interventions.

Chatham County would now have rolling MASH units and ER services on wheels.

To oversee the county's operation, the county police chief had agreed to provide 24/7 dispatching services; Civil Defense provided some of the initial berthing areas for crews downtown and near the airport; the local Red Cross would provide supplies and medications.

Chance worked nights and weekends for Gelding. The private ambulance service jumped and prematurely responded to calls meant for Chatham County EMS. Savannah drivers suddenly found themselves paying the ultimate price with ambulances literally racing anywhere there were two or more lanes: Victory Drive, Drayton Street, Abercorn Extension, Bay Street, Tybee Road – what a mess. And dangerous!

Five o'clock traffic jam on Abercorn or DeRenne Avenue? No problem.
"Jump that median, traffic coming the other way ain't got no excuse they can't see us."

Drayton, Price, Victory Drive, and both Henry and Anderson Streets all have large "humps" where they cross connecting streets. The average driver could get a little jostled at normal speeds, spill his drink, or bump the car's undercarriage over these rises. These crazy guys were such insanely devilish drivers that they'd take these rises well above the speed limit tossing medics, equipment, and patients around like gumballs in a pill box. Countless times city residents witnessed those ambulances, both Geldings and EMS, running neck and neck through congested city streets, just to be first to get to an accident on Island Expressway, out Ogeechee Road, or to someone sick in East Savannah.

Where President Street crosses Randolph, the road passes through Hitch Village, a low-income project heavily populated by mostly black folks. At this point, the street takes a deep drop in elevation, maybe 50 feet or so, and angles down about two blocks to join

McIntosh Blvd. That converted, white '68 Ford ambulance of Geldings could hit that sudden drop just right or come up that rise from
the other direction at just the right speed and get airborne: quite the
site to see unless you were an unsuspecting parent trying to walk
your kid across East President about that time.

Those county EMS "cracker-boxes" were simply unstable for city
use to say the very least. The manufacturers and engineers for these
companies had gone to great lengths to design a leveling and stabi-
lization system, including gyroscopes, to help keep the top-heavy vehicles upright at highway speeds. I said *"highway speeds,'* not
daredevil cornering, rapid acceleration/deceleration, or sudden dart-
ing maneuvers through heavy rush-hour Savannah traffic. Those
gyros simply proved to be no match for these wildcat drivers and the
city's unsuspecting public, attempting to get out of their way. The
Savannah Morning News was ripe with photos and accounts of
county ambulances on their sides, content, and sometimes passen-
gers spilled out onto the streets. Besides the obvious frequent repair
and replacement costs, Chatham County faced huge risks of significant liability from injury or property damage caused by such foolishness.

Speaking of the news media, the circus was not confined to vehicle mishaps. Oh, no. These guys were super competitive, especially
those working for Gelding, and they had been instructed to *"get
there, get that patient, no matter what, get back to the hospital as*

quick as possible.” And that *“no matter what”* was taken more than figuratively; by both sides and crews.

There were fist fights over patients at traffic accidents; some very serious fights, some seriously delayed emergency care. At times, these attendants fought as they dropped patients off at hospital ER entrance ramps. On several occasions, the news captured and published shots of still-stretchered patients rolling across or down ramps at Candler and Memorial Hospitals while attendants fought hand-to-hand. Hollywood could not have scripted events any better in Chatham County for the first five years of this fiasco.

Eventually, Mr. Gelding retired, then he passed away, and his business fell into disrepair under poor control by his heirs.

The county commission had devices called “governors” installed on the existing vehicles and upgraded computer programs on newer models, which they publicized under the guise of "control of fuel consumption costs," but, in actuality, they were specifically to control the speed of these vehicles. Technicians were required to undergo safety and driver's education classes, including skid pad exercises and defensive driving tactics. By 1980 the streets of Savannah were under much better, much *safer* emergency medical service.

Chance was right in the middle of all of this. First with Geldings, then hired on with a crew for the county EMS. Ecstatic barely describes what he was feeling about that time. He partnered with an ex-Marine who was to be his best man at his wedding to Kathy, and that same guy later became the toastmaster for his divorce party. The two partners were rather irreverent about the whole ordeal, and they'd hang at times during their off days, drinking PBR and Harry sharing his tales from Vietnam and exploits with the Corps.

It didn't take long to learn that these ex-military guys with the county were crazy, fun-loving, and hard-living, but also very dedicated men who loved what they did and the men they worked beside.

What EMS had that Gelding or any other service in the area, in the state, and likely the whole rest of the country didn't, and likely never would have, were their incredibly well-thought out uniforms these men and women had the pleasure of donning before the taxpayers and tourist of the Hostess City. I say that very tongue-in-cheek because they were simply - horrid.

One piece, single zipper, 100% cotton, untailored jump suits — bright (and I mean *bright*) canary-ass yellow.

YELLOW jump-suits!?!

Could have picked black (very professional), green, navy blue, even brown. Nope – neon frickin' yellow.

What the hell were they thinking?

These guys - these retired veterans of Vietnam, skirmishes around the world, former members of groups like the Strategic Medical Airlift, the Strategic Air Command, the Marines, Navy Hospital Corps, and Army Special Forces - were paraded around Chatham

County in huge white cracker boxes on wheels, easily tipped over with the slightest miscalculation, Christmas lights up the wazoo with reflective bright orange striping and manned by grown men clad in loud, obnoxious, lemon yellow "onesies." How silly.

Now, THIS would have been really great, scripted into the movie, Mother Jugs & Speed; what a hoot!

When these crews gathered at an accident or a mock disaster drill, the scene could easily have been mistaken for a Tweety Bird convention rather than a group of professional, highly trained medical personnel. In the dead of winter, it got no better. Imagine poo-brown, nylon short-sleeved shirts paired with baby-shit orange pants and Eisenhower jackets; short, midriff-baring jackets that hadn't been in vogue since the 1940s.

Where on earth did the county commission find the catalog for this mess?

It was downright sad, really. A damn shame, in fact. The guys; well, all men at the time; were actually top-notch at what they did. They deserved so much more respect than the absurd outfits they were forced to wear. They did their jobs, driving like bats out of hell, performing under pressure; and they did it all well. But those in charge, the county powers-that-be, seemed to be living in some bizarre fantasy world of their own. Meanwhile, these destined-to-be EMS dinosaurs existed in the stark, harsh reality of the world, a world where every day counted and professionalism was needed more than anything.

***

EMS – A Real World Drama

The tone alert sounded; the dispatcher's voice rang out with a frantic clarity.

"EMS one, EMS two. President Street at Randolph, multiple vehicle, accident with injuries....respond 10-18"

***

The graduation ceremony that night was a far cry from the grandiose events one might expect; just a hearty salutation from the instructors and an informal handout of their State certificates. Yet, that red, white, and blue patch, proudly displaying the words "Emergency Medical Technician – Ambulance" along with an official certification number from the State of Georgia Department of Health and Human Services, was a badge of honor to each graduate. It symbolized an achievement hard-earned through hundreds of hours of study, countless drills, numerous practice sessions, and seemingly endless lectures. This moment, this piece of paper, was the long-awaited payoff.

All of Chance's previous accomplishments; those Boy Scout first aid merit badges, the Red Cross safety courses; were now a distant

169

memory. No longer would he rely on the rudimentary techniques he had learned over the years. These new EMTs were equipped with cutting-edge medical technology and clinical skills far beyond anything he had imagined. They were ready to deliver care faster, cleaner, safer, and with more precision than any traditional ambulance service had ever provided. This was the dawn of a new era in professional pre-hospital care, now officially under the banner of Emergency Medical Services.

Chance spent countless hours driving up and down Interstate-16, between Savannah and Statesboro, sometimes in the very late afternoon and often well into the night. Those long, lonesome drives could have been excruciating, but the only thing that kept him awake on the way back was the late-night talk show on his AM radio. The signal from WBT in Charlotte, North Carolina, came in crystal clear most nights on 1110 AM. The program was always thoughtful, informative, and entertaining, offering a welcome distraction from the humdrum of the highway.

In his mind, Chance had envisioned a very different life as an EMT or paramedic. He expected to work in a pristine hospital emergency room or maybe join a glossy, well-organized fire department rescue squad, much like those heroic scenes on TV shows like *Emergency!*, *Medical Center*, or the like. He was 18, the year was 1975, and the world was full of possibilities. His future seemed as bright and promising as the headlights shining down the road ahead. Or, so he thought.

In actuality, he found himself caught in something of a limbo between his aspirations and the reality of the moment. Here he was - a fresh, newly graduated, head-strong Emergency Medical Technician ready and eager to take on the world in delivering of the latest in care and treatment of the sick and injured - working as an "attendant" for a private ambulance service. The owner could care less about all that hype, get to the call fast, and the patient to the hospital. That's it!

Many days he spent just transporting sick people from nursing homes to their clinic appointments, sometimes to the emergency room, other times picking a body up from the morgue and transporting it to one of several funeral homes. He found himself sorely disappointed, often pouting like a child with a broken toy because he was hampered in testing his newfound skills in this place with this employer. It simply wasn't fair, not an affirmation of his achievements or talents. But on this hot, sticky humid Saturday night in August, it would not be long before his whole outlook would change – drastically.

At 9:30 p.m., right on the nose, just as he was polishing off a plate of homemade pasta, the police monitor in the front room of the ambulance service office exploded to life. An ear-piercing high/low tone came across the monitor quickly, followed by the voice of a clearly excited dispatcher.

"EMS unit 1 and EMS unit 2....President Street at Randolph. Signal 5 signal 30. Multiple victims reported, Rescue 6 enroute. Advise on the fire department."

Signal 5 was the police code for a traffic accident, signal 30 for injuries. This was some serious stuff. But this was <u>not</u> a call intended for Geldings Ambulance Service. This call for assistance was dispatched by the county police to the county EMS crews. To take this call meant to "jump" the dispatch and deny Chatham County revenue for the care and transport of these injured victims, profiting only from this private service.

Mr. Gelding stood up, pointed to four crew members, and instructed them, *"Hit it, boys! Get out there".*

Two of the well-dressed men hopped in that '68 Ford parked against the curb, flipped on the lights, hit that old rotating siren, and gunned the super-charged 351 engines down Habersham toward Henry. The other two, Chance and Stan, jumped into the freshly washed, highly polished, bright red Olds ambulance parked nose out in the alley. His partner floored the gas pedal; their heads and bodies violently thrust back against the seats.

Chance feverishly worked to fasten his seat belt while flipping every switch he could reach; lights, flashers, that new electronic siren.

"What happened to 'proceed with caution" and '15 miles an hour over the speed limit'?", he thought.

At that moment, the other important mantra of "remain calm" was just – gone!

Instead, he found himself experiencing an overabundance of nerves, excitement, and fear all in an instant – an *adrenaline over-load*.

Right behind them, less than a block away and closing fast, the large white silhouette of EMS unit 1 turned sharply off Drayton and onto Anderson Street.

Stan, a rather large, stout man with eyeglasses that looked like the bottom of a Coke bottle, buried his right foot in the floorboard. All four hundred horsepower of their Olds 98 lunged forward again, galloping down Anderson toward East Broad at full tilt . Right over his head, a pair of highly polished, double-horned speakers repeatedly pierced the night air with a gut-wrenching "WAH-WAH-WAH" warble. This thing sounded like something from a science-fiction movie blasting through the dark, near desolate streets, disrupting the still of the night. To bystanders, this rig was nothing more than a sudden streak of red and white and blur streaming by at break-neck speed: passing, then gone nearly as soon as they looked up.

The flashing lights, the speed, the sounds, the tension of the moment, all nearly overwhelming to Chance; he lay in there. At this moment, in this place, he found himself experiencing sheer panic for the first time in his life. But he didn't show it; at least, he thought he wasn't.

In training, the typical scenario for an automobile accident was two cars, maybe three, with two or three victims at the most. There were set protocols for specific conditions: closed and open chest wounds, closed and open or compound fractures, impaled objects, and critical spinal injuries. They spent hours and hours on repetitive drills, splinting, bandaging, and immobilizing mock patients for just this type of incident. They practiced cutting a victim from a vehicle using the Jaws of Life, a large and very heavy piece of equipment that cut doors and roofs off their stantions, spread bent or collapsed doors apart, and untangled crushed metal to free the bodies of mangled occupants. All of that, all of it, paled in comparison to this moment in time right now.

As the two units of Gelding ambulance arrived, so did the two EMS units and their crews. The scene was horrific.

In an instant of pure engineering inspiration, someone had once called these two masses of twisted and tangled metal, rubber, and cellulose *automobiles*. Here, before his inexperienced eyes, were two nearly unidentifiable masses of metal. In the middle of President Street was an older station wagon bearing a family of four returning from an afternoon at the beach. Down the hill, about 60 yards near McIntosh, was a yellow sports car. He couldn't make out what kind, occupied by two teenagers just joy riding on this still Saturday night.

Something or someone - maybe one of the teens, maybe a distraction of the man behind the wheel of the wagon – caused one of the drivers to twitch or one of the vehicles to zig instead of zag. Who cares? The result was the same. These two 2500 pounds of metal, traveling at least 40 miles an hour, suddenly and violently collided: head-on. Minutes before – just seconds before - six living, breathing, happy individuals were in a moment of joy, maybe laughter. Then, in the blink of an eye, each were instantaneously thrust into this nightmare out of the very depths of Hell, twisted and contorted metal, entangled limbs, blood and water, broken bones, and broken glass.

The strong smell of gasoline enveloped the scene; the odor of blood, bowels, and motor oil burned his nostrils and sickened his belly. To say that Chance was shaken would be a gross understatement. There was little need for the essential element of TRIAGE usually employed in these circumstances. Only two categories of victims were present here; the dead and the dying. Two of the crew with EMS vomited as they approached the station wagon.

A small child, maybe 4 or 5 years old, had been trapped in the back seat: tangled in the very device meant to save its life, strangled to death by the nylon belt. Firemen freed its body just as sparks threatened to ignite the explosive liquid leaking from under the car. Some ten feet from the passenger's side of the vehicle, ejected on impact, the baby's young mother was lying in the road. She was obviously dead from an open chest wound. An older brother lay nearby, his little legs bent in opposite directions from open fractures to both thighs. Only partially conscious and breathing erratically, he was quickly attended to by the crew from EMS Unit 2. They covered his wounds, secured him to a backboard, whisked him aboard their vehicle, and sped away. The dad had died on impact, his chest crushed by the steering wheel and then impaled by the column.

What happened to the near-sterile sanctity of the well-triaged, well-organized movement and treatment of these people? Where was all the order he had expected, the organization of starting intravenous fluids and neatly splinting simple fractured bones, minor cuts and abrasions?

THIS was unimaginable.

Dazed and shaken, Chance and Stan turned their focus to the chaos unfolding at the bottom of the hill. What was once a sleek Mazda Miata was now a twisted, mangled mess, nearly unrecognizable. The vehicle had flipped and crumpled beyond repair. Rescue 6, the other unit, spent over an hour battling to free the bodies from the wreckage using the Jaws of Life, cutting through the jagged metal like a butcher slicing through bone. It wasn't enough. The boys in the car were gone. A half-empty bottle of Malibu rum lay on the floorboard, a chilling testament to the reckless decision that led them here.

The harsh screech of an ignored pager sliced through the grim quiet as the coroner confirmed the inevitable. The crowd of bystanders, their bright car lights flickering like a swarm of fireflies, quickly descended upon the scene. News crews arrived, cameras flashing, eager to capture the horror. The bodies of the mother and child from the back seat were loaded into the other EMS truck. It seemed the night had no room for anyone but the dead. Geldings wouldn't be getting any of these patients.

Back home the next morning, Chance stood in his living room, staring at the clean, nearly untouched yellow textbook he had once cherished. Now, it seemed no more than an overpriced first-aid manual. Useless. Just like the oxygen tank with no tubing, no mask, no purpose. The grief of the night before weighed heavily on him, leaving him feeling empty, betrayed by the harsh realities of his work. Anger bubbled up inside him at the callousness of the bystanders, the onlookers who had treated the scene like some kind of morbid spectacle. He had trained for this. He had studied for this. But there were no opportunities to apply the skills he'd worked so hard to master. There were no IV fluids to be administered, no splints to apply, no vital signs to measure, no comforting drugs to offer, and no oxygen to deliver.

Instead, he stood there, feeling like a ghost in the room, knowing that all his expertise and training had been rendered irrelevant in the face of death's cold indifference.

What had he truly learned, he wondered, if none of it had mattered when it came time to put it into action?

The words of Mr. Gelding that night towering over him in his crisply pressed white shirt, seersucker pants, and Florsheim wing-tips stung his ears and angered him beyond reproach when he uttered;

"Young man, you don't need all that training you went through to do this work. All you need is a clean sheet to change that stretcher and a white towel to wipe your hands. Welcome to the real world, my boy."

"What an arrogant ass", he thought.

This insensitivity from a man whose highlight of the day was dispatching his ambulance, lights and siren, to pick up a box or Russell-Stover candies from the drug store down the block and deliver them, full tilt, to his girlfriend across town. A former mortician, owner of several very successful local businesses, always well-dressed and well-groomed, the old man waited several hours in the afternoon for the opportunity to show his hidden level of perversion in the early evening. This guy would walk up behind a certain young crew member, have someone a significant distraction, pull out his rather large penis, stick it in the boy's pocket, and piss all over his leg. Sick bastard.

Chance resigned his position with this company right there. Not a problem, he had already applied and been interviewed for the county service.

As I mentioned earlier, Chance was hired on the spot with EMS after that harrowing incident with Geldings. It marked the beginning of his involvement in a groundbreaking effort to provide pre-hospital care to the sick and injured, transforming the way emergency services were delivered. The program became a vital, revolutionary presence in the county, and thanks to a close collaboration with Memorial Hospital, it quickly gained momentum.

The doctors and nurses at Memorial played a crucial role in the training of EMS personnel, and with additional funding from the State, the local medical board approved the first specialized emergency care units focused on cardiac emergencies. This was the dawn of a new era in pre-hospital care, and it was nothing short of transformative. The teams were trained to intervene immediately in cases of heart attacks and strokes, delivering life-saving care in those crucial early moments that could mean the difference between life and death. They were there to save those precious minutes when every second mattered; moments that could prevent irreparable damage to the heart muscle and brain tissue.

EMS was now working in full force in Savannah, and the crews, including Chance, quickly became the unsung heroes of the city. The work they did was groundbreaking, and lives were saved every single day thanks to their skills and dedication. The efforts of these men and women were recognized and celebrated, earning them the admiration and respect of the community. In the world of emergency medicine, they were a new breed; trained, focused, and capable of providing the kind of care that made a real difference.

***

Easy Distractions, Too Much Time

After Kathy left, Chance was a bit shell-shocked by the whole affair. Mom and dad raised the boys with the understanding that marriage lasted for life, so this was a major failure for him. Divorce also left him with the entire responsibility of a new mobile home and the payment, and he found himself quite lonely and depressed most of the time. By now, he was also working with a partner for the county EMS, 24 hours on-duty and 48 hours off. This schedule left him with a considerable amount of time on his hands: too much time to waste, far too often.

In 1976 Savannah was experiencing a surge of "girlie bars," places where young women danced topless for expensive fake "cocktails" and tips. The girls performed their sultry, suggestive moves for men while they drank; the more they drank, the more they tipped. Sometimes the guys would pay extra for a special attention, called a "lap dance," where the girl would get particularly erotic during the performance, really rubbing against his erection and teasing him with the false hope that she might go home with him. Chance found himself taken in by the temptation of these women, and he spent a fair amount of time and money in these dives. Although only 19, dating was neither comfortable nor an attractive option for him, even though the loneliness was nearly overwhelming at times. He never got into drugs, but the sexual arousal of these encounters and the increasing frustration of being unable to satisfy his urges normally led Chance into the world of porn and masturbation.

One of his favorite places to hang out then was the Korean Village in East Savannah, and he became enamored with a tall, very sexy blonde named Teresa. This dancer seemed to always single him out within minutes of his arrival, and she'd usher him down to the edge of the stage for a first-hand experience. She gets a couple of dollars from him for the jukebox, picks something appropriate, and returns to the stage with this plush white carpet, wearing heels and nothing else but a tiny G-string bottom. Once in a while, she'd disappear to the back dressing room and come back out in a short T-shirt, and that G-string would be sheer, hiding absolutely nothing from Chance's lusting eyes. And then, she'd dance and gyrate her hips, up and down, spreading her legs as if giving her show for only him. To Chance, there was no one else in the place in those moments. He lusted for this young woman with all he could imagine. Many nights he'd hang around, and somehow, she'd slink out the backdoor before they'd close, again leaving him to go home alone, frustrated.

Chance recalled those girlie pics he'd seen in the bottom of his Dad's dresser years before and the drawings that seemed so life-like. He'd learned to draw as a child, but usually, his work was bowls of fruit, anatomical drawings for school, plans for building something, and the like. So, it was only a slight leap in technique to take carbon paper, trace the outlines of the girls' pictures in the magazines, and then pencil the images onto plain white paper. From these tracings, Chance quickly learned that he could draw these girls in any pose he could imagine, later even to appear to be actively engaging him. Over time, he'd find himself devoting far too much time to this new habit to the point of obsession with his "girls." He eventually acquired an extensive collection of drawings that he'd view in the privacy of his home to satisfy his natural urges, unaware or unappreciative of how unnatural this behavior was quickly becoming; or eventually problematic.

Occasionally, he'd meet a dancer at one of the clubs and take her home. They'd have great sex (sometimes not so great), and he'd feel so much more of a man, normal in his desire and the satisfaction from real physical contact. For a time, he'd even forget about the drawing habit and spend more effort in the prolific dating scene of the times. In 1976, a nightclub called Stonehenge was the quintessential discotheque in town. Chance would meet up with one or more of his former classmates; they'd dance and drink the night away; sometimes, he'd get lucky and score. Other times, he'd leave early and wind up at one of the bars looking for a cheap thrill with a lap dance instead.

***

One night, he met a dancer named Tonya; she was tall, with shapely legs, long jet-black hair, and very attractive. She revealed that she was new in town and had no place to stay. Chance had a spare, empty room at the far end of his home, so he didn't think before offering to rent the room to her. Concerned about unwanted men in his home, she agreed that she would not entertain anyone with his express permission at any time; besides, Tonya professed to be a lesbian. When he asked her, she accepted the invitation and moved in later that same night. One morning, very early, she made sure he knew how much she appreciated his gesture by sharing her body with him for several hours.

Things seemed to go well for a while. She seemed genuinely trustworthy to him, considering everything he thought he knew about her, and he found himself leaving her to attend to his property while he worked his shifts in the ambulance.

One morning he came home after a long shift, took his usual shower, drank a cup of coffee, and laid down in his room to take a nap. Around 9:00, he was startled by a sudden **BOOM**, like something suddenly hit the end of the house or fell. He lay in bed for several minutes, waiting to see if anything else happened, then got up, slipped on his pants and robe, and entered the living room. After a few minutes, he put on a pot of coffee and walked out to get the paper.

Sitting at the table, drinking his coffee, Tonya's bedroom door suddenly opened and closed. Within a couple of moments, this thin, short-statured man emerged from down the hall wearing only his underwear and a wife-beater. He came bouncin' down the hall and promptly announced himself.

"Hi, I'm Scott. You must be Chance", he said.

"Yeah", Chance said, *"...d'you hear somethin' fall earlier?"*

Scott laughed. *"Oh, yeah, that was just me. I think I touched something that really turned her on. She screamed and slapped me, and I fell off the bed"*.

Good grief, he thought; he could not allow this to continue. Enough already. Tonya offered to find another place to stay and assured Chance that Scott would be gone within an hour. Chance had business to take care of in town anyway and agreed with the offer.

Right next door lived a girl Chance had gone to school that lived two blocks behind him most of his life. Her name was Demi Tidwell. He'd given her his number when he first moved in, just in case there was an emergency of any kind with his property. She lived there with her husband and their 3-year-old little girl.

Around 3 pm, Chance returned home to find Scott's car still in the driveway. Walking up the concrete stones toward the front door, he suddenly caught Demi standing at the backdoor, the 3-year-old in her arms, weeping softly. At one point, he walked across the yard and thought he saw the curtains in his living room rustle as if someone had been looking out. For the next 20 minutes, Demi had his undivided attention, and she relayed a horrific incident that happened while he was gone.

Sometime around noon, she saw Tonya leave the house, get in her car with some boxes of clothes and drive off. He thought she saw someone looking out through the curtains of his house a couple of minutes later but couldn't be sure. About an hour later, with her little one taking a nap, she slipped on a pair of shorts and a little halter top, then went outside to hang some clothes on the line. After a few minutes or so, she felt like someone was watching her; to her horror, there was.

Over her shoulder, she looked back toward Chance's front door, and there, standing in the window with his pants around his knees, Scott was standing at the window – masturbating. She screamed and ran back inside the house. Her first inclination was to call the police, but she worried that it might cause problems for Chance. She'd just wait and take up the issue with him when he got home.

Chance apologized for the incident and the risk that Scott posed. He then turned sharply and walked briskly up to and inside the house. Adult magazines from his collection and several of his better drawings were strewn out on the dining table and kitchen floor. A couple of moments later, he heard the toilet flush, and Scott came down the hall and into the kitchen.

"Hi!.....I...."

Chance hit that boy so hard - right in the mouth - that he thought he may have broken his neck in addition to knocking out all his front teeth.

Scott flew back against the counter, striking the back of his head against the cabinet, and fell to the floor. Chance went over, picked him up by the scruff of his neck, and pushed the squatty little man against the wall – his feet no longer touching the floor.

"Unless you want me to kill you right here and now, you have 10 minutes to get your shit and get the hell out of my house!"

Scott just nodded, and Chance slowly lowered him to the floor. It took 10 minutes, maybe 5, for this pervert to gather his things and disappear.

Chance looked around at the filth spread on his floors and table; tears came to his eyes, and he thought, *"What in hell have I done?"*

He fell to his knees and prayed for what seemed like an hour. He prayed for forgiveness, repentance, and wisdom to renew his life and faith. Feeling the Spirit and a full sense of hope, he knew what to do.

It took an hour or so to put everything in a good-sized plastic trash bag, and he cleaned his home of every piece of pornography in his home that very day. He couldn't just dispose of that mess in a public trash receptacle or a dumpster, but he knew a place to dispose of it completely.

He had a friend who still worked at a grocery store downtown and had a flash incinerator on the property. After several calls, his friend agreed to let him bring the bag in, and they watched as this hellacious collection burned into thin air, appropriately, in smoke.

Several months passed; Chance got used to living by himself; at least, that's what he told himself. He was lonely. What a horrendous mistake he'd made with Katy. Sitting around the house on his off time, he only listened to old country records, which were so depressing. He did a little D.J. work spinning records between band sets at the September Club down the road. He just wasn't used to living alone.

The nail in his coffin came one morning on his way to work at the EMS site next door to the county police station on Hodgson Memorial. He was driving a used 1970 Dodge Coronet and traveling down Montgomery Crossroads when he thought he heard something grinding in the rear. Over the last six months, he'd replaced the universal joints on the drive shaft, first the front, then the rear, twice. The last time the rear went out, it stuck him on the side of Quacco Road until he could walk down to a parts store, borrow a few tools and buy the part, install it on the shoulder of the road – one hell-of-a mess. He probably should have sold the car after the first set went out, but it drove well, and he liked how it looked.

He got to Mall Blvd and stopped at the light. It was 7:40 am, and he had to be at the station by 7:55. He was one block away from his destination. The light turned green; he pressed the gas, and the car lunged forward a bit; there was a loud BANG, and the rear of the car bolted upright about 3 feet and slammed back down on the pavement. She wouldn't move. The engine ran, but the transmission wasn't engaging.

Frustrated and pissed off, he opened the driver's door, leaned way over, and looked underneath the car. Yep, the front part of the drive shaft was lying on the street and stuck in a pothole – the only pothole for miles around – in the middle of Hodgson Memorial Boulevard at 7:45 on a Wednesday morning. Embarrassing.

Luckily his partner came along about 10 minutes later, helped him wire the drive shaft back up, and they pushed the car to the station. He paid for a tow truck to take it away and sold it for salvage the next morning. Then he accepted an offer to move back home and sold the mobile home he and Kathy had bought just one year before.

***

Though the grandeur or the glamour, maybe, of working as a paramedic – a would-be labeled *first responder* – diminished greatly in the boredom of playing cards and watching TV reruns while waiting for a call, the glitz and glitter returned abruptly every time that alert tone sounded and dispatch called the unit Chance was assigned to. That adrenaline rush was both intoxicating and addictive – for day one – and it never got old. The downtown unit, Unit 1, was at Bull and 31st Streets. The was the busiest site in the county, sometimes running as many as 20 calls in a single 24-hour span. The next busiest site was Unit 2, down behind St. Joseph's Hospital and near the Forrest River bridge. Unit 3 was at Travis Field, covering all the county's west side, and Unit 4 ran out of the Island Fire Department on Johnny Mercer Blvd, Wilmington Island. During summer months, this ambulance crew was stationed on Tybee Island; man was *that* ever boring.

But occasionally, all hell would break loose, and emergency work in the county would become anything but glamorous.

***

Rollin' On the River

Working in EMS undoubtedly changed Chance's perspective on life and his views on the people he encountered daily. In those early days, there was a system in place to help medics navigate the tricky world of liability, particularly when it came to deciding who should ride and who shouldn't when someone called for assistance. It became clear early on that not every call was a real emergency.

Medicaid patients were often the source of frustration. Many would call simply because they wanted a ride to the hospital or their clinic appointment. The county, however, wasn't interested in turning their emergency medical services into an expensive taxi service for the indigent. When they received such calls, the medics would arrive, take vital signs, perform a physical exam, and then relay the information via radio to a physician on the other end of the line. The doctor would review the details, make a diagnosis, and advise whether the call truly constituted an emergency. If not, the medics would leave, no transport necessary.

There were, of course, far too many instances where the ambulance would arrive, only to find the patient sitting on their front porch, suitcase in hand and Medicaid card ready. In those cases, the lead medic would simply cancel the call, mark it as non-emergency, and get ready for the next one. There was no point in wasting resources when there was no real emergency to address. Sometimes, to ensure that procedures were being followed properly, the Medical Director would ride along with the downtown unit to observe firsthand how the medics were handling the calls and how the public was responding to their services.

One Sunday morning, Dr. Matt popped into the downtown site, Unit 1, with his medical bag and small backpack in hand and announced he was there *"to ride with you guys for a couple of hours."* Well, it was Sunday, and things were very quiet for about three hours. Just when he thought he'd just load up and go home, the two-phase tone on the card table blasted to life:

"EMS Unit 1 and EMS Unit 4....on the Carolina side of the Talmadge Bridge, signal 5, signal 30 involving a semi-truck and a motorcycle...Rescue One enroute. Timed out 1330".

That sure didn't sound good: two units to an accident scene, motorcycle, and semi. But Dr. Matt was now stoked and nearly ran to the ambulance in anticipation. They pulled out, lights flashing and sirens blaring, and turned up Drayton Street toward downtown; Matt had his face sticking through the access window between the front and the patient care box so he could see.

Unit 4 had to come from Wilmington Island and would take some time to arrive. EMS 3 was on the move to get some lunch, and somewhere around the traffic circle on Bay Street, they took the call from Unit 4 because they were much closer. The police monitor in the cab of Unit 1 was now going wild with vehicles en route, units being dispatched, and officers directing incoming traffic to the scene: chaotic.

Oglethorpe traffic was backed up to Bull Street because traffic was at a standstill going up the bridge. There was no traffic from the other direction, though, because they had all been blocked at the accident scene from the other end and across the expanses of the river. Once they got to the center rise of the bridge, they could see traffic backed up for miles into South Carolina.

They also got their first look at the horror they would dive into.

"EMS 1 10-23 (meant they were on scene)".

Within just a moment they were joined by EMS 3, Rescue One, a pumper from Savannah Fire Department, and everybody got busy.

***

It looked like the semi, a fairly new, bright green Peterbilt long-nose pulling a reefer (refrigerated trailer), was coming down the Carolina side of the bridge when a couple on a big Harley-Davidson cruiser pulled out to pass. Witnesses said the bike had been following an old Buick station wagon for a few miles as they came up the causeway over Back River, a secondary channel on the other side of Hutchinson Island.

The station wagon was filled with a Black family of six (Mom, Dad, three kids 6 to 10 years old, and an infant) returning to Savannah from a family gathering in Hardeeville. The couple on the bike was a middle-aged Dad and his 16-year-old daughter just making a loop on his new bike in Port Wentworth, through the Savannah Wildlife Preserve, into Carolina near Hardeeville cut-off on US-17 Bypass, and back south on US-17 into Savannah.

***

The rider on the bike must have simply misjudged his distance, not been paying attention, or something seriously distracted him to make him think he could pass that wagon on the Causeway before the truck barreling down the bridge got to him.

By the way, that stretch across the river - NO PASSING zone.

Troopers guesstimated the semi was traveling 55-60 mph but couldn't tell for sure – there were no skid marks, except those streaks of rubber on the road surface from the sudden jolt of impact. Pretty much the same story with the motorcycle. It looked like he tried to cut back just before impact but way too little, way too late.

That station wagon full of family, and that unsecured baby on his mother's lap sucking a bottle, were drawn into the collision as the trailer jack-knifed and tore the roof away. It decapitated both parents instantly. Two of the three children were ejected and lay on the pavement, dead. One was in the very back compartment under a piece of the roof, missing one of his arms and part of his face; he was dead.

Chance, Dr. Matt, one of the engineers on the fire truck, and the lead medic on EMS 4 all vomited several times at the initial site of the catastrophe. So did that young Carolina Trooper working the accident. By now, there were dozens of rescue personnel, police officers, tow trucks, fire personnel and equipment, television news crews, and bystanders everywhere.

US-17 was covered with fluids from the truck, the car and that bike all running downhill together: fluids mixed with pieces of brain matter, blood, body fluids, and baby formula.

The truck driver survived, horribly shaken, sitting in the middle of the road, his face in his hands, crying uncontrollably. His wife was still unaware of his involvement in the accident. She'd have to wait until the next day because he retired to a dingy room in a motel at the foot of the bridge to reflect on the event and the value of his own life. He'd need serious counseling for some time.

The driver of the motorcycle was dead, crushed on impact by the front of the rig and his bat-wing fairing. The right handlebar was impaled in his chest, his head nearly torn away. The passenger, his pretty young blonde daughter, dressed in shorts and a tank top, was now a tangled mass of distorted limbs. Her head was missing.

That was the second gut-wrenching curiosity about this horrific scene; the first was when rescue crews realized they couldn't locate that baby from the station wagon. He was nowhere to be found. The Marine Rescue Squad even sent divers to scour the river for its little body; they found nothing.

Just as they were pulling the bike out from under the fifth wheel of that truck, a black helmet came slowly rolling down the bridge toward the Carolina Trooper standing in the road. As it rolled; end over end; the clear facemask, now shattered and missing, revealed the battered face of that pretty little blonde; her ponytail flipping against the pavement from underneath the helmet's confines with each rotation.

The coroner became violently ill this time.

Chance, the other medics on the scene, several firefighters, and Dr. Matt took several days off to reflect on this tragedy. Matt never asked to ride again.

Three weeks later, South Carolina Law Enforcement Division (SLED) investigators reported they had located that infant. Someone in the salvage yard was inspecting the nose of the tractor, trying to locate a still-tracking GPS device. The inspector spotted something flesh-colored through the grill. That baby; a fully developed little boy about six months old, still in his diaper and onesie; was pressed through a screen behind the front grill and the radiator.

One sunny Sunday afternoon. Three destroyed, tangled masses of metal, glass, and rubber. Eight dead. One surviving driver, in a manner of speaking, now trapped inside overwhelming guilt for something entirely beyond his control. God took all those souls to their appointed resting place in the same instant to wait to greet Jesus. At least Chance was convinced they made it all together: simultaneously, lifted to heaven's gate at once. No passing.

***

Enter .... Eve

With 48 hours to kill twice a week, Chance found himself frequently searching for something else to occupy his time. He'd always been interested in radio, and one day, right out of nowhere, he got word that a little AM station downtown was looking for part-time help on the weekends. He interviewed, then auditioned, and got the job working as a radio announcer, a D.J., on weekends at WGGT. The station manager offered him the opportunity to learn the business, how to work the soundboards, check the transmitter, play a few records here and there, announce the weather forecast, and monitor a 4-hour pre-recorded broadcast. Easy peasy. After a couple of weeks, he got the hang of talking into the microphone, how to control his voice quality and diction, got used to hearing himself in the headsets, and developed a "style" all his own. To his listeners, however many there were, he was Jay Hanson.

Radio station WGGT played country music in Savannah. The year was 1977. *Star Wars, Close Encounters of the Third Kind*, and *Saturday Night Fever* were monster hits in theatres. Burt Reynolds, Sally Field, and Jackie Gleason blasted across the nation's movie screens with *Smokey and the Bandit*, and country music was hot. Artists like Eddie Rabbit, Johnny Duncan, Ronnie Milsap, Donna Fargo, The Oak Ridge Boys, and Alabama came into their own and were all very big that year. What a thrill it was for Chance to spin those vinyl 45s from the station playlist, cue those records, then start it at just the right moment to keep the music tight and on time. He introduced the Bellamy Brothers to Savannah one weekend and debuted the band's new single, *"Let Your Love Flow,"* to his listeners.

Chance picked up extra shifts as often as he could and soon became quite good on the air. In fact, he found himself a bit of a celebrity in the community and did a little casual dating from time to time.

The crews with the ambulance service didn't even know he was a radio personality, and he kept things that way for a long time.

Unfortunately, there was still a bit too much time to waste and too many of those topless bars in town he still hadn't explored yet. Boppin' around downtown one night after being sorely disappointed by the "talent" at the Emerald Lounge a couple of blocks away, he found himself downtown and waltzed into the first place with good music he found. Where he stopped at 110 E. Congress Street was The Gator Lounge.

The usual assortment of pretty young ladies with long legs, spiked heels, and tiny little outfits strolled the floors and gyrated against the big chrome pole on stage. A long wooden bar ran the length of the wall as he walked in; mirrors lined the walls, and the lights were little more than an afterthought.

Several seedy old men were seated throughout the bar, some with girls sitting right up close or in their laps, teasing them out of another "champagne cocktail."

These drinks were $5 a piece, and the girls expected the guys to tip both the waitress and the bartender with each refill. They contained neither champagne and nor cocktail. They were simply fruit juice and a splash of soda. But I will tell you that a horny man with lust on his mind, looking at these scantily clad and very attractive young women with long, shapely legs sure suffers a severe tug on his wallet. It doesn't get easier when she accidently "brushes" against that bulge she's caused in his trouser, either.

The place smelled like sour fruit juice, stale alcohol, urine, and the fragrance of cheap perfume mixed with sweat and bad breath. In an instant, he experienced the unmistakable waft of pheromones: the scent of a woman.

It was nearly overwhelming, and he found himself terribly excited at the night's prospects.

There he sat, alone at a table in the middle of a darkened floor, waiting for someone to come over and offer to take his order.

The top of the little table was sticky, and the chair wobbled gently against the uneven wooden floor.

A very tall, very leggy black girl was on stage, and she certainly was working that pole.

An older but still young woman was behind the bar. Shapely with short brown hair, hazel eyes, a big smile, and a rack to write home about she was easy to watch. When he caught her eye she signaled for someone to attend to him.

In the shadows at the end of the bar he could barely make out the silhouette of a rather large man dressed all in black seated up behind a turntable. He guessed that was the bouncer. It wouldn't be a problem for him; he knew how to behave.

Then, out of the corner of his eye, he saw her.

Out of the shadows, through the smokey haze and fake smoke from the DJs fog machine he could see a short but very shapely figure walking across the floor with a slow and sultry stroll. As the dim light slowly cast a subtle glow on the gentle curves of her body, he could just begin to make out her short hair and her legs. She looked to be a little over 5 feet, but at least 3 feet of that was leg.

The music became more "rhythmic," more beat intensive as the DJ placed the needle down on the song "Black Velvet."

The spotlight suddenly pointed to mid-stage, and now reflected off the huge mirror on the wall and illuminating this beauty in all her glory.

Her short, medium brown hair curled inward just above her shoulders. She wore silver hoops in her ears that sparkled like rings of diamond against the smooth, silky texture of her neck. Those eyes; like a cat. Her eyes opened wide. A big, brown center like huge buck-eyes against gleaming white globes, and she looked into his eyes from the shadows like she was searching for his soul.

A small, thin silver herringbone necklace hung loose around the base of her neck and gently turning into the upper cleft of her breasts. The gleaming necklace immediately drew his eyes to the prominent rise and fall of her small but obviously firm globes. The thin fabric of her blouse barely concealed fully erect, eraser-sized nipples.

He was mesmerized. As she inched ever closer, the detail height-ened his anticipation, not to mention that suddenly and not surpris-ing the rise in the pressure against his zipper.

She wore a short, tightly fitted tank top that buttoned down the middle and exposed a firmly toned mid-drift. She left three buttons open from the top and only a single white pearl at the bottom to barely secure its treasures. Not much else encompassed those firm puppies except his imagination. If he thought there was even the slightest hint of anything under that top, she moved ever so slightly to allow a narrow sliver of light to cross her torso. That move subtly but effectively exposed the dark circle of her left breast and areola, about the size of a quarter.

She looked down at the light across her breast, then up at him as if to say she knew exactly what just she revealed to him.

The more he watched, the more *she* seemed to enjoy the game. As she moved more he noticed the material over her breasts began to heave gently. He hadn't imaged those pert nipples could press any tighter against that fabric – until now.

She had a single piercing that he could just barely see; a simple gold bead through the lower border of her belly button. The top of those little white shorts covered just enough to tease.

Her very tight, bright white terry cloth shorts hung low around her waist. A single cotton cord at the top left open untied, only the light weight of the garment and its firm cling to her waist and hips hide her candy. The snug fit of the legs rode high against the perfect shape of her thighs, barely covering the perfect turn in the upper, inner cleft of leg where it met the lower recesses of her mound. Not much more than the seam covered the fullness of her wound.

Playfully, fully enjoying her show and its obvious effects on him, she slowly turned to back to him revealing the finest, tightest little bum he had seen since high school. He could now completely see those cheeks were as firm as a fully inflated ball - high and tight. She was driving him crazy, and she knew it. To let him know she acknowledged the play she even kicked her chin skyward a little and flipped her hair like a mare enticing a stallion into her pen. Then, to make absolute sure she had him dead to rights, this beauty slowly turned to face him again, this time lifting her heel to the seat of the chair and turning ever so slightly in the opposite direction. The movement or her leg and torso opened the fold at the top of her leg as those little shorts pulled slightly up and inward. Chance got a glimpse of the tiniest G-string he'd ever seen riding tightly within lips the of her little treasure. Nothing else – nothing.

The lower half of her firmly developed mound was now fully exposed, for just a fleeting moment, revealing the freshly shaved peach begging him continue the dance to tastes all the pleasures it offered.

This pretty little thing was <u>HOT</u>!!

A pair of white patent leather, single-strap heels completed her ensemble, making her calves "pop" to attention when she walked. A dainty, silver chain encircled her left ankle drawing his eyes to her nicely sculpted legs. A black lacey garter caressed her firm, full upper right thigh. This was one incredibly sexy gal.

He guessed she was probably no more than 18, maybe 19. That was fine since he was 20 at the time, about to turn 21.

Damn! What a sight for sore eyes.
It wasn't love; it sure was pretty serious lust, though.

Without speaking a word, never mentioning her name, she walked over to his table.

She reached out, slid the empty chair up next to his, and slowly, purposefully slithered down into it. Her leg brushed gently against his as she batted those long lashes at him and softly whispered, *"Excuse me. Is this seat taken?"*

She reached out for his hand, placed it on her supple thigh, gently rubbing her bare flesh, smiled, then signaled for a girl to come to the table.

Holy, moley...... as if he need any MORE of a turn-on!
This woman was some kinda' hot!

He stood slightly from his seat, stretched out his hand as if to take hers. She reached out, gently pushing it to the side, and leaned into him. In a soft, breathy tone, she whispered in his ear, "I'm Eve." She sat down.

He stood there for a second or two, not knowing what to make of her yet, then slowly lowered himself into his chair.

"Extraordinary," he thought to himself.

He ordered the champagne cocktail she asked for and they talked. It was small talk, but every once in a while she'd reach over to caress the back of his hand. After a couple of hours, she changed that gesture to stroking the length of one of his much larger fingers with her long, slender nails.

He thought she was just so erotic, so... sensual: unlike almost any other woman he had been with or around. This girl knew how to work her charms and certainly how to keep him buying those cocktails.

Her sister, Selena, was the cute brunette he'd eyeballed earlier behind the bar. These girls had worked this joint since she was just turning 16. The owner was a family "friend" who called himself "helping the girls" take care of their mom. Eve was single, though she most certainly had plenty of suitors and potentials lining the bar every night. Here tonight, at this moment, these two appeared to have struck a chord of some type in each other that was palpable. Or should I say, at the very least, now pulsating. At least from Chance's perspective.

At closing time, and over $100 later, he offered to take her to breakfast. She accepted on the condition that her sister could join them; okay, he thought, whatever.

They ate breakfast, and he drove the girls back to the bar where they were parked. He didn't carry her anywhere else that first night, partly because the opportunity simply didn't present itself; mostly because he lived back home with his parents right then and didn't even have one red cent left from the night's events to even think about a motel room. The second time he saw her would be a completely different story.

Right Time, Wrong Place

Eve was the youngest of 5 kids. She had four sisters – Donna, Allison, Rebecca, and Selena. Her mom, Glenus, had terrible emphysema and she coughed frequently, near incessantly at times. Despite the ashen grey tone of her skin and the thick, pale yellow sputum she coughed up several times a day she continued to smoke non-filtered cigarettes like an old wood stove.

This pretty little thing, two of the sisters and mom lived in a low-rent housing project just off the main drag in Port Wentworth, a tiny suburb just west of Savannah. Four adults were sharing this two-bedroom apartment with a single living room, a tiny eat-in kitchen, a two-burner gas stove, a single-floor furnace, and an antique coil refrigerator nearly as old as Glenus.

There were clothes strewn everywhere. The living room looked like a glass menagerie full of old glassware (cups, glasses, ashtrays, figurines, plates) and junk from all over, mostly flea markets, and many items with the small handwritten tags still adhering to their dusty surfaces.

Glenus turned out to be one serious hoarder.

A TV and a heavily stained denim couch were in the rooms off to one side of the living room. One of her sisters, I think it was Allison, was in the side room, huddled under a couple of blankets with a much older man. He was drunk, the room was freezing, and they definitely weren't sleepin'.

Eve took him by the hand and led him down a narrow hallway into a back room. Like the others, this room was deep with old clothes, blankets, towels, stuffed toys, broken and discarded pieces of furniture, and junk. Around the corner, up against a wall, was a hastily made double bed; two pillows with dingy white cases, and an old patchwork quilt that probably *was* as old as her mom covered lumpy, dusty mattress.

Tonight, Eve was wearing a pair of tights and an old Lynard Skynard concert T-shirt. No sooner did they reach that dank, chilly room but she peeled that outfit off in less than a minute and quickly crawled under those covers.

Suddenly his whole outlook on the situation changed dramatically; he might as well have been in the Taj Mahal, and, damn, that room was becoming warmer by the minute.

Out of his jeans and T-shirt, he slipped under those covers as well.

She peeked under the blanket, looked up at him and whispered, *"Ah, ah"*, pointing to his briefs.

He slipped them off and hastily threw them to the side in the direction of his clothes.

Eve reached down, took his hand, and put it on something very moist ... and very warm. She turned into him, moaning softly now, and gently nibbled his ear. Then she slid her hand down his belly and around what *she* anticipated. Neither of the lovers were disappointed.

Over the next few weeks he spent several nights with her in that setting, somewhere between a hoard nest and a vagabond camp, noticing a little more each time: more trash and filth under more damp, partly mildewed clothing and blankets. More plates, pots, pans, and dried food and mold in the sink and on the counter. In the bathroom, the toilet and the tub likely never got wiped out, let alone cleaned or sanitized.

There was food in the refrigerator that had gone bad days or weeks before. When he moved a plate or bumped a picture on the wall dozens of tiny red German cockroaches scurried in every direction. Hell, they were even in the freezer and the microwave.

One night, Chance's mom dropped by to check on him because she hadn't seen or heard from him in a few days. This was certainly not like her son to do this sort of thing. After all, he was living with her and she was, understandably, worried: where was he bathing, getting a change of clothes, or even eating?

Years later she confessed to him that she regretted not just killing him right there that night. She couldn't believe he would lay his head in such filth.

And mama was right; he couldn't continue to do this.

So, he married Eve and moved her into a nicely furnished, very clean, double-wide mobile home in South Savannah.

Chance worked his shifts with EMS; she continued to B-drink for tips at the Gator until they closed their doors. They seemed to be happy, as far as Chance was concerned anyway, but he'd sometimes come home to find a note on the table telling him that she "needed to think."

She'd be gone a week or so, usually taking her mom to one of the sister's houses or one of her siblings places somewhere around the country. If never knew for several days where she'd wind up. There was family spread out like so many flies on soured watermelon: in Florida, Carolina, Tennessee, New York, Virginia, and Louisiana. When Glenus got tired of staying here or there, she'd call Eve, and Eve would go pick her up, take her where she wanted to go for the next few weeks or months at a time. This happened far too many times over the first couple of years. It began affecting his schedule, he couldn't concentrate on his duties, and it was showing on his performance evaluations.

Much to his chagrin, he now sought other options.

Chance's dad had been a police officer for a time, both for the city and later the county: maybe that was an option for change. Anything was open to discussion, and nothing was out of the question to save this bond with Eve that he wanted so genuinely, so deeply.

Maybe as a cop, he'd have regular shifts and make better money; they get into a routine and anything would certainly be a change of pace.

By this time, he'd also come to know many of the county police officers well and they were encouraging him to consider coming on the force. Unfortunately, the county policy required officers to be 23 years of age at the time of application.

Within a couple of months, as if by fate or through the graces of his guardian angel (or maybe just a gift of God) the Savannah Morning News ran an ad recruiting for the city police. He applied, they hired him, and he started the police academy within a couple of weeks.

Ten weeks later he completed the Academy and was a State-certified police officer.

Eve never seemed comfortable with that but they stayed together through the couple of years he was with the city police. Even still, she would continue to leave periodically weeks at a time without warning or apology on return as was her custom.

They moved into a comfortable apartment in Savannah Gardens. The rent was easy at just under $120 a month, and very comfortable because he was only making just over $8,800 a year. It wasn't long before he did get tired of coming in after a shift, just knowing she'd be there ready to enjoy time together, only to find a note again: a never-ending cycle of cat and mouse that was, by now, quickly waxing fatal for their marriage.

Now when they were together during those first few months, they were together. Mmm, yes, they were. As far as Chance was concerned his girl had the body of Venus. She was the perfect little package for him. Eve didn't need any special lingerie; whatever she wore was sexy to him. She'd come home, put on Aretha Franklin or Gladys Knight, dance around the house teasing him incessantly, and they'd end up entangled – in the bedroom, on the sofa, on top of the kitchen table, in the shower. Throw on Cheryl Lynn's "*Got To Be Real*" or The Emotions "*Best of My Love*," and this little thing would go wild.

Every now and then, Chance would invite or bring her mama over for a few days. She loved old music and they'd have coffee all day, sitting around going through his collection of vintage country music vinyl 45s and albums; Bill Monroe, Hank Williams, and lots of bluegrass. Eve would eventually find something to do outside or suddenly forget that she needed something from the store, disappear for a couple of hours, and return with little or nothing.

She'd bat those long lashes, look into his eyes with those big brown doe eyes, whisper that she thought he *"might need a cookie,"* and he would find a way to quickly pack things up and get Glenus back across town to her place before rushing back into Eve's waiting embrace. Those were some really hot nights, they just didn't that often or weren't quite strong enough to spark the baby machine. *That problem,* turned out to be a Godsend.

Chance tried so hard to be faithful to her, although she was gone with Mama more frequently than with him. He was a young, well-built police officer, not too bad looking; that uniform sure fit him well.

There is something, a great deal actually, to be said about women and their attraction to men in uniforms. The temptation was too much for him at times, and she was not around.

What could she expect?

That pretty young thing across the street with the long blonde hair sure was a lovely lass. The porn thing came back then, too. He had far too much time on his hands, and it was easier just to entertain himself in the privacy of his home when he felt the urge anyway.

He found a source of material in a little bookstore on DeRenne Avenue, spent a couple of hundred bucks a month on magazines, and quickly built up another collection of tracings and drawings. When he knew she was coming home, he'd simply wrap up the collection and his drawings, bind them in doubled-up trash bags, and hide them under the apartment in the crawl space.

Eve finally found the collection and confronted him. Of course, she left again and he thought he'd never get her back that time. But she did come back.

Mama and dad raised this guy to stay married when he got married and, damn it, he was trying. Chance kept reassuring her that he'd get rid of that trash, and he did try – several times. Then she'd up and leave again, and he'd stop by a store, buy another magazine – you get the picture.

Intimacy became nearly non-existent between them, usually only happening on a single night after she'd be gone for a couple of weeks and come home horny. Otherwise, she told him she didn't feel sexy with him because she didn't know if he was making love to her or one of his drawings.

Nothing good can come of those thoughts. Sex was amazing, it came naturally for them both in the best times; so awkward in the worst. Shame, really.

To an odd portion of Chance's mind, of course, there were a couple of other points to ponder...

He understood his wife's poignant observations, he really did, but, considering *his* needs – the "girls" were always there, always ready, never said 'no' to his advances, and there was "zero" risk of acquiring or suffering or putting her at risk from a sexually transmitted disease. How could she argue with that reasoning?

Only <u>one</u> jester could incite those feelings, twisted justifications for filth or impure thoughts – that was the Devil himself.

Chance really did try to rid himself of this liability and what he knew was his *dirty little habit*. He prayed diligently about his feelings of guilt and mortal weakness so many days and nights. At times the feelings of guilt would consume his thoughts to the point of occasional distraction in his duties. Such a distraction in this profession could be life-threatening at the wrong times.

He'd take hold of the Word, put this thing aside for weeks and months at a time, sure this was all behind him. Then, in a moment of weakness or vulnerability, most often when she would leave again, his mind would backslide into lust and temptation. But they were just excuses: unlocked windows of the mind for the Devil to infuse perversion.

Strangely, at other times, Chance found himself thinking, *"Hell, I'm having the time of my life"*. A healthy, active police officer with a large, modern department in Savannah, Georgia in 1978.

"How could life be any better for a man in his 20s in these times?", he'd question.

Were it not for these couple of distractions from the failing marriage and his dirty picture collection, bein' a cop was a blast!

***

Chapter Seven

A Lot of City to Police

Under a portion of the Crime Control Act of 1976, then-President Jimmy Carter revitalized and restored funding for the Law Enforcement Education Program (LEEP). This program would vastly increase the size of many police departments nationwide and the number of officers patrolling those streets. For the first time in history, this program also offered government grants to departments that implemented policies consistent with affirmative action, where advances in leadership and rank in funded agencies would be tied directly to degree programs in criminal justice. A two-year degree would now be worth a 2-step increase in rank (patrolman to corporal); a four-year degree, a 4-step increase (patrolman to sergeant; corporal to lieutenant) – all regardless of seniority or time in grade.

Nearly simultaneously, the Department of Education and the National Education Administration under Carter increased educational funding, Pell Grants, and federally guaranteed student loans to colleges and universities that would agree to increase their admissions criteria under federal affirmative action guidelines.

In plain language, there were simply not enough Black police officers, and overwhelming statistics indicated unacceptable numbers of Black officers being passed over for promotion due to race alone. These federal incentives would severely affect many departments in the deep South; Savannah was on the radar.

In 1978, the Savannah Police Department expanded dramatically, adding over 75 officers to prepare for the upcoming enlargement of their patrol areas. That fall, the city would annex the incorporated portion of Chapman County, stretching from DeRenne Avenue south to the Forrest River.

Chance, eager to take the next step in his career, took a leap of faith. He applied to the Savannah Police Academy and was accepted into the grueling ten-week Peace Officer Standards and Training program. Along with his academy training, he would continue to work occasional shifts with EMS, but his focus would now be squarely on becoming the best police officer he could be.

One question during the interview before the officer's eligibility committee would stay with him for years: "Which current police-related TV program most accurately represents what you think a police officer should be?" At the time, the airwaves were filled with popular police dramas; *Police Story*, *Hill Street Blues*, *ADAM-12*, *Dragnet*, and *Ironside*. Chance immediately responded with *Hill Street Blues* and was asked to explain why.

He wasn't a fan of the other shows. *Police Story* was well-crafted, but too sensationalized, written by Joseph Wambaugh, a former police lieutenant and suspense novelist. *Ironside* was pure fiction, *ADAM-12* felt too simplistic, and *Dragnet* was written by former LAPD officer Jack Webb, whose sterile, monotone storytelling made it feel more like a documentary than entertainment. To Chance, *Hill Street Blues* struck a chord because it balanced the gritty, realistic portrayal of law enforcement with compassion for both victims and criminals. The committee was impressed.

The ten weeks of training at Travis Field were grueling, but Chance embraced every challenge. Between classroom lectures, range practice, gym sessions, and driving drills on the skid pan, he learned Georgia state law and Savannah's municipal ordinances. He studied basic police procedures, hand-to-hand combat, courtroom etiquette, case presentation, evidence preservation, and crime scene protection. Law enforcement radio protocols, defensive driving, pursuit tactics, and the ethical use of force were also part of the curriculum. It was intense. It had to be.

Even amid the seriousness of the training, there were moments of levity. Like the cadet on the firing range who, preparing to "lock and load," picked up the wrong ammunition.

For the uninitiated, 9mm ammunition doesn't fit in a .45 caliber semi-automatic.

Officer Nix picked up the weapon, loaded the clip with the ill-advised rounds, secured it, depressed the safety, and activated the slide to load a bullet into the chamber. Only, that's not exactly what happened.

The line was ready. The range captain's voice rang out, "The line is hot!" All cadets had their weapons at the ready; guns drawn, pointed downrange. Nearly every cadet activated their slide at the same time, a synchronized motion. The weapons moved a round from the clip into the chamber; except for Officer Nix's. His bullet, still nestled in the clip, shot out the end of his barrel and; *PLOP*; landed about three feet in front of him, as if in slow motion.

"What the hell was that?" the Sergeant barked, his voice cutting through the air. "Nix, that's twenty push-ups, and you're inventorying the ammunition locker this afternoon." His day was over, and not just in the literal sense. Pardon the pun, but his reputation took a hit too.

***

AC ? - I See.

One morning, his lieutenant showed up to class with a massive bandage wrapped around his forehead, both eyes swollen and blackened. We hadn't seen him for a couple of days, and it was clear something had gone down. He didn't offer much in the way of explanation, but Sergeant Edwards did.

Many of the residences in midtown Savannah are occupied by low-income families, primarily Black. A significant number of these homes are what we call "shotgun houses." These narrow, wood-framed dwellings are usually no more than twelve feet wide, with rooms arranged one behind the other, and doors at each end of the house. The term "shotgun house" has its origins from Civil War times and refers to the idea that you could fire a shot through the front door, and it would exit the back without hitting anything in between. These homes are a staple of historic antebellum Savannah, and there are so many of them crammed together that developers have stacked them nearly on top of each other.

How close?

You could flush the toilet in one of those shotgun houses, and the neighbor next door might not have had time to wipe their butt yet. Yep, that close. Maybe eight feet between houses.

For the most part, these homes feature gas floor furnaces and either no air conditioning or just a window unit here or there, typically on the first floor. They all sport spacious front porches and large, multi-section thin glass windows. It's crucial to keep these details in mind because Savannah's finest frequently find themselves in "tag" races with innocent bystanders; people who would rather stay out of sight than answer any unassuming questions.

Police officers refer to these "races" as foot pursuits, and those so-called "innocent bystanders" have usually committed some crime or were strongly contemplating one when they make a run for it.

About five days before the lieutenant showed up to class with his black eyes and bandaged forehead, he was on duty with B-watch as commander when an armed robbery occurred on Montgomery Street near 37th, just after dark; around 8:30 pm. Several officers responded, including the lieutenant. As they arrived, three suspects did the usual and "bolted"; all three, of course, in different directions.

Not one to be left out, and wanting to maintain his reputation as an active commander, the lieutenant took off after the closest suspect.

They ran down Montgomery Street, then turned sharply down 37th, heading west toward West Broad, then on to Burroughs; him and a junior officer, guns drawn, in hot pursuit. Radios blared nonsense from other officers as more pursuits were underway in the area.

Just before they reached 37th and Florence, the suspect darted sharply to his right, leaped over a short iron fence, and slipped between two of those shotgun houses.

The lieutenant thought to himself, "Damn, that guy can run."

What he should have been thinking was, "Hmm, maybe this guy lives here," because the suspect knew something the lieutenant obviously didn't.

The lieutenant followed, making the same sharp right, leaping over the same little fence; proud of his agility; only to slam into the off-white sheet-metal window AC unit protruding about three feet into his path.

"SAFE!"

"Shit, that hurt."

That wasn't exactly what the lieutenant had in mind. He was out cold, flat on his back, sprawled across the alley.

The junior officer, who nearly tripped over him, wasn't sure whether to laugh or help. The poor guy ended up with a dozen stitches and spent two days in the hospital with a concussion. Of course, with no malice intended but plenty of opportunity, this incident became a "teaching moment" for our class. It was hilarious; at least to us. The lieutenant, however, was less than amused.

Oh, and yeah, the suspect got away.

(;o)

***

They graduated, and Chance was near the top of his class, quickly assigned to C-watch. Back then, police officers worked what was called a "swing shift." It went like this: one week working 11 pm to 7 am with two days off; a week of 3 pm to 11 pm with one day off; and a week of 7 am to 3 pm, then four days off. Easy peasy, right?

The starting salary for Savannah Police officers was about $10,000 a year, including insurance, paid time off, vacation, and all the other perks. Pretty sweet for those days.

Now, with the new job, Chance and Eve could finally settle into a routine. They'd have someone else shuttle Glenus around, and maybe, just maybe, they could start that family he'd been dreaming about. They moved to a spacious apartment on the other side of The Gardens. It had a real yard, a front porch, a two-car driveway, and a couple of decorative cedar trees out front. Too cool.

Eve seemed all-in for the time being.

As per city policy, Chance was required to ride with a Field Training Officer for 3-4 weeks, and he drew Officer Dorsey Stinson. Officer Stinson, a seasoned veteran, showed him the ropes. He taught Chance how to check out a patrol vehicle, inspect it for damage, make sure all the equipment was accounted for, gas it up for the shift, and of course; wipe it down.

Wipe it down? Really??

The steering wheel; especially the steering wheel; the microphone, the shotgun, the knobs on the radio and siren, the inside door handles. Every little detail had to be spotless.

Geez. Are you kidding?

Much to Chance's amazement and surprise, he quickly learned that police officers are pretty nasty. They dribble chewing tobacco on the seats. They let ashes fly all over the inside of their vehicle, sometimes burning holes in the ceiling, seat, or door stantions. They tract dog poo in the floorboard.....**AND THEY WIPE <u>BOOGERS</u> ON THE BACK OF THE STEERING WHEEL!!**

I shit you not – absolutely dis-gusting.

Chance gagged. How revolting. Who would ever think? ADAM-12; Officer Milner, Officer Reed. Really? Which one of them.....damn.

Was that why Officer Smith always had a handkerchief on duty with Sergeant Friday?

Did the arms of Chief Ironside's wheelchair – OMG, no way.

Chance was ready to go solo much sooner than the required four weeks, and the lieutenant cut him loose. He was assigned beat 34, which was from East Broad to West Broad, 37th Street to DeRenne Avenue. He was allowed to cruise anywhere within Zone 3 but was primarily responsible for answering calls and patrolling Area 34.

So cool. I mean, how boring can riding around in a marked police car all day be, flirting with passing women, getting to flip on flashing blue lights from time to time, and playing with a siren when he felt the need without asking anyone's permission? Not to mention strolling into quick marts and restaurants in that sharp, freshly-pressed, tailored navy blue uniform, shiny brass all over, highly-polished leather gun belt and walnut-gripped .38 revolver; he wore Corfram shoes so highly polished that he could see his reflection.

My goodness, this guy looked sharp.

He hated to work dayshift (7 am to 3 pm) – just too much brass on the street, too much chatter on the radio, and traffic was terrible in his area all the time.

People in Savannah cannot drive. They are disrespectful to each other to the point of being utterly rude and largely have no respect for rule of law or common courtesy. They pass on the right, back without looking, turn without using their signals, fail to yield to each other, fail to stop at the sign, and go wherever they want whenever they want and however they want to get there.

Did I say, "people in Savannah can't drive?" I thought so.

Most of the radio calls were somebody stole somebody else' somethin'; two cars bumped into each other; two guys got drunk and punched each other, or somebody else. Yada yada.

But he *loved* working the night shift (11 pm to 7 am). That's when he worked his magic.

Chance would check out his area, all the business on his beat, mostly on Habersham or Waters, then cruise over toward Skidaway, east Victory, and Bee Roads. There were a lot of businesses and places to get coffee and several bars to keep an eye on, and his mama lived on the far eastern part of that beat.

Right in the middle of that area was Daffin Park. Now, although nothing was usually going on there, it was the place where several officers, pretty frequently, liked to cruise to after around 4 am and get a little shut eye.

They'd pull their units up close to one of those big oak trees so it'd block some of the street lights, leave the vehicle running to keep warm or cool, turn the radio down, open their window, and slump down in the seat. You could always find a couple of officers somewhere in the park this time of night. Sometimes they'd hide from the sergeant behind Grayson Stadium itself. That's where Officer Claude Weavers liked to park.

***

Rockets' Red Glare

One night, Chance and Officer Iny Valdez decided they'd play with Claude a little. Earlier in the week they planned out a prank, if they got the occasion, involving bottle rockets and whipped cream. They never got the opportunity to use the whipped cream. That's another story.

You oughta watch "The Choirboys" for a better perspective on police humor.

All was quiet. They found him, as expected, behind the stadium: window down, engine running, radio on low. Claude's head was thrown back, mouth wide open, fast asleep. At that moment, Chance and Valdez felt less like respectable police professionals and more like mischievous kids. Whatever; it was too good to pass up.

Chance slipped a firecracker rocket into a Coke bottle (hence the term "bottle rocket"), angled it just right toward the open window, lit the fuse, and... *WHOOOOSH – BANG!*

The rocket landed squarely on the passenger seat; a perfect shot. But in hindsight, maybe not the best idea.

Claude jolted awake with a start, his revolver already in hand. Half-conscious and pure reflex, he came up fighting; and shooting. He fired off two rounds before anyone could calm him down, both shots going straight into the side of Valdez's patrol unit.

Right on cue:

"C34, 36, and any available unit; shots fired; Grayson Stadium at Bee Road; code 4."

Sergeant Travis, their unflappable supervisor, had already spotted Claude's unit parked behind the stadium about 20 minutes earlier. Knowing Chance and Valdez's penchant for antics, he suspected they were up to something. Sure enough, the commotion didn't surprise him one bit.

With impeccable timing, the sergeant's voice came over the radio:

"Units, use 10-0 (caution). I hear there may be a dangerous suspect in the area."

Radio mics clicked all over as officers laughed at the jab. Then, with a more serious tone:

"34, 36, see me when you clear from that situation."

Busted.

Finally, he added,

"Oh, and how about checking on 32 (Officer Claude)? I hear he might need some assistance over there. He seemed a little 'anxious' earlier in the shift."

Well, damn. Now he tells them.

Turns out Officer Claude Weavers had been dealing with some "nerve" issues lately. The guy had been moonlighting as a security guard, popping uppers (amphetamines) to stay awake, and running on fumes. Toss some caffeine on top, and you've got a recipe for disaster. None of them had known this before their little prank.

They cleared the call quickly, of course, reporting the disturbance as unfounded. Then, the four of them cooked up a story about Claude half-asleep, showing off his weapon when he accidentally dropped it, causing it to discharge; twice; into the other patrol car. The captain was skeptical, but their spotless records bought them some leniency.

The fallout? Mandatory gun safety classes for all involved. And as for Chance, the sergeant confiscated his beloved bottle rockets.

Lesson learned... maybe.

***

See? The Devil was there, too.

A few weeks later, his dad went nuts again and threatened to kill mama and himself. She had him committed to Georgia Regional for a week. It took his mother, Mammie, to sign him out. Now, although they all knew better and knew the man, his whole family was mad as a nest of hornets at her and threatened physical harm if she came around them. What a mess.

Things can always get worse.

***

The Paperback & "The Fence"

It was a quiet afternoon, and Chance was on the evening shift, cruising along DeRenne Avenue, trying to avoid the midday traffic. Turning into the parking lot of the Globe Shopping Center, he found his eyes drawn to the towering globe behind the building; a recently refurbished relic of Savannah's past.

Originally a massive natural gas reservoir, the metal globe once belonged to the Savannah Gas Company. Back then, the surrounding area was sparse, with a handful of businesses and base housing for Hunter Air Corps. Hunter was an Air Force base at the time, home to B-47 Stratofortresses under the Strategic Air Command (SAC); the very folks responsible for the rapid deployment of nuclear weapons along the East Coast. These were also the ones who "misplaced" a bomb near Tybee in the '50s.

But that's another story.

Chance's attention drifted back to the present. A sign caught his eye: **The Paperback.**

Needing to make a few rounds through the local businesses anyway, he parked his cruiser, turned on his portable radio, and stepped into the store.

At first glance, it seemed like a standard bookstore; walls lined with paperbacks and large wooden tables neatly arranged in rows. The owner, a thin, smirking man behind the counter, greeted

Chance, who nodded in return and began to browse. There were a few other patrons in the store, both men, and nothing seemed out of the ordinary.

Until Chance noticed the shelves at the back. They were positioned just off-kilter enough to suggest they were hiding something. Curious, he walked closer.

The store radio crackled faintly, but otherwise, all was still. Rounding the shelves, Chance found what was being concealed: the back walls were lined with adult magazines, sealed in clear cellophane, bundled in discounted packs.

Every major title was there; **Playboy, Penthouse, Oui, Swank,** and others. But some of the material was far more explicit than Chance expected to find outside an adult bookstore.

It wasn't exactly a kid-in-a-candy-store moment. More like a cop-in-a-spotlight situation. Still, he couldn't resist. Glancing around to ensure no one was watching, he quickly picked out a few bundles. The smirking owner stood behind the counter, ready to make the sale, his eyes gleaming with amusement.

Chance wasn't two minutes out the door when his radio blared:

"C34, what's your 10-20 (location)?"

"DeRenne at White Bluff," he replied, trying to sound casual.

"10-4. Do you see anything that looks like an explosion back toward Staley Avenue?"

Chance stiffened. He tossed the magazines into his briefcase, started his cruiser, and backed out of the parking lot. As he turned onto DeRenne, he glanced over his shoulder and froze.

A massive, coal-black and fiery-red mushroom cloud was rising above the rooftops near Montgomery Street.

"What the hell?"

The radio came alive again.

"All available units, vicinity of Staley and Temple; explosion and fire. Respond code 4. Fire Department, EMS, and Savannah Electric en route."

Chance floored it, racing up DeRenne, then Montgomery, and onto Staley. Turning a corner, he saw the source of the chaos: a brick house fully engulfed in flames. The roof was gone, the front wall blown outward in one solid piece, and standing in what had been the front doorway was a man; completely ablaze.

Chance barely shifted his car into park before leaping out. As he sprinted toward the burning man, two neighbors pulled the victim down, covered him with a blanket, and smothered the flames. One of the neighbors' clothes caught fire in the process, and Chance tackled him, rolling him on the ground to extinguish the flames.

The scene was hellish. As firefighters doused the blaze, they found the bodies of the man's wife and youngest child in the back room. She had a head injury, and both were burned beyond recognition. Investigators later learned the husband had poured accelerants; gasoline mixed with fuel oil; throughout the house. He'd argued with his wife over burning it down for insurance money to save his failing junkyard. The wife had resisted, and in his rage, he struck her, causing her to fall onto the baby.

The explosion occurred as their older son fled the house, the vacuum from the open door pulling fumes into the gas stove's pilot light. The boy, miraculously unhurt, gave the first account of the tragedy to Chance: a harrowing tale of a father consumed by desperation and a family destroyed in seconds.

Chance left work early that day, shaken to his core. He drove home in silence, parked in the driveway, and stepped inside, his briefcase still in hand.

The house was quiet, save for the hum of the refrigerator. As he set his gun belt on a chair, the phone rang.

"Hello? ... Hi, Mom... Did you call the police? ... I'll be right there."

Another family crisis; his father and younger brother had come to blows. He sighed, grabbing his keys.

But as he turned toward the door, his eyes fell on the table. There, out of place and somehow accusatory, was the envelope containing those magazines.

Chance stared at it for a long moment, the weight of the day pressing down on him.

"Well, if that's not the perfect end to this day…"

***

Music played a pivotal role in Chance's life during this time. When he wasn't patrolling the streets, he was back on the airwaves as Jay Hanson, spinning records and finding solace in the soft rock of Air Supply, Little River Band, and the Eagles. The station's rotation was a mix of timeless hits from Michael Jackson, Madonna, and Aerosmith, filling the air with melodies that tugged at the heart.

But those songs cut deep, especially during the late-night shifts when the tempo slowed and the lyrics hit too close to home. Lonely as he was, the music became a mirror, reflecting his struggles. More than once, he found himself pulling back on the mic, speaking less than he should. It wasn't long before the station manager started noticing; and raising concerns.

Then came a rare opportunity: a chance to work at **WSGA**, the station he'd idolized as a kid. They were undergoing a massive shift, transitioning from Top 40 rock to **The Music of Your Life**, a format featuring classics from the 1920s, '30s, and '40s played on reel-to-reel tapes.

One weekend in 1979, Chance took on two 12-hour shifts, saying goodbye to the station's rock-and-roll identity as he signed off its final broadcast at midnight. For the next couple of years, he juggled weekends at WSGA, alternating between nostalgic standards and the Hot 40 rock station down the hall.

It was an exhilarating experience, filled with music, long hours, and no shortage of young women eager to meet the DJ behind the voice.

But Eve remained the constant wild card in his life. She appeared and disappeared with the unpredictability of a summer storm; intense, fleeting, and leaving chaos in her wake. She knew exactly which buttons to push, how far she could go, and when to stop just short of breaking him.

They had a rhythm, toxic yet familiar. She'd show up in that baby blue dress, the one she always wore when she wanted something, and Chance would give in. It was better than being alone, better than nights spent with just himself and his thoughts.

Yet when she left, the void was deeper. Sometimes, as he sat in the booth spinning records, a song request would come through; **Gladys Knight's "Neither One of Us Wants to Be the First to Say Goodbye."**

That was *their* song. He'd seen Eve cry to it too many times during their fights, and it never failed to hit him like a gut punch. He'd choke back the lump in his throat, set a stack of carts to auto play, and let the station run itself while he stepped away to collect himself.

Eve's hold on him was undeniable, but it was wearing thin.

The final straw came with one of her calls. She had been gone for over six months, reportedly in Florida with her mother. When she called, her voice was raw and desperate. She was crying, saying she'd had a miscarriage, begging him to help her. She was alone, bleeding in a rundown motel, out of money, and out of options.

But Chance had nothing left to give. The cycle of fire and ice, pleasure and pain, had burned him out. He was done.

It wasn't anger he felt; just a hollow sense of resolve. Her chaos wasn't his to fix anymore.

And besides, life was pulling him in another direction. He was about to change jobs, move forward, and, finally, leave Eve in his rearview mirror.

***

Chapter Eight

❦

Boys Will Be Boys

W hen the City of Savannah annexed the "southside" portion of Chatham County, it acquired a significant new tax base: sprawling residential neighborhoods, thriving commercial developments, and high-end properties that poured millions into the city's coffers. Recognizing the importance of this new addition, the mayor and city council went all out, ensuring every effort was made to present the city in its best light to these new taxpayers.

From a law enforcement perspective, the transition marked a notable shift. Before the annexation, the county police, under the capable leadership of Chief Ed St. Laurens, had managed the nearly 100-square-mile area with just four patrol officers. The chief had even moved the central office and communications center to a location between Mall Boulevard and Eisenhower Drive, a clear demonstration of his commitment to the residents of the southside.

Now, Savannah PD would take over, and they wasted no time making a statement. They established a new sub-station at Oglethorpe Mall, signaling to the community that they were serious about their presence in the area.

To staff this new precinct, Chief Gallop selected a squad of Savannah's finest; officers who were polished, presentable, and highly decorated. The team would include four officers and a sergeant on every shift, all driving brand-new, state-of-the-art '79 Plymouth Gran Fury patrol cars equipped with the latest technology.

The officers selected for the C-watch were an impressive bunch: seasoned corporals with the experience and demeanor to represent the department in this prestigious assignment. To lead the squad, the chief chose Chance's favorite supervisor, Sgt. Tyson; a well-respected and steady leader.

Chance wanted in. He was sharp, meticulous in his appearance, and well-spoken; qualities that had already earned him the nickname "a police officer's policeman" among some of his peers. It was a distinction that meant the world to him.

But with less than two years on the force, he didn't make the cut. The decision stung, especially when one of the chosen officers turned out to be Corporal Nicky Gardo.

Gardo was, by all accounts, a character. Handsome and confident to the point of arrogance, he fancied himself a ladies' man, and his colleagues never missed an opportunity to rib him about it.

Gardo, however, had a way of turning the tables; and one night, he did just that, leaving the squad with a story they wouldn't forget.

Almost.

***

Burgers and Thighs

Tom's Restaurants were the Mel's Diners of Savannah in the early 60s to mid-70s. The restaurants hired some of the best-looking college-aged girls in town as car hops. The girls had to be attractive, have shapely legs, look good in little outfits and short skirts, and maneuver with trays full of food on roller skates.

This one young thing named Vanessa at Tom's on Victory Drive was so attractive and playful that she had guys from all over swooning for her attention.

Gardo claimed he had her "in his sites," and she would fold to his whims whenever he wanted.

A rather cocky "butthole".

Whenever someone brought up Vanessa's name, Gardo would carry on about his latest exploits with the girls and how much she cared for him. Nobody believed him. Gardo was definitely not nearly the best-looking guy on the department. He was also a couple of fries short of a Happy Meal when it came to women, much more frequently than he liked to admit.

Chance and the rest of the watch demanded proof. So, they made a bet to get to the bottom of this fiasco once and for all.

On this certain, otherwise uneventful Friday night during their week of overnight shifts, Gardo arranged for Vanessa to meet him after she ended her shift around 11 pm. He was working her beat that night and would have her wait until around one in the morning, when things usually slowed down a bit before the bars closed. No problem.

By prior arrangement with the officers in the radio room - and several others on the street that night - Gardo would meet up with the girl and turn his radio to the secondary channel for private communication. Just as she was to get in the car, he would take the microphone, depress the "talk" button, tie a rubber band around it to hold the button down and hang it back on the dash. This way, everybody could hear everything going on in the car and know that he had, in fact, met and caroused with the beauty.

What Gardo was not expecting was that Vanessa had gone home and taken a short nap after her shift ended around 11 pm. An hour later, she got up, showered, put on a special little outfit just for him, and headed out the door. She chose a little white T-shirt sans bra, a pair of tight-fitting denim shorts, and a pair of nylon mesh slippers. He also didn't know she had dropped by the restaurant again before they closed at 12:30 to have the cook make him a hot hamburger and fresh steak fries.

This meal was his favorite combo, and she had memorized the condiments and fixin' he liked down to a tee. A couple of the guys had also let slip the description of an outfit or two that really turned Gardo on earlier in the week.

Well, he parked where they agreed, and, right at 1 am, she pulled in behind his cruiser.

He checked the mike again; yep, everything was ready to go.

She approached the door, he reached over and unlocked it. She slide into the seat and closed the door.

"Damn, girl, you are lookin' fine tonight", he said.

It sounded like they may have bent over and kissed, there was a brief period of shuffling around in the car.

"Thanks, Gardo. Hey, I put this together just for you."

The guys in the radio rcom were sure she was talking about her outfit, and they giggled like school girls for a few moments.

"Oh, honey, I really like that. I can tell something very nice is waiting for me to put my hands around tonight".

Damn, he's getting' right to the point, they thought.

He was really looking at the large white paper bag with that Tom's logo on the outside, usually reserved for large orders.

"Hell yeah. I worked these puppies for several minutes to get 'em nice and plump for ya."

She pulled out the large order of thick, freshly cooked steak fries, still piping hot. Proud of what she had prepared for him, and overjoyed by his reaction, she let out a nice long sigh of relief.

"Mmmm, I can see you're really excited. I'm glad you like these, big guy".

"Hell yes I do", he said. *"So damned firm and warm…"*

(shuffling, muffled sounds like they might exchanging an embrace again)….

"….. look how these things just stand straight out, waiting for me to pop them in my mouth. Mmmm."

She was, of course, referreing those large fries.

"My goodness, honey….hmm….I had no idea.", Vanessa whispered softly.

Mikes started clicking all over the radio; this was getting good.

"Open that a little farther, baby, I can't get to them like that."

"Oh Gardo", she whined. *"Let me help, darling."*

Then he made some guttural sounds like he was really getting into the heat of the moment. Actually, it was the fries in the bottom of the box he was desperately trying to get to.

They were now 10 minutes into this ordeal – <u>what</u> <u>a show</u> the boys *thought* they were getting.

As she turn in the seat, twisting her legs towards him, he suddenly noticed her slippers and commented.

"Dang, girl, I like those! Love to see a woman wearing mesh".

They could hear her shifting in the seat,

"Here, let me take these off" she said in a low, sultry voice (as she slipped out of her shoes).

"There, now....is that better?" She put her feet up on the dash, showing off her freshly painted toes.

Then she threw back her head, arched her back slightly, took a deep breath and then exhaled a very sexy sigh. After what seemed like several moments, they heard him reply, *"Oh, yeah.. Get comfy, baby."*

She reached into the big bag again and pulled out the large, foil wrapped hamburger.

"How 'bout this, big boy. Want this?" she asked.

"Are you kidding me? Hell, yeah." Now obviously quite enthused, he raised his voice to add, *"Bring it on, girl."*

The clicking of mics across the police radio was suddenly near frantic.

Vanessa reached down, unwrapped the burger, and moved in a little closer to him. Her arm bumped the microphone, *"I thought you'd like it this way. I had it trimmed up just right so you wouldn't get it all over your chin – or your uniform."*

OMG! These burly cops were going crazy: cat calls, wolf whistles, mouths drooling.

"That's a beautiful thing, honey. Warm, moist, ready for me. What a woman."

She sighed again, softly, obviously acknowledging his gesture. Proud she could provide such a pleasing meal for her man. That was not, obviously, what the boys in the booth were thinking.

"Do you know how much I thought about you all day? Just know-ing you'd be coming tonight, made my mouth water."

What an erotic thing to say to a woman at a moment like this, his colleagues thought. Even on a secondary channel on the police radio.

"You do look good right now", he continued.

"Alright, tiger..." They could hear rustling again; they were moving around. Imaginations were no running wild. She unwrapped the burger and moved it toward him, *"Ssss...get some of this."*

Hot damn!! The radio room was deathly quiet. Nobody moved.

Just as she leaned forward, and he was about ready to bite that big juicy sandwich, it slipped out of her grip and tumbled onto the floorboard on her side of the car. Gardo leaned over, mumbled something they couldn't understand, she moaned softly as he squeezed her bladder while reaching over to pick it up.

"Honey..." she said softly, *"you're not gonna eat that nasty ole thing now, are you?"*

Reality suddenly hit about that time, and he remembered what was happening.

He shouted back, *"Say hamburger! SAY HAMBURGER!!"*

***

The boys in the radio room really should've sprung for plaque or a special trophy or something. Gardo was now a bonafide star worthy of their respect and admiration. Not because he was such a stud but his quick wit and ability to save his stuff when the time was right. This man could be Chance's wingman any time. And he frequently was.

***

The camaraderie Chance had envisioned among the city officers wasn't always there, but he made sure his shifts were lively. The force had its fair share of characters, as most jobs do when people work closely together. Over time, quirks, eccentricities, and habits became well-known among the ranks. Cops, it seemed, had plenty of all three.

The officers were, in many ways, like the vivid personalities in Joseph Wambaugh's *The Choirboys,* though without the infamous after-hours parties. Some supervisors, however, weren't exactly in on the fun. Strictly business, they had little patience for humor or antics, a sharp contrast to the otherwise colorful environment.

Chance and his classmates got their first taste of trouble just before graduation. In celebration of their accomplishments, four men and one fiery redhead decided to hit the town. They'd been warned to leave their police IDs and weapons behind if they went out drinking, and they got it *mostly* right.

The night began innocently enough at the Holiday Inn lounge in Midtown, near the foot of the Talmadge Bridge. Spirits were high, laughter was louder, and the group felt invincible. Emboldened, they made their way down Ogeechee Road to one of the roughest, most notorious dives in the county: Duggen's Lounge.

It was the kind of place where trouble didn't just find you; it had a seat waiting. Fortunately, the bar was nearly empty, save for a couple of old-timers nursing their drinks and a weathered bartender with a no-nonsense demeanor. Sensing they were out of their depth, the group didn't linger long.

Later that night, Chance discovered he'd lost his police ID. Panic set in when he realized where it might be: Duggen's. The thought of it lying around in that place, potentially in the wrong hands, was enough to make his blood run cold.

Despite these early stumbles, the force had a way of bringing together people from every walk of life; men and women, a mix of races, personalities ranging from wild to reserved. What united them was the shared responsibility of upholding the law and protecting one another, no matter the cost.

Chance would learn just how unbreakable that bond could be one terrifying night, a moment that tested their resolve and proved the depths of their loyalty.

***

Bridge Play'as

Sgt. Travis called the watch to order at exactly 2:15 p.m. The team reviewed BOLOs (Be On The Lookout bulletins) and requests for extra patrol, with special attention given to a recent string of armed robberies near the Welcome Center at the base of the Talmadge Bridge. Detectives suspected another attempt might occur that evening, keeping everyone on edge.

Chance was late for roll call that day; why, no one remembers; but it meant he couldn't ride his usual beat. Instead, he drew cruiser duty, otherwise known as prisoner transport or the "paddy wagon." The vehicle was a beat-up '75 Pontiac Le Mans, its size unsuitable for narrow city alleys. It rattled with every bump, reeked of stale odors, and was an assignment nobody wanted.

As sunset fell, Chance had already crisscrossed downtown and the southside several times when the emergency alert sounded.

Beep, Beep, Beep.

"All units...all units in the vicinity of Alfred and Oglethorpe near the base of the bridge..."

A pause, heavy with the weight of impending danger, hung over the airwaves.

"All units...Ramada Inn across from the Welcome Center...Signal 23 Code 4. Proceed with extreme caution. Three suspects armed with small-caliber weapons, no vehicle identified. Units responding, advise."

Signal 23 meant armed robbery, Code 4 meant it was in progress, and no vehicle meant the suspects were on foot. The radio exploded with responses as officers raced to the scene:

"13 en route...23...24...2 Charlie 16...ID 312 en route..."

Chance responded: "120 in the vicinity, standing by."

The dispatch supervisor interrupted with details:

"All units...three suspects, all Black males. First suspect: 5'8" to 5'11," white tank top, black shorts, no shoes, armed with a blue steel revolver, last seen running toward Augusta Avenue. Second suspect: 5'4" to 5'5," short red hair, blue T-shirt, white shorts, white shoes, armed with a shiny handgun, last seen running toward Fahm. Third suspect, possibly female: 5'2" to 5'5," tan baseball cap, sunglasses, black top and shorts, sandals, armed with a large hunting knife. Use extreme caution."

By the time Chance reached Louisville Road near Martin Luther King Jr. Boulevard, a detective radioed in: they'd stopped a female suspect matching the third description a few blocks from the scene. Moments later, as Chance approached West Boundary, gunshots erupted nearby.

BANG! BANG! BANG!

The shots came from multiple directions, echoing in the night. Chance scanned the area, spotting the high embankment of an old railroad overpass. Visibility was poor. Grabbing his radio, he prepared to call it in when:

BANG! BANG!

The shots were closer now; too close. As Chance reached an intersection near a cluster of small homes, he looked to his right. On the embankment, two suspects; one in a white tank top, the other in a blue T-shirt; fired at pursuing officers, who returned fire.

"Shit," Chance muttered. "I'm in the middle of this."

Just then, the redheaded suspect in the blue T-shirt broke away from the embankment and sprinted toward Chance's car.

"Unit on Louisville," a voice crackled over the radio. "Suspect is heading your way! Get outta there, Brogdon!"

Sgt. Travis's voice rang out, urgent and commanding. Chance froze for a split second, then hit the brakes hard. The microphone flew from his hand, clattering onto the passenger floor.

The suspect, soaked from the dew-covered grass, darted in front of the cruiser. Chance grabbed his revolver, cocked it, and stepped out, his left leg bracing against the car door. The Pontiac, still in gear, rolled forward, nudging his calf. Ignoring the pain, he focused on the suspect, aiming his weapon squarely at the man's chest.

The world seemed to hold its breath.

The suspect's wild eyes locked with Chance's as he raised his weapon. Chance's finger tightened on the trigger.

BANG!

Gunfire erupted again, this time from behind the suspect. Officers tackled the man in the tank top on the railroad tracks while others sprinted toward Chance's position.

The redheaded suspect veered toward a nearby AME church, screaming something unintelligible as he ran. Just as he rounded the corner, Officer Claude Weavers and two others intercepted him, taking him down in a flurry of shouts and flashing lights.

Chance lowered his weapon, adrenaline surging as he caught his breath. The radio crackled back to life, filling the silence. The chaos was over; but the memory of those moments would linger far longer than the echoes of the gunfire.

***

In the fraction of a second it took to decide, Chance almost pulled the trigger. The suspect's life; or perhaps Claude's; could have ended in that instant. But the hammer didn't fall.

His hands trembled violently as he slowly uncocked the revolver and lowered it, his arms heavy and unsteady. He stepped on the brake again, shifted the car into park, and collapsed into the driver's seat, letting out a long, shuddering sigh.

A weight, like a hammer, struck him square in the chest. It wasn't physical, but the realization hit just as hard. Sweat drenched his uniform, his hands shook uncontrollably, and tears welled in his eyes.

"What just happened?" he whispered to himself, his mind racing.

The suspect had been unarmed when officers tackled him. Unknown to Chance in the heat of the moment, the man had tossed his weapon after firing his final shot, just before descending the embankment. When he ran across Chance's path, he turned, shouting back at someone; his brother, maybe; and pointing in Chance's direction.

It looked as though he was aiming to shoot. He wasn't.

Chance's finger had been on the trigger, and his mind had screamed for action. Yet, by what could only be described as divine intervention, something; something beyond his control; stopped him.

In the blink of an eye, a higher power had made the decision Chance couldn't fully comprehend. That moment wasn't his to command; it belonged to God.

The rookie officer sat there, his breath uneven, his spirit rattled. He had come within a heartbeat of ending an unarmed man's life, and the thought of what could have been shook him to his core.

The following day, Chance took a leave. He spent most of it in solitude, kneeling in prayer. He thanked God for the miracle, for his restraint, and for the chance to reflect on the fragility of life and the mercy he'd been granted.

***

Only the suspect and God; knew why his life was spared that night. He and his accomplices had committed armed robbery, fired shots at pursuing officers, and caused chaos. Yet, by some divine intervention, no one was injured, no lives were lost.

In that split second before Sgt. Travis's voice intervened; just a breath before the hammer on Chance's revolver would strike the firing pin and send a bullet into the young man's chest; perhaps the Lord was listening to a mother's desperate plea for her son's forgiveness. Who could say? But if that night was a miracle, it was fleeting.

Six nights later, less than a quarter mile from where the chase had ended, tragedy struck. While on patrol near West Broad Street and Louisville Road, Sgt. Travis confronted a young man, erratic and wild; whether from drugs, alcohol, or the chaos of a fractured mind, no one could be sure. Before the sergeant could even draw his service revolver, the man pulled a sawed-off shotgun from under his overcoat.

Two deafening blasts.

The first struck Sgt. Travis in the chest; the second, to his head. The sergeant never had a chance.

The squad was shattered. Chance and the other officers mourned their leader deeply. Travis wasn't just a supervisor; he was their rock, their guide. His loss left an emptiness that lingered long after the funeral.

For Chance, the tragedy reinforced the weight of every moment in their line of duty; how quickly the tide could turn, how fragile their lives truly were. It was a sobering reminder of both the miracles they prayed for and the heartbreaks they couldn't escape.

***

Life as a police officer seemed to fit Chance quite well. He really enjoyed the lifestyle, and he felt well accepted by his fellow officers. His schedule of regular, rotating shifts didn't leave either much time or opportunity for extra work.

Eve continued to play her game of hide-n-seek despite his pleas for her to settle down. He desperately needed her to be the kind of wife he had hoped for and deserved. But her mom continued to pull at Eve's heart strings, always at just the right moments when Eve's willpower was at its lowest.

Those times were most often when she and Chance were having trouble. The strain was becoming too much, too frequent: something had to break.

Not only was she legitimately bothered by the bundle of pictures he still kept hidden under their new apartment - most women certainly would be - but she seemed jealous of his new commitment and love for the job he was now so actively involved. *She* was having trouble conforming to, even simply adapting to any job that involved the discipline required to maintain a regular schedule. And her mama's *trips* were now becoming far too frequent, too "convenient" for Chance.

Glenus' Escapades

Glenus' health was deteriorating rapidly. Frequent bouts of bronchitis often escalated into pneumonia, fueled by her relentless habit of alternating between puffs on a half-empty inhaler and a Marlboro Red, all while sinking into a fog of self-pity. She had no reliable transportation, no stable home to call her own.

The pattern was predictable: when the Florida heat became unbearable with one daughter, she'd plead with Eve to let her stay, then move on to a sister in New York. She had two other sisters— one in New Jersey and another in California—but those relationships were strained and rare. Glenus smoked heavily, lost weight alarmingly fast, and leaned heavily on her inhalers as her daughters, despite their concern, unwittingly supported her habits by supplying her with cartons of cigarettes. Two cartons a week became the norm.

When they had first met, Chance remembered Glenus as a robust woman, somewhere between 180 and 200 pounds. Now, she struggled to hit 120. Her skin had taken on an ashen, leathery quality, and she reeked of stale smoke and the unpleasant odors of neglect.

Eventually, Eve and her sisters persuaded Glenus to settle in one place. Dana, one of the daughters, had a small home in Green Cove Springs, Florida, a quiet town south of Orange Park. With pooled resources and Glenus' modest savings, they managed to buy her a used single-wide trailer within walking distance of Dana's house. The predictable weather and cleaner air seemed like a good fit for her declining health—at least outside the walls of her home.

When Chance visited six months later, he found conditions worse than he had imagined. The trailer was cluttered with items Glenus had compulsively collected from garage sales and flea markets. Food was scarce; instead, she spent every spare penny from her Social Security and Medicaid on trinkets she'd never use or, worse, on lottery tickets that offered nothing but false hope.

The home was a disaster. Dirty dishes and cookware covered every surface—the sink, counters, stove, and even the microwave hid rotting food. Insects swarmed everywhere: tiny German cockroaches, massive palmetto bugs, flies, and even maggots. The air was heavy with the stench of decay, and yet her daughters seemed to tolerate these horrifying conditions, as long as Glenus seemed happy.

"How could anyone live like this?" Chance wondered in disbelief. "How could anyone in their right mind let their mother live like this?"

Desperation drove him to make one last effort to save both his marriage and Glenus. In the fall of 1979, he offered to bring her back to Savannah to live with them. For a brief moment, it seemed like a solution. But within two months, both Eve and Glenus were gone again—back to Florida.

After three years of trying everything he could think of to keep his wife grounded and their marriage intact, Chance was left with nothing but heartache. In the end, he filed for divorce. Yet, even as he signed the papers, he remained hopelessly in love with Eve..

The afternoon they signed the papers, the last moment he saw her walking away from the courthouse, Alabama's *"We Can't Love Like This Anymore"* was playing as he started the car. Those words just resonated - so deeply, so true. He just sat there for a bit, and he cried.

***

Dream Girl

In the void of two failed marriages, lonely and aching, Chance was desperate for something real. Tonight, the Korean Village seemed to promise just that.

He parked his car and took in the quiet night. Even for a Wednesday, it was slow. Just a handful of men scattered at the bar, nursing their drinks. The usual buzz of chatter was subdued. Tonya was on stage, but her performance seemed half-hearted, more a distraction than a show.

Chance ordered his usual—a Cuba Libre—and sank into the rhythm of the night, resigned to the slow pace. He had come here for a bit of fun, but tonight felt different, something in the air told him he might just get what he needed.

As Tonya wrapped up, she walked off stage, her body stiff from a performance no one seemed to appreciate. But then, as if the night had something else in store for him, a new figure appeared.

Terri.

She moved with the kind of confidence that made time stand still. The tall, blonde beauty was a vision in the dim lighting, her presence commanding the room. He hadn't seen her before—not like this. She locked eyes with him, her lips curling into a playful smile.

"Did you come to see the show, or are you just here for me?" she asked, her voice teasing yet filled with an invitation he couldn't ignore.

Chance leaned in, intrigued. "I think it's you I'm here for."

Terri didn't break her gaze. "Good choice." With a mischievous glint in her eyes, she walked toward him, her long legs swaying with each step.

She came to a stop right in front of him, her heels clicking on the floor. The air between them felt charged, alive.

Without a word, she guided him down to the front, positioning a chair directly in front of the stage. She slid a dollar into the jukebox and selected a few songs, the familiar hum of music filling the space.

The moment "Stranglehold" began, she gave him a wicked smile and began to move. Slowly at first, her body rolling with the beat as she stood before him, teasing him with every sway of her hips. Chance felt the heat rise between them. He was captivated by her every movement.

She leaned in, close enough that he could feel the warmth of her breath on his skin. Her eyes held his, dark and filled with intent. "You like what you see?" she whispered.

"I like a lot more than what I see," he said, his voice low and almost a growl.

Terri's lips curled into a knowing smile. Without a word, she reached for his hand, guiding it up her leg, her touch light but firm, coaxing him closer to the heat of her skin. He could feel the tension building, the electric pull between them undeniable.

But just as quickly as it started, she withdrew his hand, her fingers brushing over his chest. Her smile was playful but dangerous. "Not yet," she said softly, before moving away, her body rolling back into the rhythm of the music.

The air in the club seemed to thicken as Terri's movements grew more sensual, more deliberate. Her body undulated to the beat, her eyes never leaving his. The other men watched, but it was clear she wasn't performing for them—she was performing for him.

As the song reached its peak, Terri took a few steps back, giving him a fleeting glance that sent a shiver through his body. She leaned forward once more, her fingers grazing the fabric of his shirt before she whispered, "If you want me, you're going to have to show me."

Chance's pulse quickened. "How do you want me to show you?" he asked, the words slipping out before he could stop them.

She gave him a sultry grin. "Get a little closer," she said, before guiding him forward, her hips swaying as she beckoned him with her finger.

Terri dropped to her knees, her movements graceful and fluid. With a flick of her wrist, she slipped the edge of her dress down slightly, revealing just enough to make his breath catch.

She looked up at him, eyes smoldering. "This is what you wanted, right?"

Chance swallowed hard, his mind racing with thoughts he couldn't quite control. "This is... exactly what I wanted."

She stood again, pulling him to his feet with ease, and led him toward the back of the club, her hand brushing over his as if marking him for something more.

Outside, the night air felt cooler, a stark contrast to the heat building between them. She led him to his car, her lips meeting his in a kiss that was urgent, hungry—like they both couldn't get enough.

Once inside, they barely made it past the front door before the pace quickened. The room, dim and quiet, became their private stage. They undressed in silence, each movement a promise of what was to come.

Terri slid into bed beside him, her body pressing against his. She kissed him deeply, the taste of her intoxicating. Their hands explored, tracing paths of fire over skin. Chance could feel the intensity of the moment build as their bodies moved together in a way that felt natural, as though they had been doing this for years.

But this wasn't just physical—it was a connection, an unspoken understanding of what they both needed, of what they both craved. Every kiss, every touch sent sparks through them.

Terri's breath hitched as he touched her in all the right places, her body arching into his. "God, you feel so good," she moaned, her voice thick with desire.

Chance's mind spun, his hands following the curves of her body, his fingers lingering on the places that made her gasp. He had no idea how long it would last, but he didn't care. All that mattered was the way she responded, the way their chemistry seemed to deepen with every touch.

Finally, their bodies came together in a frantic union, a dance of raw need and pleasure. Terri's lips found his neck as her hands gripped his shoulders, her legs wrapping around him tightly. She urged him on, her voice a whispered command.

"I want you... now," she breathed, the intensity of her desire mirrored in every word. Her body shaking with the intensity of the moment. Without any warning, her entire body stiffened, and she let out a scream—loud, raw, and completely uninhibited. It was as if the world around them had stopped, and everything was centered on that moment of release.

Chance felt a rush of heat pour through him as he too reached his climax. The pressure in his body built to an overwhelming peak, and when it finally broke, it felt as though everything in him exploded at once. His orgasm was so intense, he thought he'd ruptured something. His entire body trembled as his release overtook him, and for a fleeting moment, all he could focus on was the sensation of their connection, of their shared ecstasy.

But just as quickly as the passion had surged between them, it dissipated.

Terri's grip suddenly loosened, and her body went limp in his arms. The intense heat of her had gone cold, and her breathing became shallow, ragged. She was no longer responsive, her body lying still, her pulse weak beneath his fingertips. Panic surged through Chance as he looked at her, unsure what to do.

It hit him then—she had been drinking heavily at the bar, had taken shots of Stoli's, had popped "ludes" and downed a double shot of Everclear. He hadn't known about the cocaine, but now it all clicked into place. The combination had been too much for her, and in that moment, he feared the worst.

His first thought was to take her to the hospital, but he immediately dismissed the idea. The thought of explaining the situation to Internal Affairs, or anyone else for that matter, made the hospital option impossible.

Instead, he stayed with her, watching her carefully. His experience with EMS told him to let her sleep it off. So, he did. The hours dragged by as he sat there beside her, the room quiet except for the sound of her uneven breathing. Chance didn't sleep at all that night, his eyes trained on her, unwilling to let her out of his sight.

It wasn't until the next afternoon that she finally began to stir. Her eyes fluttered open, but there was no recognition in them. She looked at Chance as if seeing him for the first time. Her voice was thick, confused. "Where... where am I?"

Chance said nothing, his heart heavy with the silence between them. She had no memory of what had happened, of the night they'd shared. Not even a hint of the incredible connection they'd experienced. He carried her home to her small place near Forsythe Park in silence, the weight of everything unspoken hanging between them.

As she climbed out of the car, he offered her a few extra dollars to help her through the weekend, but she refused, her face unreadable. She didn't even offer him a kiss, not a thank you. Just a quiet, unceremonious departure.

Chance watched her disappear into the distance, and as she turned the corner, he felt a pang of loss. Terri, his dream girl, the one who had made him feel alive again after everything he'd been through, had vanished as quickly as she had appeared.

He never saw her again.

She was gone, just like that. And though he would never forget the passion they had shared, it was a memory that seemed to belong to no one but him. A beautiful, fleeting dream that slipped through his fingers without a trace.

***

Chapter Nine

Three Shades of Brown

In June 1979, just a few months past his 22nd birthday, Chance found himself stepping into a world he had always admired from the sidelines. Thanks to an old bond between the Chief of Police and Chance's father, forged many years earlier, he was granted an early opportunity to join the county police force. The favor came with some murmurs of approval in the tightly knit law enforcement community and plenty of chatter in the CCPD radio room. By all accounts, Chance was well-liked, his charm and earnestness paving the way before he even put on the uniform.

The Chief, perhaps seeing a spark in Chance, made sure his entry into the force was nothing short of special. He was issued the best of everything—a set of new basket-weave leather duty gear, perfectly tailored uniforms, and the crowning piece of the county's identity: a brand-new, hard-billed, brown trooper-style hat. This wasn't just a piece of headwear; it was a symbol of pride, discipline, and the county's law enforcement legacy. Chance took every detail seriously, down to the pair of Corofram dress shoes he polished to a mirror shine.

When the department handed him the standard-issue Smith & Wesson blue steel revolver, Chance respected its heritage but felt it didn't quite match the image he envisioned for himself. He wanted something personal, something that felt like an extension of who he was. So he bought himself a Smith & Wesson Model 67, a stainless-steel Combat Masterpiece adorned with heavy-grain walnut competition grips. The weight of it in his hand, the cool sheen of the steel, and the precision of its craftsmanship—it felt right. "Damn, this thing is sharp," he thought, admiring his choice.

His uniform wasn't the only thing that spoke of new beginnings. Around the same time, Commissioner Bob McCormack spearheaded a groundbreaking policy aimed at making law enforcement a visible and constant presence across the county. The new initiative provided every officer with a personal patrol car—no more signing out a different one every shift. Under this policy, officers were expected to use their patrol vehicles everywhere, both on duty and off. Family trips to the store or community events became part of the job. If an emergency call came in, officers were required to drop their families off and respond immediately. They were to wear their service revolvers and display their badges at all times, projecting an image of preparedness and authority. The effect was striking; the sight of a patrol car in every corner of the county sent a clear message to would-be criminals.

The cars themselves were as formidable as their drivers. Many were brand-new Plymouth Gran Furys and Dodge Monacos, fitted with four-barrel carburetors, heavy-duty transmissions, and police interceptor engines. The county's contract with the Chrysler dealership on Abercorn ensured these vehicles were the best money could buy. In the driver's seat sat officers who were more than capable of handling them—many of the department's personnel were former military police, Marines, or Special Forces veterans. Their crisp tan and brown uniforms, combined with their disciplined demeanor and top physical condition, only added to the department's commanding presence.

Behind the scenes, the department's reputation was steadily rising. Several staff members had attended the prestigious FBI Academy under the LEEP grants, and the Chatham County Police Department had earned a national reputation for professionalism. While the FBI affiliation helped raise its profile, it was the respect and trust the officers had built with the community over the years that solidified its status as one of the region's most respected agencies.

For Chance, stepping into this polished, disciplined world was more than just a career move—it was a call to be part of something bigger. Every polished shoe, every gleaming patrol car, and every proud salute he gave in that sharp brown hat reminded him he was now part of a legacy, one that demanded both honor and excellence.

Did I say these guys were sharp? You damn right!

Second only to Ga State Patrol, but not by far.

Chance was, without question, thrilled to be part of the department. It wasn't just the reputation of CCPD and its members—it was the feeling of belonging to something bigger, something respected. The department had earned one hell of a reputation, not just for the way they carried themselves on duty, but for their camaraderie, the way they connected with businesses around the county, and their dedication to community service. And let's not forget the Christmas parties—those were something else entirely.

For the single officers, life was especially sweet. Many lived in the apartment complexes along Abercorn Extension or in the condos out on the islands, where they'd take on property security roles in exchange for reduced or even free rent. It was a win-win. The owners got peace of mind, and the officers got to live comfortably among friends. These complexes loved having county officers around, and it showed. Before and after annexation, they'd regularly host county watch parties, opening their entertainment kiosks at no charge. It wasn't just practical; it was a point of pride for both sides.

There was no denying it—life as a "county mountie" was good. Whether it was the sense of community, the respect of the public, or just the satisfaction of knowing they were part of something that mattered, the officers had every reason to hold their heads high.

Chance felt it too. He was in the right place, surrounded by the right people, and he wasn't taking a second of it for granted

**

Winds of Change

On Saturday, September 1, 1979, Chance woke up that morning to the phone ringing, unanswered, in the living room. It was about 10 am, he'd planned to spend time doing pretty much nothing during his 4-day shift break.

Ring, ring....ring, ring....ring, ring.....

After several minutes, now realizing Eve must not be home, he got up and answered it.

"Hello....yeah, wha's up?....No, I was just laying around."

The caller was his buddy, Iny Valdez, and he was a little worried about what he and his family would do if the coming hurricane, David, was bad enough to damage their home. Where could his wife and kids go to ride it out. He was calling to let Chance know that his wife was calling him.

"Hey, no prob, lil' brother. I'll listen out for her call....yeah, later."

Chance hung up the receiver, looked around for his cigarettes.

He found the TV remote instead so he turned it on. The Weather Channel was still in its early days but highly efficient, already, at these types of forecast and weather emergencies. It just happened to be the first thing he saw.

"Man, that is one damn big hurricane".

Hurricane David was spinning away, winds at 90 mph, sitting right over the Bahamas. A near-perfect spiral, a well-defined eye wobbling just off dead center. This storm was a monster.

This day was the third of Iny's afternoon rotation with the city police and he was about to start getting ready for work. His wife and kids were at her mother's house.

The phone rang again.

Chance down and picked it up on the second ring;

"Perkins Pancake House....What? Yeah.... The Big Stack, heavy on the butta and extra meat (LOL, gesturing to himself)...I got'cha sausage.... Wha's up, my girl?"

It was Janice, laughing nervously. He could tell in her voice that she was in near panic about the storm and where they might need to go to be safe. The couple lived in a single-wide home in west Savannah, under a bunch of huge old oaks with two small children and a puppy; they'd need someplace to ride out the storm.

"Think you guys might want a little company while our shack gets pummeled, Honey". She could get away with calling him that 'cause they were such good friends: Iny would do anything in the world for Chance.

"Of course. Need me to come pick you guys up, or you just wanna drive over?" he asked.

"Well, Iny's got the car to go to work and I ain't got no way to get there. The wind's beginning to pick up a little now and I'm scared of those danged oak trees around the house" she insisted.

His comforting words settled her down like the reassurance from a big brother. *"Not a problem, babe, I'll be right there".*

Eve was at work downtown. She was now manager at that restaurant in the hotel on Bay Street and they were very busy with guests. Apparently, the approaching hurricane had done less to quell enthusiasm of visitors and curious Savannahians than either the news media or Civil Defense and FEMA had hoped.

Hurricane David was forecast to travel north skirting the Florida coast over the next 24-48 hours and predicted to turn northeast toward he Carolina's by Monday.

OK, still be off then. We'll be fine, ride it out.

He and Eve had stocked up on extra canned and dry goods a few days earlier. The next-door neighbor had a large generator they had agreed to share, Chance would provide several cans of gasoline.

Like most people in Savannah, these *happy campers* were primarily concerned about two main issues: flooding, and the overabundance of huge oaks and tall pines throughout the city. While they didn't have either within the immediate vicinity of their apartment building, his mama had a couple of pines in her backyard and one big oak growing right beside and underneath the front corner of the house.

The couple had a big, beautiful Alaskan Malamut now that they had spent months, and several hundred dollars, treating for mange. He was fine now and certainly wouldn't be a problem around the kids during the storm. Besides, Iny's kids loved the big guy.

"C'mon, boy". He grabbed the leash from the hook next to the back door. *"Gotta take you for your morning business"*.

It took about 10 minutes, just a little walk around the block. Chance found his cigarettes, reached over and picked up the kettle of water he set to boil just before he left, and poured it into the waiting cup of instant Folger's on the table. Then he lit one of his Kool's and walked outside on the front porch, coffee in hand, pooch by his side.

As he and Barks sat there on that little 5 x 10-foot concrete porch, enjoying the fresh morning air and now increasingly brisk winds, he suddenly realized something he needed to be a bit concerned with. On either side of their porch were two hefty cedar trees, one abutting each corner of that timid veranda.

As he flicked his cigarette butt out into the yard and reached down to pet his pal, he nodded his head a little and confessed to Barks, *"Lil buddy, that right there might be a problem"*.

Chance put the dog in the crate, grabbed his keys and headed out the door. Then he climbed into the red '69 Chevy van sitting in his driveway and fired it up.

He and Alden had spent many hours customizing this baby. It had shag carpet on the floors, a double bed across the back, knotty pine paneling on the inside walls, a small fridge and a really boss stereo system. Janice and the kids fell in love with it right away.

***

Every now and then, he and Alden would swap cars, giving Chance the chance to take another beauty they'd been working on out for a spin. This one was a firecracker red '71 Mustang Mach 1 with a 351 Cleveland big block engine and an automatic transmission. The white interior, accented with sharp black details, made it as much a showpiece as it was a muscle car. Chance had driven that beast a few times back and forth to the Police Academy, and each time, it was a struggle not to let the speedometer creep higher than it should. He'd come dangerously close to racking up a ticket or two—a situation that would've been more than a little embarrassing and could've cost him plenty in demerits while climbing the ranks.

The car was a masterpiece. Alden kept it spotless, polishing it religiously with Rain Dance until the finish gleamed so bright you couldn't lean against the sides without sliding right off. That thing wasn't just fast; it looked like it was moving even when it was parked.

***

Janice and the kids were starting to settle in, and even Barks had made a couple of new friends. By Monday afternoon, September 3rd, the wind had picked up enough to make its presence known, gusting every now and then with a feisty whistle. The kids, though, were getting quieter, their usual chatter replaced by uncertainty. A new place, their daddy on duty, and the relentless news of destruction from the Bahamas—it was enough to make anyone uneasy. Eve and Janice tried their best to keep the little ones occupied, but the updates on the Weather Channel were grim: catastrophic damage, hundreds dead.

The county had already called all emergency personnel to standby, putting watches in place, and authorized overtime for any officer willing to take it. Chance didn't mind. He had no problem working extra shifts in bad weather—besides, the overtime pay would help. He'd heard Eve was planning to bring Glenus over to stay with them for a bit. He wasn't sure how he felt about that, but he'd deal with it.

By 5 p.m., he was back on the porch with a glass of bourbon in one hand and a cigarette in the other. The misty rain had started blowing sideways, carried by the restless wind. His eyes were fixed on the two old cypress trees swaying out front. Every now and then, a gust would catch them just right, and they'd let out a low, mournful creak, like they were arguing with the storm itself.

Chance called to check in on his mom and dad. Everything was fine for now. Surprisingly, the old man hadn't decided to start a project on the roof this time, so they should've been in the clear. Still, it felt strange to hear that for once, the roof wasn't a problem.

Around 6 p.m., Iny called. He'd gotten soaked helping a stranded motorist and needed a change of uniform. With the supply clerk nowhere to be found, Janice had smartly packed a couple of spares, just in case. Chance agreed to drop them off, though by then, the wind had picked up enough to make driving dicey.

In the old '69 Chevy, Chance roared down Gwinnett Street, dodging flying debris and trash tumbling across the road. At one point, a massive green metal dumpster rolled across Wheaton Street like it weighed nothing. It was enough to make him tighten his grip on the wheel. The drive back wasn't any better—gusts were getting stronger, and the van rocked and swayed like it was being tossed by invisible waves. By the time he got home, in one piece thankfully, one of the cypress trees out front had already come crashing down.

He called his mom again to check if Dad had made it home yet. He hadn't. Where in the world could the old man be? Everything seemed fine—until around 8 p.m. when the rain, which had been falling steadily for hours, turned into a relentless downpour. His mom called, her voice edged with panic.

"Can you come help Alden with a leak in the ceiling?" she asked.

Apparently, a bulge had formed in the dining room ceiling from water pooling above it, and she was terrified it would burst and flood the room. Dad was still MIA, so Chance grabbed his coat and braved the wind and rain to help Alden figure it out.

It didn't take long to find the problem. A pine tree limb had punched a hole clean through the roof. The rain was coming down harder by the minute, gravity working against them as the water stretched the sheetrock ceiling to its breaking point. The bulge was growing bigger by the second.

While Chance and Alden scrambled to cover the dining room table and floor with towels and plastic, the front door slammed open. In bopped Dad, full of ideas and unsolicited opinions.

"What are you boys doing?" he asked.

"Well," Alden started, "I was fixin' to head up top and patch that damned hole. Chance was about to—"

Before Alden could finish, the old man pulled out his penknife and cut him off—literally. "Here," he said, walking up to the bulge in the ceiling. Without a second thought, he stabbed it with a single, confident strike.

"What a bonehead," Chance thought. "What a maroon," Bugs Bunny would've said.

The result was instant chaos. The ceiling gave way in an explosion of wet sheetrock and drenched fiberglass insulation. Along with it came a six-foot section of pine limb, bits of bark, shingles, and roofing debris. It all came crashing down in a soggy heap.

Chance, Alden, and Mama had stepped back just in time to avoid the worst of it. Everyone, except Dad. He stood there, dumbfounded, covered in wet insulation, shingle dust, and bits of ceiling, his freshly buzzed crew cut now a nest of fiberglass fluff.

"That's where he went in this weather?" Chance thought. "To get a damn haircut?"

A man has to have his priorities.

For a moment, no one said a word. Then, as if on cue, they all burst out laughing. It was dumb. It was ridiculous. But it was exactly what they needed. Amid the storm, the stress, and the sheer absurdity of it all, they found a moment to just be family again.

***

Back home, weather and condition concerns were building ever stronger.

Around noon on Tuesday, September 4th, Iny asked Chance to give him a ride to work. The wind was now blowing steadily 20-30 mph with occasional gusts to around 50. The hurricane was coming up the east coast and the leading edge somewhere east of Brunswick; not at all a good time for anyone to be out on the streets but Iny had to get to work.

The two got in that Chevy van and off they went. Up Gwinnett again to Wheaton, up Wheaton to E. Oglethorpe. A strong gust, they had no idea how strong, hit the side of the van and nearly blew it over. The boys watched another large metal dumpster in the parking lot at Randolph and Wheaton roll across the pavement and across the street like so many other boxes and large debris by this time. Gusts were certainly 65 miles an hour or more. They did take note that there were no other idiots out on the street now.

Obviously, Angel Earl was working overtime looking after this nut.

He dropped Iny off at the precinct on Habersham Street and headed back home. As he was pulling up in the driveway, he looked up toward the front of the house just as the other cypress tree was cracking at its base. It fell only feet from his patrol car parked in the yard and lifted that corner of the front porch about 3 feet.

That afternoon, sometime around 5 pm with winds of 90 mph, Hurricane Hugo turned suddenly inward near Hilton Head and the storm's most destructive edge inundated the Coastal Empire. CCPD called Chance in around midnight and he covered several extras shifts that week during clean-up efforts.

Iny, Janice and the kids went back home to find an oak tree down right through their living room. They would certainly have been injured severely or even killed had they stayed. And in his home, Glenus was mostly concerned because she couldn't get a pack of cigarette that next day because nothing was opened.

***

Chance worked long, grueling days, clocking in overtime hours patrolling the streets and businesses, keeping looters and trouble-makers at bay. The aftermath of the storm had left the roads in a terrible state. Debris was everywhere—fallen trees, broken signs, pieces of roofs—and in some places, the streets were completely im-passable. Tybee Road was flooded and shut down, leaving the is-landers stranded for at least 48 hours. It wasn't just inconvenient; it was a pressing concern. They'd need water, power, and lights long before that.

For days, Chance pushed through exhaustion, doing his part to restore order. The patrols were relentless, with officers from both city and county working around the clock. Slowly, though, things started falling back into place. By the end of the week, the watch shifts returned to normal hours, and the personnel rotation settled back into its usual rhythm. It wasn't perfect, but it was close enough to normal to finally exhale.

***

Zotz

On the south side of Savannah, Montgomery Crossroads used to be the southern city limits before the second phase of annexation of the city from Chapman County in the 1970s. Running south from Montgomery Crossroads, and across the street from Mayfair subdivision, was Whitfield Avenue. Whitfield ran south for about three miles to intersect Ferguson Avenue, then turning into Diamond Causeway and connecting Skidaway Island residents to the rest of the free world. South and east from that area was Rio Vista, the old Camp Strachan for Boy Scouts, Burnside Island, Pinpoint, Isle of Hope, Bethesda Boys Home, Wormsloe Plantation, Dutch Island, Nottingham Woods, and as far east as Savannah State Campus.

It's important to picture this area because it encompassed about 80 square miles of then unincorporated Chatham County. Unincorporated meaning that the area was largely residential, without industry or large commercial interests, and under the services of only the county government. In other words, there weren't enough residents at that time to generate the additional tax income needed for the city of Savannah to take an interest. That was fine with the residents of those areas, too—it was quiet, peaceful, and life was good.

Southside folks had recently seen the city annex a large portion of their neighboring residents from DeRenne Avenue east to Skidaway Road, south from Montgomery Crossroads all the way to Coffee Bluff, including Windsor Forest, and west to the Forrest River and the eastern side of Hunter Army Airfield. Those residents now belonged to the City of Savannah, relying on city services like police, fire, water, and sanitation while falling under the governance of a city council.

In those days, the county police station had been moved from the old county jail on Habersham Street between Oglethorpe and Liberty to what would later be known as Hodgson Memorial Drive, near Mall Boulevard. At the time, Oglethorpe Mall had recently opened, access to Skidaway Island had just been completed, and the county government wanted its police department represented in the most populated, highest tax-income area that required high visibility. Of course, they couldn't have known then that the entire area, including the police station, would be incorporated into the city by 1975.

Nonetheless, the "southside," as the department referred to it, was a very peaceful, well-behaved area—for the most part.

On a good day during an 8-hour shift, there were two patrol officers responsible for covering the entire southside area. Their duties ranged from answering calls for assistance and filing reports of missing or stolen property to breaking up domestic disturbances and investigating the occasional automobile accident. That was on a *good* day. More often than not, there was just one officer covering the entire area.

For an officer on day shift, working 7 a.m. to 3 p.m., the airwaves were cluttered with nonstop radio chatter. Traffic squad units were often stationed along the main roads, their radar traps primed for speeders. The Chief himself monitored the radio traffic. The Lieutenant was out patrolling, while the small municipal departments contributed their own brand of gibberish to the mix. With so many voices fighting for airtime, simply responding to calls and staying low-profile in the chaos was often the best approach.

It was one of those mornings, early in his shift, when Chance got a call over the radio to head to the Church of God on Whitfield Avenue. There'd been a break-in overnight.

Now, as I mentioned before, Whitfield Avenue is a long stretch of road, running about three miles from Montgomery Crossroads to Ferguson Avenue. Along its route stood two churches—St. Luke United Methodist and the Church of God—and Hesse Elementary School, all neatly lined up on the same side of the road, directly across from the Halycon Bluff subdivision.

When Chance arrived at the church, the pastor was waiting at the door of the administration building. They exchanged a firm handshake before crossing the sandy parking lot toward the office.

As police officers often do, Chance took a moment to inspect his uniform, checking his appearance from his badge to his boots. Everything was in order. He reached down and gave the tops of his shoes a quick brush with his handkerchief. That's when something caught his eye—a small yellow-and-black candy wrapper lying in the sand. It stood out against the otherwise pristine parking lot. The brand name "Zotz" was printed in bold white letters, accompanied by a cartoon lightning bolt.

Chance frowned slightly. It seemed out of place. The grounds were clearly well-maintained, save for the occasional bare footprints and scuffs left in the sand. Someone had clearly cleaned up recently, yet here was this lone wrapper. He smirked to himself—it was hard not to. Zotz had been a childhood favorite of his. He remembered the hard lemon and orange candies, each with a fizzy baking soda center that popped in your mouth when you bit into them.

When he followed the pastor inside, the acrid smell hit him immediately. It was the unmistakable stench of a recently discharged chemical fire extinguisher. The sharp, bitter scent of baking soda and lime burned his nostrils and made his eyes water. A fine white powder blanketed the carpet and walls, stretching from the sanctuary to the pastor's office.

Chance's sharp eye noticed two distinct sets of footprints in the powder. One belonged to a pair of flat-soled tennis shoes, marked by squiggly patterns across the sole. The other? Bare feet.

The pastor led him into the office. On the desk, in the corner, was a candy dish. Sure enough, it was filled with lemon and orange Zotz. Chance raised an eyebrow, a half-smile creeping across his face.

"Man, I used to love these things," he said.

The pastor chuckled. "Yeah, I still do. Go ahead, take as many as you want."

Chance glanced back toward the sandy lot and the wrapper. "Looks like your visitors already helped themselves. Left us a little marker, too."

Further into the chapel, the chaos became more apparent. Musical instruments on the platform seemed undisturbed, but the deacon would have to confirm whether anything was missing. Everything else, though, was covered in the extinguisher's fine chemical residue. Pews, Bibles, hymnals, even the pulpit—all coated in that devilish dust.

And in that layer of powder, as clear as a trail of breadcrumbs, were those same two sets of tracks: one pair of tennis shoes and one pair of bare feet.

He took the information from the clergyman, called it into the detective's office, but didn't reach anyone. He asked the supervisor to come out and take a look.

"Nah," the corporal told him. "Just take the report and let it go."

It was only 7:30 in the morning. Too early for anyone to be in the detective duty room, and there wasn't enough urgency to bother the on-call detective.

Standing outside his police car, Chance glanced across the sandy parking lot. Now that he was paying attention, he could see the tracks from the pair of bandits much more clearly. They came from the church's softball field, heading in from the direction of the elementary school, and went back the same way.

"I wonder," he thought to himself.

With some time to kill and nothing pressing yet, he decided to follow the trail. He drove over to the school, curious to see where the tracks might lead.

"Damn it, look at this shit! Little bastards."

Sure enough, they'd struck again. The glass on the door to the administrative wing was shattered, fire extinguisher dust coated the floor, and two adjacent wings had been broken into and ransacked. He had no idea what was missing, but the signs of their handiwork were clear as day—those same footprints, one pair of tennis shoes and one pair of bare feet.

Chance placed another call to his supervisor, this time pointing out the pattern. He tried to stress the urgency of the situation, but once again, he was dismissed and told to take the report and turn it over to school security.

By now, it was about 8:00 a.m., and the radio chatter was starting to pick up. Street traffic was getting heavier on Whitfield Avenue, particularly from Waters Avenue extension south. But the quieter sections branching toward the crossroads were still light. It was mid-June, and the cold front that had passed through the night before left the morning air cool and crisp. The marsh grass near Casey Canal had mingled with the warm ground air, creating a fine mist that clung to the sand and sidewalks, leaving them damp.

The neighborhood itself remained quiet, oblivious to the chaos of the early morning hours. The stillness was only interrupted by the distant barking of a couple of dogs and the faint sound of traffic. Chance pulled the police cruiser into the driveway of the little Methodist church and stepped out. As he walked along the concrete sidewalk toward the school, he spotted more tracks. There they were again, going in both directions.

"Mm-hmm. That's what I thought," he muttered to himself.

As he turned back toward the cruiser, something caught his eye—a lemon Zotz wrapper lying right in the driveway. It looked like it had been deliberately placed to grab someone's attention. Well, it had.

He also noticed a fresh set of tire tracks leading into the church parking lot. Nearby, an older model Chevy was parked by a side door. The footprints in the lot were scattered, closer together as they entered but spaced farther apart heading out. Something might have startled them, forcing them to leave in a hurry. They were brazen, maybe even still out as late as just before sunrise.

By now, it was 8:30 a.m. The sun still hadn't risen fully over the treetops, and the cool morning air carried the faint scent of bacon from someone's kitchen. The neighborhood behind the church was beginning to stir as people got ready for work and school.

Chance drove back up to the church, parked, turned on his portable radio, and walked inside. In the doorway, he saw the preacher sitting on the edge of the choir stage, his head buried in his hands.

"Look what they've done to my little church," the pastor said, his voice heavy with emotion. "We just bought this equipment last week for the revival coming up, and now, this!

He pointed around to the stage where microphone stands were left with their mikes and guitar stanchions were unattended by their finely tuned instruments. One of the missing items was a very expensive Stern's microphone purchased exclusively for the big baritone member of the church's little gospel quartet. The sound of that voice amplified by and through the mics ultra-sensitive coils was well worth the $1500 that had been raised especially for its purchase, part of only $5000 they could raise from baked goods for the group.

Several drums were damaged in the new, pearl blue Ludwig set. Big, expensive, Peavey amplifiers had their faces kicked in. One had the large woofer snatched out, its cord dangling to the floor.

More fire extinguisher residue. Purely childish behavior, but much more serious, this was heinous.

The preacher's office had been turned upside down, and someone had obviously tried to get into a floor safe. Thankfully, they were unsuccessful.

Wow, another candy wrapper. This one orange.

In their rounds through the building, they quickly identified a glass in the rear of the church had been broken from the outside. Chance rushed out and around to see if, by some miracle, they had left yet another calling card.

Nope. No wrapper.

But only God himself could have left the next amazing illustration and indictment that left them both breathless, in absolute awe. It wasn't enough that the two terribly inconsiderate juveniles had left a nice path of retreat in the dark of night, unlike that of Hanson and Gretel, but now a higher power appeared to have intervened in their discovery.

Violating a house of worship and burglary therein is a felony in the State of Georgia. They had violated two this morning. Criminal damage and burglary of a school is a felony as well. Much worse, though, these idiots had violated the sanctity of the church – twice – and stole from the temple of the Lord. By His hand they would be delivered.

The back lot of the little Methodist church was covered in a thick lawn of freshly mowed grass. This grass was the fine, small grain of fescue that held water droplets with perfect definition. There, across the half-acre lawn from the church to a canal lining the neighborhood of Cresthill, was the beautiful outline of a pair of familiar prints leading grass in the glimmering sunlight – one pair of sneakers, one pair of bare feet.

Crossing the canal, the two sets of prints made their way alongside a house and carport into a little side street. The tennis shoe crossed the wide bladed, dew-soaked St. Augustine grass in the yard and left its impression on the concrete driveway toward the house next door. The bare feet left their marks on the asphalt in front of the same house for a short distance and up that sidewalk to the front doorsteps.

"Well, I'll be damned", he said to himself.

This time he had the preacher call the department and asked them to send a detective to the church lot right away.

About that time the supervisor also called him on the radio.

"Dispatch to 153. Are you out at St. Luke's with a complainant?"

Chance answered right away, *"10-4."*

The corporal chimed in, *"153, you want to explain what's going on out there?"*

Chance just could not resist nor hold back any longer.

"You might want to send the detectives to me now, I have a pair of suspects identified. We have two churches, and a school burglarized."

That went out over the radio for everyone, including the news media, to hear.

Within minutes two detectives arrived, one of them was the Sergeant for the squad. Chance explained what he had and showed them what he'd found. They readily agreed with the conclusion that these two individuals were likely where the footprints clearly terminated at 1864 Crindlewood.

They stealthily approached, then knocked on the door.

Within a few moments a tall, lanky, dark-haired young man, probably early 20s, opened the door just enough to see two men in suits and a uniformed police officer standing on their stoop. Peering just inside the doorway, sitting on a corduroy covered sofa, with his dirty bare feet, propped up on the coffee table, was a pudgy younger boy in a dirty, wet, white T-shirt.

As the detectives and Chance stepped inside, there, on the top of the table, were a new Sterns microphone and a large black woofer with the contact splayed apart. Beside the sofa were a pair of wet, sand-covered Keds tennis shoes, with squiggly lines all across the bottom. And thrown up on the tabletop, as if planted there by the hand of God himself, two unopened lemon and one orange *Zotz* candies.

The two suspects, one only 15 years old, were later convicted as adults and sentenced to 15 years in prison of their dirty deeds.

Chance got a Chief's Letter of Accommodation for that one and, for a brief moment, he thought he saw a glint in the captain's eye for a position with the Investigation Unit.

That didn't happen.

***

It didn't take long for Chance to realize that the rumors about fun times and wild watch parties weren't just true—they were a regular occurrence. Those county mounties worked hard, but they played just as hard. The camaraderie was real, the laughter was loud, and the good times came often. But, as with anything in life, the good times were balanced by their share of hardships.

During Chance's time on the force, they lost several officers. Each loss cut deep, a sobering reminder of the risks that came with the badge.

The first officer's death was a gut punch to everyone. Driven by his concern for his fellow officers, he ignored direct orders for his own safety. As he ascended an attic stairway, he was shot in the face by a mental patient armed with a sawed-off shotgun. The killer narrowly escaped death himself, appearing at a window just above a crowd of news reporters and two police chiefs, one of whom was the fallen officer's own.

Another loss came when a female officer was struck and killed while directing traffic away from the scene of an accident. The driver who hit her was intoxicated, a repeat offender on bond for being a Habitual Violator—someone with far too many drunk driving and reckless driving arrests.

One officer died in the line of duty while diverting traffic from an obstruction on a viaduct. He had leaned down to pick up a large traffic barrel when a distracted driver, rubbernecking the scene, struck him.

Another tragedy hit close to home. An officer, just blocks from his own house, lost his life to yet another drunk driver. He had just left his wife and a warm meal, returning to patrol on a major highway. A drunk driver crossed the center line and slammed into his cruiser head-on. He died instantly, so disfigured that his wife couldn't recognize him.

The parties lost their importance after that. Sure, they still played the occasional prank on one another—boys will be boys—but the lightheartedness wasn't the same. These men and women carried themselves with pride, but they couldn't maintain such erect posture all the time. The losses weighed on them, a constant reminder of the fragility of their lives and the gravity of their work.

***

Chance enjoyed his career with the CCPD so much that over the years, he was always looking for ways to improve himself and everything he could offer to his fellow officers and the people he served in patrol areas. He took it seriously, but not in a way that came off as stiff—he genuinely cared about getting things right.

One of the things he spent time on was mapping out every trailer park and apartment complex that didn't have maps of lot numbers or room layouts. He figured it wasn't just about saving time; it was about making sure everyone who responded to a call knew exactly where they were going. It wasn't long before other officers noticed and started asking for copies. He gladly shared.

Chance didn't just stay cooped up in his cruiser, either. He made a point to walk the shopping areas, talk to business owners and patrons, and even sit down with travelers for a cup of coffee. He'd hand out maps to visitors who needed better directions. People appreci-ated it. He wasn't just a good cop—he was *the kind of cop you wanted around*. And, of course, he always looked sharp doing it.

His uniforms were dry-cleaned and pressed with double starch, sharp enough to impress a drill sergeant. Every crease on his shirts and pant legs was perfect. About every six months, he'd request a couple of new uniforms, keeping everything fresh. His leather gear was polished to a shine, his shoes were mirrors, and his brass in-spection was always spot-on.

His cruiser got the same treatment. It was washed before every shift, waxed at least weekly, vacuumed, and searched for contra-band after every shift. Everyone on the force knew about his metic-ulous care. New officers would line up, hoping to get assigned one of Chance's old cars whenever he got a new one because they knew it would be spotless.

From a former officer named Calfo, Chance learned a thing or two about patrol car lighting. Calfo had gone overboard, with lights on the grill, roof, and even the trunk. Chance wasn't about all that, but he decided to tweak the setup on his Gran Fury. The patrol cars came with a big blue light on the roof, housing four 1,000-watt in-candescent bulbs. But Chance wanted more. He installed two 10,000-candlepower runway bulbs in alternating positions. Every other sweep of the rotating light sent out an intensely bright flash—so bright it was impossible to miss.

It was effective, sure. But as with all things, there was a catch.

Those 10,000-candlepower bulbs gave off an incredible amount of heat. And, as you might have already guessed, the dome covering the roof light? It was made of plastic.

Yeah, I think you see where this is going.

***

The Ladies and the Man

By this point, Chance had been divorced for several months. He was happy, dating occasionally, and taking plenty of extra classes at the State Academy in Forsyth. Life was fun, plain and simple. He'd met several attractive women along the way—married women, even—some of whom seemed more than interested in a man in uniform. But he knew better than to get too tangled up. He didn't need trouble, and he wasn't about to go looking for it.

Still, some of those domestic calls had their perks. The ones where the husband had stormed off to the bar or been hauled to jail for slapping the wife or kids? Well, let's just say those situations occasionally filled the pages of Chance's little black book. He couldn't help himself. It was fun, and he knew how to take care of himself.

Then there was Carole.

Carole was tall, sexy, and drop-dead gorgeous, with long legs that drove him crazy from the moment they met one night at a trailer park on Ogeechee Road. Her husband had a habit of getting drunk, slapping the kids, and threatening her before heading off to spend the weekend duck hunting with his brother. Carole didn't want to press charges, but she was all too eager to press herself against Chance.

That night, she called her mom to come stay with the kids. When Chance rolled up in his '77 brown Bandit-Edition Trans Am after his shift, Carole came out barefoot, wearing a short T-shirt and a pair of the tightest, shortest shorts he'd ever seen. The shorts had the American flag printed across them, and all Chance could think about was getting her back to his place. Let's just say he was saluting Old Glory all the way across town.

Then there was Paula.

Paula was tiny, with a small frame and frizzy brunette hair. Chance met her one late night escorting her out of a bar on Wilmington Island. She had a ride—her sister—but insisted Chance follow them to make sure she got home safely. Her sister left, and Chance ended up staying for a couple of quiet hours. She was much more than okay.

But things changed when he learned her little girl had absence seizures caused by Fetal Alcohol Syndrome. That was a line for Chance—he wanted no part of that situation.

Another time, he responded to a call about a prowler at an apartment complex off LaRoche Avenue. Two stunning college girls from Savannah State greeted him at the door. One of them recognized him from earlier that day, when she'd seen him getting coffee. They'd taken a shine to him and invited him back for some bar-hopping later that night. But first, they needed a shower—and someone to help wash their backs. His shift ended at 3 p.m., and you better believe he took them up on it.

And then there was Amazing Amy.

Amy lived alone in a little alley off Rio Vista. She had an orange-and-white tabby and a knack for needing "help" late at night. The first time Chance met her, she called him to check out a sound outside her apartment. She answered the door wearing a fluffy bathrobe, pajama pants, and furry slippers. By the second call, things changed. She offered him coffee, a brownie, and some conversation, this time wearing short terry-cloth shorts instead of pajama pants. Chance didn't mind—he even told her those were his favorite.

By the third call that night, the sound outside had gotten "louder." There was nothing there, of course, but Amy invited him in anyway. This time, she was lounging on the couch, the bathrobe open just enough to grab his attention. At 7:30 the next morning, she answered the door in just the robe—for a few minutes anyway. She wasn't worried about someone taking her kitty anymore.

Finally, there was Sue.

Sue worked at a convenience store across from Mammie's Kitchen, a barbecue joint on Highway 17. Her iridescent green eyes could stop a man in his tracks. They certainly stopped Chance. The first time he saw her, he was mesmerized. But there was a catch—his best friend on the watch, Jerry, was sweet on her, and Chance didn't want to muddy the waters.

Still, he'd drop by occasionally while working the area, just to say hi. Over time, her smiles became a little more inviting, but every time he made a move, she'd shy away. Eventually, he gave up.

But Chance figured she'd be back around.

***

More Than One Way to Soil the Uniform

Chance came on that night ready for whatever the shift might throw at him—good, bad, or otherwise. Two weeks earlier, he had traded in his Fury for a brand-new Dodge Diplomat. The car was smaller but a lot more fun to drive, with a peppy engine and plenty of speed. Unlike the big bench seat of the Fury, the Diplomat came with corduroy bucket seats, which were great for comfort but left no place to stash his briefcase or report files. He solved that problem by building a custom case to hold his gear, perfectly sized to fit between the seats, keeping everything within easy reach.

Back then, patrol cars didn't have computers—just the essentials: a radio mounted in the floorboard, a siren, and a shotgun rack.

Riding with Chance that night were two new officers. Tom McNair was from a small town in North Georgia, where he'd worked for a tiny municipality before joining the CCPD. Bob "Skeeter" Casini had been an assistant chief in a little South Carolina town and was already known for his reputation as a practical joker. This might be an interesting shift. Acting as their Field Training Officer for the night, Chance was ready—new car, fresh uniform, and the usual sharpness in his stride.

Making his usual rounds, Chance stopped by a Quik Mart on Ogeechee Road to grab a cup of coffee and a pack of cigarettes. He greeted the girl working the overnight shift, then headed back to his patrol car. Coffee in hand, he turned off his portable radio and started to back out of the parking lot. He planned to cruise down Highway 17 to Dean Forest Road and then pass through Suburban-ite Village.

As he approached the road to turn, his radio crackled.

"167 to 143... busy?"

Chance froze for a second. Was someone watching him? It was McNair's voice, but he couldn't see him anywhere.

"Negative, 167... meet you somewhere?" he replied.

"10-4," McNair said. "Arrow Sales, right below Buckhalter."

Arrow Sales was a mobile home lot just off the main road. The radio was quiet, with nothing urgent happening.

"Be right there," Chance answered.

He pulled into the circular drive in front of the little office.

Always gotta know your exits in case of an ambush, Chance thought.

But where was McNair?

Sitting in the car, Chance reached over, placing his Styrofoam cup of coffee in his right hand. His foot was still on the brake as he pressed the button to roll down the power window.

The moment the window clicked to the bottom of its track, there was a sudden, deafening **BOOM**—followed immediately by a second **BOOM**. The sound was so close it felt like it was right on top of him.

Instinctively, Chance's right hand let go of the coffee cup mid-air and shot toward the grip of his combat masterpiece. At the same time, his left hand reached across his body, trying to catch the falling coffee. Unfortunately, he squeezed the Styrofoam cup much harder than he intended. Hot, sweet coffee erupted like a geyser, spraying onto the tan felt lining of his brand-new cruiser and rebounding all over his freshly pressed tan blouse.

For a moment, Chance sat there, motionless. Coffee dripped off the brim of his glasses and the tip of his nose. His right hand hovered over the grip of his still-holstered revolver, while coffee stained everything around him.

"What the hell is that sound?" he thought.

Out of the corner of his eye, he saw them—McNair and Skeeter, just out of range and doubled over in laughter. They had been lying in wait for him to grab his coffee, get back in the car, and lower the window. Armed with M-80 firecrackers, they had timed everything perfectly, tossing the explosives under his car from two directions as soon as they saw him roll down the glass.

"Bastards," Chance muttered. "Come out here before I shoot the shit out of both of you!"

The two pranksters were rolling on the grass, laughing so hard they could barely stand. As Chance got out of the car, trying to regain his composure, McNair reached out to help Skeeter up. Instead, he lost his balance, and the two of them tumbled forward—right into the area where the sales manager's German shepherds were chained during the day.

They landed squarely in two fresh, soft piles of dogshit.

Chance couldn't help but grin. Sometimes revenge didn't require his help. His guardian angel, whom he liked to call "Earl," seemed to have handled this one for him.

"Way to go there, Earl," he said, wiping the coffee off his glasses.

(what he calls his angel).

***

The Straw The Breaks The Camel

About a year after he thought he'd heard the last from Eve, enjoying life again, getting plenty of – work – she called him one afternoon. They talked a bit. She convinced him she still had feelings for him and really, really, wanted to see. It wouldn't be, couldn't be, just a convenient drive by or sit-down meal over coffee.

She and Harriett had been offered free rent if they would come up to Niagara Falls, New frikin' York at the invitation of sister Selena if they would stay at least through the winter. Well, hell, you could not have engraved an invitation as readily accepted as that offer had obviously been. She offered to have him stay for a couple of weeks, see if they could rekindle something, then come back home. Sounded OK to him.

"What the hell", he thought, *"can't hurt nothin'."*

He had plenty of time off on the books, so he took a couple of weeks and headed up state. Up I-77 through Charleston, West Virginia, he picked up I-79 into Erie, Pennsylvania. The roads were icy as hell but that brown Trans Am was doin' a pretty good job of sticking to the road. From Erie to Buffalo the snow was falling harder and faster all the way. By the time he got to the city limits of Niagara Falls and turned onto Sheridan Boulevard the drifts were several feet high.

***

Buffalo – More Falling Than Niagara

Chance came on that night ready for whatever might be thrown at him—good, bad, or otherwise. Two weeks earlier, he'd swapped out his old Fury for a brand-new Dodge Diplomat. It was smaller, but with a peppy engine and plenty of speed, it was a lot more fun to drive. Instead of the typical bench seat, this model came with corduroy bucket seats, which were more comfortable but left him without a place to stash his briefcase and report files. He'd solved that by building a custom case for his gear, which fit perfectly between the seats and kept everything within easy reach.

Patrol cars back then were simple: just a radio mounted in the floorboard, a siren, and a shotgun rack. No computers, no fancy tech.

Two new officers were riding along with him that night. Tom McNair had come from a small municipality in North Georgia, while Bob "Skeeter" Casini had previously been an assistant chief in a little South Carolina town. Skeeter came with a reputation for being a practical joker, so Chance figured the night might be interesting. Acting as their Field Training Officer for the shift, Chance was ready—new car, crisp uniform, and his usual sharp sense of humor.

As part of his routine, he stopped at a Quik Mart on Ogeechee Road to grab a cup of coffee and a pack of cigarettes. He exchanged a quick greeting with the girl working the overnight shift before heading back to his cruiser. Coffee in his left hand, he turned off his portable radio, shifted into gear, and pulled out of the lot. His plan was to head down Highway 17, cut over to Dean Forest Road, and cruise through Suburbanite Village.

As he approached the road to turn, his radio crackled to life.

"167 to 143... busy?"

Chance paused. Was someone watching him? It was McNair's voice, but Chance couldn't see him anywhere.

"Negative, 167... meet you somewhere?" he replied.

"10-4," McNair said. "Arrow Sales, right below Buckhalter."

Arrow Sales was a mobile home lot just off the main road. The radio was quiet, and nothing else seemed to be going on.

"Be right there," Chance answered.

He pulled into the circular drive in front of the little office, as always making a mental note of a quick exit route—just in case.

Always gotta know your way out, he reminded himself.

But where was McNair?

Sitting in his car, Chance reached over to set his Styrofoam coffee cup in his right hand. Keeping his foot on the brake, he pressed the button to roll down the power window.

The moment the window hit the bottom of its track, a deafening **BOOM** erupted, followed immediately by a second **BOOM**. The sound was so loud it felt like it was right on top of him.

Instinctively, Chance's right hand let go of the coffee cup mid-air and darted to the grip of his revolver. At the same time, his left hand tried to catch the falling coffee, but instead of grabbing the cup, he squeezed it—harder than he meant to. Hot, sweet coffee shot straight up, splattering the tan felt interior of his brand-new cruiser before rebounding all over his freshly pressed uniform.

For a moment, Chance just sat there, motionless, coffee dripping from the brim of his glasses and the tip of his nose. His right hand froze over the grip of his holstered revolver, while coffee stains spread across his shirt.

"What the hell is that sound?" he thought.

Out of the corner of his eye, he saw them. McNair and Skeeter were just outside the car, laughing hysterically and rolling on the grass. They'd been waiting for him to grab his coffee, roll down the window, and pull into the lot. Armed with M-80 firecrackers, they'd timed it perfectly, tossing the explosives under his car from two directions.

"Bastards," Chance muttered. "Come out here before I shoot the shit out of both of you!"

The two pranksters were laughing so hard they could barely stand. Chance got out of the cruiser, wiping coffee off his glasses and trying to regain his composure. McNair reached out to help Skeeter up, but they both lost their balance and fell forward—right into the spot where the sales manager chained his German shepherds during the day.

They landed squarely in two fresh piles of dogshit.

Chance couldn't help but grin. Revenge, it seemed, didn't always need his direct involvement. His guardian angel, whom he liked to call "Earl," had handled it for him.

"Way to go there, Earl," Chance muttered, shaking his head as he looked at the mess.

**

Revisting Old Wounds

Eve came back down to Savannah just long enough for them to get married a second time. Chance gave notice and worked it out, though he regretted it almost immediately. One of the guys from the AC business bought the T/A from him, and his new brother-in-law helped him secure financing for a front-wheel-drive Ford Tempo. It was more practical, better on gas mileage, and supposedly ideal for seasonal weather. Two weeks later, the mechanic totaled the Trans Am. That stung.

Suffice it to say, as Chance expected, things didn't work out well for him back under Mama's roof. Nearly a year of his life was gone, wasted. He'd walked away from the career he loved for this vagabond crew of losers, and for what? Nothing. He was right back where she wanted him—flat on his ass, with nothing to show for it.

This time, he laid it out clearly: she could change her life, move back to Savannah with him, let him return to the job he loved, and start over together. To his surprise, she relented.

That third shade of brown I mentioned earlier? Well, here it comes.

It's the greasy, putrid brown of pure excrement—the kind Chance was wading into as this relationship spiraled from bad to far worse.

It gets deeper, my friend. Be patient.

By some stroke of luck, his position with CCPD was still available. The Chief, eager to have him back, welcomed him with open arms. For a short time, Chance even managed to secure them an apartment in a high-end complex on Eisenhower at no charge in exchange for providing security for the residents.

For a while, things went surprisingly well. It was entirely out of character for her, but they seemed happy. Still no baby, but that was alright. Chance was in his late 20s—there was still time.

If he could be patient, maybe—just maybe—they could pull this off. Maybe they could make it work this time.

If...

***

Roger Wood – Tracks of His Tears

When he was on the city police department, Chance had a Field Training Office (FTO) named Dorsey. Dorsey was a corporal, kind of portly, a bit slow to get around at times. He'd been a member of the department for about six years at the time and had a sound reputation as a very thorough field training officer.

According to department rules, new graduates from the police academy were required to ride with an FTO for a period of at least 90 days to make sure they were indoctrinated to as many scenarios and customs as possible before going solo. They didn't teach reports, forms, booking slips and the like in class. These administrative but highly essential tasks could only be learned over time and through repetition or rote memorization.

Suffices to say that "common sense" is always, apparently, a finely tuned personal commodity - and that don't get issued in the sea bag neither. Common sense is a trait of vital importance to men and women who are armed and absolutely need to know which end of the pistol is pointed toward the suspect, and when not to spray mace into the wind. The answer to the latter, of course, is never but, nevertheless, may not be automatic to some. Chance had plenty of that and so did Dorsey, so they hit it off pretty quickly. They had their adventures, looked like the city force was going to be a long term thing, then, before you know it, Chance up and changed departments.

Within a couple of years of his move, huh, here comes Dorsey. New changes in city management didn't sit well with him and the county offered him a good deal to roll over.

Crazy enough, by that time it had already been just over two years for Chance on the county police when Dorsey came over. As fate would have it guess who was who's FTO now? Yup, Ewald had to ride with Chance for awhile. Funny how life turns sometimes.

Anyway, they rode together for several weeks before Chance cut him free to do his own thing. The county had far fewer officers and frequently your back-up may be on the other side of the county....or not at all.

One winter night, while on the graveyard shift, the two comrades had to share a ride and patrol a particularly large portion of the county. Dorsey's vehicle was down for maintenance and, thankfully, the Lieutenant assigned both of them to the west side. The night would not turn out to be as long or as boring as usual for either.

In those days the county issued squad cars to the officers like their uniforms and firearms. The goal of the county commission in this endeavor was to both increase visibility and provide for more available officers on the street at any one time. The city had jurisdiction only within city limits, but the county officers were deputized by the Sheriff with jurisdiction in the entire metropolis – including the municipalities.

The city police checked their cars at the end of each shift. They had to be quickly cleaned, buggers wiped off the steering wheel, refueled, and restocked with forms and blank reports after roll call. If you were lucky, you drew a unit already parked and cleaned from the lot. Those days the city bought the shittest vehicles – damned Chevy Novas; 4-door Pontiac LeMans sedans (to drive through the alleys of downtown Savannah. Try that some time); frickin' POS Dodge Darts!

Think I'm kidding about the buggers, huh? Ask a city cop sometime.

Conversely, the county had much better deals with much larger dealerships and were providing much large, much nicer vehicles to their officers. Dodge Monacos, Coronets, Polaras, etc. The most sought after by all the officers was the Plymouth Gran Fury 440 police interceptor. These babies had a 4-barrel carburetor that made a loud, throaty "woooooom" sound when the officer floored her, turned on the rotating incandescent blue light, and the distinctive wailing electronic siren that only the county officer had at the time.

I remember think in high school, when I would date a girl from the southside of town, sometimes you could hear those guys "woooooom" and that siren – somebody's ass was in deep doodoo.

Anyway, Chance got one. Like I said, Dorsey was a bit portly.

This car was big enough to provide a bit more leg and "maneuvering" room. Even with the center console Chance had built himself to hold reports, accident diagram kits, and the shotgun mounted in the center, both could be comfortable overnight. Usually both men road alone.

It was winter, it was raining, there was very little traffic on the road due in part to the weather and in part due to the holiday season. Chance and Dorsey were assigned to the westside of the county that consisted of everything in the unincorporated county from Loop 26 (Lyons Parkway) to the Forest River, south to the Bryan County line, west to the Effingham County line, and north and east to the Savannah River. This is roughly 200 square miles of sparsely populated rural county with several main thoroughfares including Ogeechee Road (US Hwy 17), Ga Hwy 204, Interstates 95 and 16, Ga Hwy 21, US Hwy 80, and Ga Hwy 307 (Dean Forrest Road).

There was also a huge industrial area within their patrol in which the majority of railroad connections and commercial warehouses are frequented, violated by less than desirables of all walks. Amtrak, Southern Pacific, Atlantic Coastal Lines and others all traverse these strips and configurated roadways, sometimes blocking passageways for hours on end. Within this confine sits Roger Wood packing house.

Famous for their smokehouse wieners and sausages, Roger Wood was known to stock several hundred cases of smoked turkeys during the holiday season to gift to various individuals and groups within the county: government officials, prominent businesses, police departments, security companies. It was their way of saying thank you for their support and decades of good business in SE Georgia. They were well represented in grocery stores, food stores, corner markets, restaurants, roadside venues – everywhere.

But this particular year, this particular season, Roger Woods had been plagued with several break-ins and already lost several million dollars in profits from repeated burglaries and thefts. It was commonplace to get at least one drop alarm from Hollow Wells at least every other night. Usually, it was due to a large wharf rat scampering across a contact in the warehouse. Sometimes, though, is was a real thing.

Did I say it was raining? Nope. It was frickin' pouring. You could barely see anything on the road, let alone where you were going. There was literally no one on the road.

The night had been exceptionally quiet. Dorsey and Chance were on their fourth cups of coffee and they had already buzzed through most of the hot spots along Ogeechee Road. Duggers, Lonnie

Lynch's, Korean Village, Mammie's Kitchen, September Club – kind of dead for a Thursday. April was working at the Waffle House, Big Jim cooking at the DeSoto Truck Stop, Circle-K and Starvin Marvin's were all peaceful. Then, about 1:30 it happened. And all of a sudden it started pouring rain.

"Dispatch to 153/164, Roger Woods on Louisville Road. Inside alarm, code 4".

What that meant was that the alarm had been activated from the inside of the building and the officers were to proceed as fast as possible but to run silent.

On a night like this. Fast but silent. Good luck with that. But they were actually pretty close as the crow flies, about 2 miles west of the location. Unfortunately, this was well before Chatham Parkway had been completed connecting Ogeechee Road to US Hwy 80, crossing I-16 and Telfair Avenues. That would have been a great and very fast response had those routes existed. Instead, they had to go down Ogeechee to Staley, under Lyons Pkwy, traverse the entire length of Tremont Avenue and then Telfair Road to get to Louisville Road where the packing company was located. At best, this was a 20-minute drive in good, clear weather.

"Shit!"

Despite the torrential downpour, literally on the edge of their seats, they made it within just under 15 minutes. I don't know how it happened by no trains blocked their paths along the route at all that night.

Just before they got to the last set of railroad track near Tremont Road Chance cut the lights on the patrol car and eased into the front of the lot. As they crossed those tracks, they could barely hear the "blump, blump" the tires made as they rolled over the metal rails. The same sound that the trains make as they traverse the steel joints in the tracks.

"Blump, blump....blump, blump".

The exterior siren was blasting on the corner of the building. On the radio, a Garden City unit was heard telling dispatch that he was heading toward the packing house to back them up.

Dorsey picked up the mic. *"153 and 164 are 10-23"*. They had arrived.

"10-4 153, all units 10-33".

This was dispatch instruction to all units on the air to maintain radio silence for the two officers responding to this possible burglary in progress.

Chance grabbed the shotgun, entered a round in the chamber, cleared the console, and out the door. Even over the pounding rain they could both hear what sounded like a sledgehammer beating against a concrete wall. He told Dorsey to take the car, turn just on the other side of the building, and block the suspects escape route with the vehicle.

From that vantage point Dorsey would be able to see the end of the building where Chance would be coming around and the suspects would likely run in his direction. Dorsey affirmed his instruction and Chance heard him turn the vehicle around.

The closer Chance got down the end of the building the louder the hammer sounded. He checked the safety on the shotgun.

Oddly enough, in the distance, he could also hear the sounds of that big 440 - "wooooooooom" and a distinct "blump, blump....blump, blump" as Dorsey raced in the opposite direction he had agree.

Soaking wet, rain dripping from his brow, condensation on his glasses, Chance peered around the corner of the building and couldn't see anyting. His flashlight immediately came in contact with a black male standing about 3 feet away from him with a sledgehammer in his hand, looking over his shoulder at Chance in disbelief. Both now froze in respective stance.

"Freeze. Don't move a muscle. You're under arrest. Drop the hammer!"

Oops. Just then another face popped out from inside the wall. Out came another tall, young black male holding two large, frozen turkeys. And off they ran.

"Freeze!", Chance yelled. Yeah, right.

Tires screaching. *"Blump, blump.....blump, blump".*

"Wooooom". *"Blump, blump.....blump, blump".*

"What the....!

It was Dorsey.

Back and forth over those damned tracks. Completely lost track of instructions and his wits, his common sense.

Both suspects now running along a drainage canal adjacent to the back of the warehouse.

"153...I'm in foot pursuit. Two black males, medium build, one with no shirt, one with a white shirt. Running west along Dundee Canal".

"Woooooom.....blump, blump.....blump, blump" Tires screech. Vehicle stops.

"164 to 153.....where are you?"

It was Dorsey calling Chance.

Holy shit.....now he calls.

About that time, he could see one of the suspects weave slightly to the left then back to the right. The other one was now about a block away running right beside the canal.

He could hear other units on the radio, now from Port Went-worth and Garden City, coming to his aid.

Suddenly, right in front of him, a break in the canal. About 4 feet wide. It looked like a dry spot right in the middle of this break. Maybe he could jump, bounce on the spot, hoist himself back up the other side to catch at least one of these guys.

Not to be.

He jumped.

He did land on the green, grassy looking area in the middle of the slew. But that was neither dry nor solid ground.

Chance had no idea how deep the water actually was, but he went up to his nipples in muddy water before hoisting himself out of the muck and sludge on the other side. Last time he saw both suspects were rounding the distant end of the canal along the railroad tracks, one still holding tightly to two frozen turkeys.

The corporal really went up one side of him and down the other because he didn't shoot the suspect holding either the hammer or the turkey. Chance just couldn't fathom explaining to a jury why he shot a man armed only with a frozen turkey. Sounded to him like a bad episode of a sitcom, like WKRP in Cincinnati.

The two former partners never rode together again.

***

By 1983, Chance and Eve were approaching their three-year anniversary of getting back together, but life was beginning to feel rocky again. Eve was taking on some bookkeeping jobs here and there and was starting to show an interest in auditing and accounting. Chance was doing well on the county force but was starting to feel restless. While he had tried to transfer into the traffic unit, he didn't have the right connections, and despite his interest in forensics and fingerprinting, he had been passed over twice in three years for a position in the ID unit. Positions in the detective unit were highly political, and Chance hadn't been on the department long enough to have any leverage over the competition. However, the Drug Squad was beginning to look promising.

Eve's mother returned from Florida again, and they moved into a new apartment on the other side of The Gardens. Glenus quickly filled the place with her things, leaving barely enough space for furniture. Most of the time, Chance found himself confined to a small corner of the living room or retreating to their smaller-than-average bedroom. Intimacy was non-existent once again; to put it bluntly, their relationship felt flat. Chance didn't think Eve was cheating on him, but it was clear she wasn't interested in anything beyond his income.

In his downtime, Chance's alter ego, Jay Hanson, was starting to get regular work on the radio. The Weis family had converted their twin stations on Broughton Street into stations that played popular West Coast trends, moving away from the music Savannah had grown up with. For years, kids and young adults had faithfully tuned in to 1400 AM radio for Top 40 rock and oldies, but now it was "Music of Your Life," featuring taped music from the 1930s, 40s, and 50s. The music felt boring. The other station, WZAT 102.1 FM, had originally been an album-oriented station, but now it focused on Top 40 rock, playing artists like Madonna, Michael Jackson, the Eurythmics, Cyndi Lauper, and Aerosmith. While Chance's sex life at home was dead, it wasn't in short supply among the radio staff or occasional fans.

Between late 1983 and mid-1985, Chance worked in narcotics enforcement. He and a partner, who could have been his doppelgänger, became involved in everything—stings, prostitution, reverse stings, buying drugs, intercepting shipments, busting bad guys, and working cases from the streets to corporate interdiction. Chance even had multiple fake IDs to help him maintain different undercover profiles. His radio gig, a new motorcycle, and his curly perm helped the pair get into places they would never have been able to otherwise. They busted so many people in one trailer park on the Westside that rumors spread about hit squads being sent after them.

While Chance was making progress in the Drug Squad, his lieutenant was not a fan. He constantly criticized Chance's work, clouding potential cases with doubt and speculation about everything from Chance's skills to the reliability of his informants. Despite this, Chatham County was starting to get coverage in police publications.

In fact, Chance had an informant who convinced him of a covert air-strip hidden in the woods, active and ready to receive bails of mari-juana. But his lieutenant doubted the informant and was not opti-mistic about the lead. Just two weeks before Chance began develop-ing the case, an article in *Police Times* profiled a team of GBI agents who had stumbled upon an underground hot house off GA 204, which had yielded several million dollars in high-yielding sinsemilla marijuana.

***

Airfield Popsicles

The informant insisted there was a hidden airstrip in one of the highest populations of pure rednecks in Chapman County. Army in-telligence at Fort Stewart was able to confirm satellite images of the area in question as an elongated patch of closely cut fields some 300 yards long and 50 yards wide deep in heavy cover west of Georgetown subdivision. GBI aircraft were able to confirm nighttime activity through infrared camera mounted on the whis-per-quiet whirlybirds. At the same time, DEA agents were confirm-ing reports of suspected traffickers of marijuana bails had made two drops in the last month, one on Cumberland Island 2 weeks before and the other off Ossabaw that washed out into the sound just a week later. An air drop was *definitely not* out of the questions, alt-hough the airstrip still was suspect.

Information continued to develop about a possible, despite the lieutenant's best efforts to make Chance look like a fool, and they began putting together an interdiction team. Headed up by Chance and his partner, their sergeant and corporal, the team consisted of two agents from the DEA, two from the GBI, an FBI specialist in aircraft integrity, and an assistant DA.

In the early afternoon prior to the suspected drop the 10 agents met and were dropped off at an undisclosed area about 5 miles from the questionable field. This was years before drone technology or satellite feeds in real time. They were dependent on their senses and instincts.

Dressed in camo gear, backpacks full of water, radios and extra ammunitions the officers proceeded to hike into the thickly wooded area in question armed with AR-15s, scatter guns and .45mm sidearms. One of the DEA agents, a large man that looked like he could have been a linebacker for Green Bay carried a 20-foot section of large link chain. If a plane did come in and proceed down that strip the teams' objectives were clear: stop the plane at all costs. The chain was to be thrown either into the landing gear or the propeller, it didn't matter.

Just before sundown, the team reaches the edge of the thickest area of cover and an opening of waist high grass. They identified the strip of freshly cut vegetation some 40 yards or so from where they stood under cover in the shadows and progressive dusk of the evening. The informants' last message was that the drop would be some-time between 8:00 and 12 midnight. They hunkered down for the wait. It was just after 6:45 pm.

Around 9:30 they could hear noise with the Army parabolic microphone and see movement under shed at one end of the property with their infrared glasses. Then just after 10 pm they thought they would see an aircraft fly over and flash its lights. False call, it was a high-altitude commercial jet on a predictable flight path.

By now the dew had begun to fall and the temperature had dropped by 15-20 degrees. They were cold and they were getting wet. A shiver was beginning to set it as the temperature seemed to get progressively colder by the minute. Above them, not a cloud in the sky. The weather service had been consulted and indicated the night would be clear, they didn't tell them the leading edge of a cold front would be approaching by 10:30 or 11:00. They had water, one or two had small packs of granola. They were becoming miserable.

At 11:26 exactly two large 4x4 trucks sitting high off the ground roared downhill from the shed toward them. One stopped on the west end of the strip – its headlights pointing directly at their location. The other went down to the east end, turned and showed its lights across to the other side.

These burly well-equipped, fairly good-sized drug enforcement agents were now lying on their backs just below the cover of the grass some 3-4 feet tall: cold, shivering, soaked to the bone, now fearful of the sudden unknown intentions of their obvious adversaries.

Two men from either direction walked the field, just feet from where the ten agents lay; weapons locked and loaded, laying across their chests, a couple with their pistols in hand as well. As the bad guys strolled by they could hear them engage their weapons; lights panned across just over their heads.

Chance thought to himself, *"Someone may get killed here tonight"*, the informant was obviously right on target. For the first time in his law enforcement career, actually the first time in his life, he was actually terrified as he lay there shivering beyond control; frightened that his enemy might hear his teeth rattle.

As they walked the field like so many military personnel would to secure a landing one pair suddenly stopped, mumbled something, and pointed upward.

At 11:47 an aircraft with twin props circled the field at low altitude and flashed its lights – twice. That was the confirmation that the aircraft would run the field the next time around and drop its load.

The agents would have to take that aircraft down (and out), neutralize the armed suspects on the field, seize the aircraft and its cargo, then secure the field for arriving officers. People were certainly going to die; officers were be injured or killed, maybe Chance. He was petrified.

Then there was the sound of a car horn blowing three times, a vehicle flashed its light three times, the armed personnel turned and walked back to their vehicles. The plane circled halfway around then made a sharp 90-degree turn, quickly increased its speed altitude until it was out of sight. The men got in their trucks and moved back to the shed.

"Something spooked them", one of the GBI agents said.

"Holy mutha***ker", said his sergeant, *"I just knew my life was over....praise God."*

"What the hell was THAT!?" whispered Assistant DA. *"You guys are frickin' crazy. I believe you're all out of your mind. I don't make enough for this horseshit."*

They waited until all the traffic had cleared around the shed and everyone there was gone. The Squad supervisor called the extraction vans and they met up at rendezvous points within a few minutes. Chance was teased unmercifully by his lieutenant for weeks until he finally gave up and requested to go back to patrol duty. But he had achieved a lot of respect and confidence from the other members of his team that night.

The captain bought him an expensive bottle of scotch as a going away gift and a letter of commendation for his duty on the team.

***

Chance and Eve had a serious conversation about their marriage, discussing whether they wanted to save it, how much they were willing to invest in making it work, and what changes they would each need to make. Eve was having a hard time dealing with the constant opinions from Alden and Chance's mom about Glenus, her frequent moves, Eve's trips with her mother, and how her mother lived. It was difficult for Eve to swallow all of it.

Chance still had the magazines and drawings he had been holding onto, hidden away either under the house or in the trunk of his patrol car. He rarely looked at them, but they were still there. Keeping them in the trunk of his cruiser was especially risky since he could face an inspection at any time. If they were discovered, he could be fired or suspended for having pornography while on duty. His department had a strict policy on what was considered inappropriate, and even though they played hard, indecency was a line no one dared cross. He'd already seen a few officers fired for similar issues, and Eve was well aware of this.

On top of the issues in their relationship, Chance was growing increasingly frustrated with Eve's sudden disappearances, her lazy homemaking habits, her complaints about his family, and what she saw as disrespect for her mother and sisters. While she was right on some of those points, Chance still loved her. He still wanted things to work out. He remembered his Mammie's advice: "You boys marry for life, gotta make it work whatever you need to do. Ask the Lord for His blessing."

***

The county police were such a popular department with their constituents that it was almost scary at times. People didn't show anything but complete respect for these officers in their chocolate brown and caramel-colored police cars, freshly dry-cleaned tan and brown uniforms, shiny brass and direct, but openly friendly demeanor. Each of these officers were genuinely concerned with the community, involved with numerous charitable organizations and community service assignments every year. But the men and women could party and hob-knob with the best, all the politicians and all the right businesses.

So popular were these officers that the community sponsors of the police department athletic association never needed funded when it came to the annual CCPD Christmas party. Every officer was expected to be attending at least one of the events, planned at different times during the month to accommodate the swing shifts. Everybody went home with gifts, nice gifts like expensive liquor decanters, vacations, free-rent packages, clothing items, firearms, turkeys, hams, you name it.

Across town this one year the holidays weren't going very well for the profits of a particular sandwich company on the east side. For months, this company that supplied fresh sandwiches, chips, crackers, candies and drinks to several hundred work sites around the county had been the target of thieves. Nearly every truck in their fleet of some twenty-four vehicles had been broken into at least twice, several thousand dollars in sandwiches and snack goods had been stolen. These *cat burglars* were good; no traces of identification, prints, anything.

In an effort to get to the bottom of the problem CCPD had performed several surveillance events in hopes of catching the fiends. They set up overnight teams – down the road from the business, in the parking from the back of a van, in one of the vending trucks – nothing helped. During this year's Christmas party detective's had asked for a volunteer to spend the night in the shop just in case there was another break-in. Officer Gary Fetterman volunteered for the assignment. Gary was from the traffic department; Chance and his watch were off that night and he was attending the party.

Around 3am, Officer Fetterman was awakened by the sound of breaking glass from one of the vehicles our front. He had been sleeping on the couch in the manager's office, right next to the front door, but was fully awake now. Just as he approached the front, there was another noise behind him; in the bay where company stores were kept. The truck would wait, someone was going for the holy grail.

As Gary walked in the bay through a pair of swinging doors someone smacked him on the head with something hard. He went down. Not yet out, he got back up quickly and ran after what appeared to be a couple of silhouettes headed to the back of the shop.

Officer Fetterman called for assistance on his portable. Units were there within moments. The suspects were gone, Gary needed medical attention. So, the Captain had the shop secured as it was, and the officer transported to the hospital. The report would wait until the next morning when someone could see better, get an accurate inventory.

At 930 am that morning, dispatch called Chance and sent him to see about that report. God certainly moves in the most mysterious ways.

***

Tracks of Little Ones

As promised, Chance was sent to the sandwich company to gather details about an incident that had occurred the night before. This was the latest in a series of about two dozen similar episodes over the past few months. The investigators were unsure whether these were inside jobs or if a disgruntled current or former employee was involved. The thefts seemed random and petty, with only small items like packs of crackers or a few sodas being taken. One thing was clear: the incidents were becoming a headache for both the company and the CCPD.

This time, two truck compartments had been opened, and they were almost completely emptied. The day before, the trucks had been stocked with freshly made sandwiches—chicken, turkey, and ham, along with chicken and tuna salad, sodas of all flavors, chips, crackers, and candy bars. Nothing much seemed to have been taken from the warehouses themselves, as it appeared the intruders had simply rummaged through the trucks until they were spooked by the police officer who had been waiting inside.

Chance gathered all the necessary facts and started heading back to his car. As he walked to his cruiser, he noticed an empty pack of Lance Peanut Butter Crackers on the ground under the edge of his car. He wondered if it had been left from the previous night's break-in. Could the ID unit get prints from it? Probably not, so he left the wrapper on the ground and climbed into his car. As he backed out of the parking spot and started down the dirt road, something else caught his attention.

On the left side of the road, a dry Lay's potato chip bag was tucked in the underbrush near the edge. This was significant to Chance because, just before dawn, a police officer had encountered intruders inside the building. There had been heavy dew overnight, so if the bag had been there for more than 12 hours, it would have been wet—but it wasn't.

He pulled the patrol car over, parked, and got out. He walked back to the cracker pack, which was also dry. Looking around, he noticed several footprints in the sand, though it was hard to tell when or how they had been left. A half-block ahead, he spotted a couple of other discarded wrappers—within about 10 feet, there was another wrapper for Chee-toes.

"Can't be something this simple," Chance thought to himself.

As he continued around the corner, the trail of wrappers kept going: Frito's bag here, a Hershey's bar there, an empty Coke bottle, more candy wrappers, and an empty water bottle. He was about halfway down the block when the wrappers suddenly stopped. Standing in front of a dilapidated house, sitting on blocks about 3 feet off the ground, he saw a yard full of trash. Looking closer, Chance noticed a treasure trove of food products tucked under the house—Little Debbie snacks, unopened chips, and dozens of other items.

Chance called for detectives, and once they arrived and recorded the scene, they decided they had enough to knock on the door. Within moments, a very large woman, dressed in disheveled clothing and holding a small baby on her hip, answered. Both she and the baby appeared unkempt, with dried food on their faces and clothes. There were small children, puppies, and kittens everywhere.

The officers asked to come inside due to child safety and health concerns, and the woman stepped aside. Inside, Chance and the detective were shocked by what they saw. The home was completely unfurnished, with only scattered blankets and piles of dirty clothes. Three pregnant women, all roughly the same size, were living there with at least a dozen small children in various stages of undress— some in diapers, others in pull-ups. A couple of teenagers, one of whom was large enough to have possibly been the one who attacked the officer, were there as well.

The children were all barefoot, filthy, and some had dog feces on them, while others were covered in dried food. The house was littered with empty sandwich packets, chip bags, cracker packs, and candy wrappers. The kids were hungry.

The officers also noticed that the house was overrun with puppies and kittens, who had free rein to relieve themselves wherever they liked. Animal Control was called to remove the pets, while the Department of Family and Children Services arranged housing for the women and children. The house was condemned, and the landlord was cited for cruelty to children and renting unsafe housing. As a result, the vandalism and burglary reports for the sandwich shop stopped.

Departure From a Career

Patrol wasn't the same as before this time. He had drawn a hard-ass lieutenant again, his corporal was an arrogant all the time, the quartermaster issued him a piece of shit to drive; a real mechanically bad cruiser with stains everywhere. To make matters worse, he knew his marriage – the second time around – was all but done. These past four years had not been much better than the first time and Chance was frustrated to the point of just walking away. Almost.

"Oh, God", he prayed in earnest, *"what else would you have me do?"*

As if by the Lord's hand, the answer came within moments.

On his way home he passed McDonald's, Jiffy Mart, then Dairy Queen on Skidaway Road. Just as he got to the Showboat (and adult bookstore, no less) something flashed from a window directly across the street. The flickering light in the corner of his eye caused him to look in that direction. There, on the window of the US Post Office, in big bold letters and the picture of a nuclear aircraft carrier was a huge US Navy recruiting poster.

He looked up into the night sky. *"No way. Really, Lord? I'm almost 30, the average young sailor recruit is 18."*

There, as big as life and twice as high, on a billboard advertising Nike athletics right in front of him, the words - JUST DO IT - .

How does one argue with that?

Am I too *old*? Am I *fit* enough to make it through basic training? What do I *want* to do in the Navy? What *can* I do to make this a new career and a fresh start? So many questions for this 28 year old about to make a major moves in his life.

The two knew at this point, for certain, they would have to sacrifice or severely limit contact with their families' to make this life a work of their own. There was no longer any discussion or other consideration: this had to happen.

She would have to spend the time he was in basic training findings ways to break a few chains that were restraining her movement, things that were holding her here like the nieces in Florida, her sisters in several states. And then, of course, there was mama, Glenus – *her* Mama.

Chance met with the Navy recruiters: this was a *huge* move for him. HUGE.

They taunted him more than a little; *"Think you can take it, old man? Those sailors are gonna run circles around you, think you can keep up? Maybe you oughta go next door to the Marines, they can make a <u>man</u> out of you."*

Nope. He wanted to do his part in the military, and he wanted to do it the same place all other men on his mama's side had – in the Navy.

Nixon ended the war in Vietnam one year before Chance would have been drafted in 1975. He had friends who were sent over a little older than him that didn't make it back. Always felt he cheated those guys somehow: guilty.

After completing all the assessments, fitness evaluations and MEPS Chance learned that he had quite a few options for a career at this point. He chose something entirely out of his comfort zone. He chose submariner school and sonar tech rating: two of the most difficult schools and ratings to make from basic, but they were available right now. He would have to be top of the class, a real shit-hot sailor to keep those objectives available through boot camp. So he signed those papers, gave his notice to the county, and shoved off to Great Lakes Naval Training Center: 10 weeks to learn how to be a soldier / a sailor, military posture they called "bearing", and something called the Uniform Code of Military Justice (UCMJ).

Anchors Away

He thought he might get chosen to lead his company of recruits, they came close choosing him, but the Chief Petty Officer running the show had other ideas for Chance. Just short of latrine duty, Chief Smith made him Master-At-Arms (MAA), in charge of everything to do with the recruits *inside* the confines of their barracks; their military bearing, their cleanliness and "*attention to detail*", how they *lived* together on base – their *esprit de corps*. Why heck, he was in charge of everything but teaching them how to drill and wipe their butts - he taught them which hand to use, though.

For his thoroughness and dedication to his younger comrades they returned the favor by coaching him in physical endurance, running for time, military posture, and group cohesiveness. When it came time for the timed run in the gym the last week of training, he had classmates running backward around the track to help encourage "*the ole man*". He made it. Instead of graduating E2 the Chief recommended E3 and sent him across the street to Basic Electricity and Electronics training (BE&E), his pre-requisite to Sonar Tech school.

Eve came up right after basic training and the two found a little one-room apartment at a flea-bag motel in Winthrop Harbor, Wisconsin some 15 miles from the base in North Chicago.

He had an old Ford LTD his dad gave him before they left, mostly worn-out and running on about half its cylinders. He heated his coffee every morning in a microwave; she cooked their meals every night on a hot plate. Things were tough. All their possessions were now severely condensed: his uniforms, a few clothes, pots and pans, their expectations of privacy, suddenly and inconveniently all shoved into a room no bigger than 10 by 15 feet.

To make a little extra money, and to offset most of the cost of their housing, Eve worked as Front Desk clerk for the owners during the weekdays. A much older man and his wife, a Cajun couple from the bayou, stayed in a large apartment above the office during that spring and would be leaving before the first snow; Eve had her eye on the place all summer. They'd need extra space.

Three months after they officially started their new lives in the Navy, while in training, in ice country USA, she found out she was pregnant.

Pregnant!! Hallelujah, God gave them a baby!

"Finally", he thought, *"after all this time, all we had to do was nearly freeze our butts off? Get so cold we had to crawl up <u>inside</u> each other?"*

Exactly.

They didn't know it, although Chance had certainly prayed about it hard enough, they had a contract with God. Not unlike the

Israelites of the Old Testament, Chance asked for something from Him, something of great value and great reward: a new life, a child. In return God demanded something from him for each; sacrifice and the courage to step out in faith.

How like Our Father in Heaven is that not?

How many times in the Bible have we seen this same scenario, over and over.

"All things are possible through Christ."

But the final lot had yet to be cast. Chance lost his billet, or position, with submariner school to a large group of college graduates entering the Orlando training camp. Then he lost his sonar tech billet to many cutbacks that season.

He was stuck, in limbo, waiting for a fleeting opportunity to use his newfound skills in electronics for a slot in the Fire Control tech school - then it fell to the wayside. They even tried to get him into Navy Criminal Investigation Service (NCIS) or Master-At-Arms training in DC (Navy police) with his law enforcement experience to no avail.

Was this the Devil? Was God trying his faith again? Maybe he'd slipped somehow and the Lord thought he was backsliding? He sure hadn't come anywhere near to those magazines again, not this time.

Maybe it was "Earl " foolin' around.

Six months on base, 120 or more Navy correspondence course equivalent to an associate's degree outside, and he appeared to have exhausted all training options to get him out to the regular navy. Just as they were offering to send him to the fleet unclassified, they learned of his experience as an EMT and found a slot at the US Navy Hospital Corps School across the river from NTC.

His chief at NHCS promoted him to E3 with an endorsement to E4 on graduation and made him Class Adjutant. A week before graduation, with his choice of assignment to San Diego pending, his guardian angel, Earl, pulled a good one on him to further test his resolve.

A detailer in Washington changed his duty assignment after a junior corpsman had been transferred to duty on a frigate out of Mayport, Florida. The base hospital at NAS Jacksonville needed a corpsman – and he was next in line.

Remember who lives just south of Jacksonville? Uh huh. Glenus and Dana and all her kids.

"Well I'll just be a son-of-a-bitch!" he said as he read his orders to Eve. *"Would you look at this shit? Out of the frying pan, right back into the damned fire."*

She laughed so hard she started having contractions, false labor pains, but they put her in the hospital for a couple of days.

Eve was now 8 months pregnant, and the baby's head was already in the birth canal.

So, the Navy sent her ahead of him to Jacksonville where she could be monitored over the next couple of weeks. Just about the time Chance was rolling into town, she went into labor that night. Just like his mama on her fateful morning labor was tough for Eve. One week later, with the aid of an episiotomy, the doctor delivered a little boy: almost two weeks premature but healthy.

They named him Dillon because he truly was "like a lion."

Because he was in the birth canal so long the sutures in his soft skull opened, causing it to take the shape of a football. The condition, called "craniosynostosis", is not uncommon but does not occur that often either. What to do about the grossly malformed skull was the next decision. They struggled heavily with it. Doctors could perform a surgery that would split his skull, then they'd remove a strip about 2 inches wide allowing the cranium to reform and, hopefully, reshape itself normally. There were no guarantees, no half-baked promises, only supposition and conjecture.

Chance got on his knees.

Late one night he felt the presence of the Lord in his room while on duty at the clinic on base at Cecil Field. The answer was simply do nothing; he was sure he heard it; he knew it felt it. Little one would be alright in God's hands.

***

Early Warning Signs

Chance was working hard on his early career, making great gains in networking with similar aged NCOs at both the clinics and the naval hospital. These "connections" were necessary for recommendations to the next step in grade when his time came. The clinic Commander formally pinned him with his HM3/E4 chevron within a week of his arrival. By the end of his first year, he had already attained all required correspondence and physical training required for promotion to E5. Early the next year he was sent for temporary duty aboard a small combat ship out of Mayport serving with a senior chief from Cecil Field. This led to an outstanding recommendation for promotion. Then he put together a new system to intake patients at the clinics in Jacksonville, this earned him a Navy Accommodation Medal from SECNAV.

He applied for, and was accepting to, preventive med tech school in San Deigo the next year. After that school he would be assigned at least 24 months' duty with a Marine platoon out of Camp Lejeune to get ready for E6.

Near the end of his 3rd year in the Navy his Master Chief and Senior Chief had put in recommended promotion for E5, and he got it. These chief petty officers were in their 30s; he was 32 at the time, and they wanted to help bring him into the fold.

Now money was getting much better, benefits were coming left and right. Chance was at the top of his game. He had a beautiful, healthy little boy at home waiting for him every night. His wife, not quite as pretty these days as before, not so excited to see him as he had always hoped. She would most certainly welcome any possibility for him to be shipped rather than move with him to a different land duty station for a promotion. What she really wanted was to divorce him now, get the Navy benefits, take the boy and disappear. This was definitely on Chance's mind; he couldn't shake it.

From the minute they got home from the hospital, Eve was so incredibly obsessive with this baby you cannot imagine. Yet, there were frequent calls in the middle of the afternoon where she was frantic, in absolute panic when she would wake up from an after-noon nap to find that Dillon had rolled off her chest and onto the concrete floor in their apartment.

The family had found a good-sized two-bedroom apartment in old Navy base housing 15 miles south of NAS Jax. The bed sat more than 3 feet off the floor, so little one smacked that still deformed little head several times during the first year. Chance lost count of how many times he made that rushed drive from Cecil Field the 30 miles to her assistance. Dillon was always okay; he was just per-plexed as hell by her behavior.

When he was home, he couldn't seem to move with the baby, walk him outside, feed him, play with him that she wasn't right on top of them or in the middle of everything he was doing. She did permit the two to nap together, as long as she could keep them in her eyesight.

The bitch was weird, and getting weirder by the day.

Dillon was so tiny that he only took up the space between his daddy's chin and the top of his belt. Him was a little guy, but, OMG that man loved that boy so. He prayed so often and so hard for that little guy's safety and health every day and through the night.

Heaven forbid Chance would suggest or even consider taking Dillon to his mama's house without Eve for the weekend.

Absolutely not!

And don't close the door when he was taking a nap. Chance couldn't change the diaper or bathe baby at all, either. What the hell was wrong with this woman? Was she crazy?

He tried to talk to her about this behavior he considered to be bizarre, and she assured him that she was just over-protective because she had *"such a hard time giving birth to him, then I (she) made him deformed."* Neither of those was even close to the truth, but it didn't matter.

Should have taken this as a bad sign right then. But, Chance trusted his faith would see them through.

Tensions built over the next several months. Her obsession was just as strong now as the first few months, and Dillon was walking by now.

One afternoon, Chance noticed that his car was running hot on the way home. He went in and changed clothes, came right back outside intending to check the thermostat on the car: to see if it was opening and closing. If it was inoperative that would explain why the car was running hot, and he could replace the thermostat and everything would be great.

Eve came out with Dillon, put the baby down on the ground, and he began running to daddy – at the time Chance was opening the radiator cap under pressure. Just before the baby got to him, he reached down and pushed the little fella back, knocking him down. At the same moment, scalding hot water from the radiator burped out, covering Chance's entire left forearm and the top of his hand. The result was extensive second and partial thickness 3rd degree burns to the arm and hand. The baby would have died from the extent injury to his head, face, torso and more. He wasn't even sure if the baby had been pushed by him or his angel; didn't matter, little Dillon was safe.

You would think Chance had drop-kicked the baby across the yard.

She yelled, *"You bastard"*, yanked that baby up, ran back in the house, slammed and locked the front door.

Thank God the neighbor across the street saw what happened and he came over to drive Chance to the hospital on base. Twenty percent of his body surface was burned, and he was hospitalized for several days.

Like I said, Dillon would have been killed. She didn't come to see Chance in the hospital. When he came home, he couldn't hold or cuddle Dillon. For a new father, especially one as devout as Chance had become, this was agonizing. He was trying to be a good father while dealing with the breakdown of his marriage, but the stress was unbearable.

A couple of days later, he got more bad news. A detailer in Washington had changed his orders—again. Instead of going to Camp Lejeune after tech school, he was now being sent on an unaccompanied 18-month tour in Guam. To Chance, it felt like a slap in the face, pure jealousy on the part of the detailer. Chance had made rank rapidly, achieving E5 in under four years, while the other NCO, now on his second enlistment, was still stuck at E4.

The timing couldn't have been worse. Dillon was just a year old, and Chance couldn't bear the thought of missing the crucial steps in his son's development. He had waited his entire life for this special gift, and now it felt like it was slipping away. Surely not.

But it was too much.

Chance broke down. He made his way to one of the back offices, shaking uncontrollably, tears streaming down his face. And he couldn't stop. For over a week, the tears wouldn't stop. The stress of everything—his wife, his career, his orders—had pushed him to the brink.

Concerned for his well-being, they hospitalized him in isolation for a week, fearing he might be suicidal. He wasn't. But it was the breaking point, and it marked the end of his once-promising Navy career. Making E5 in under four years was nearly unheard of in the military, except during times of war. It was something to be proud of, yet it all unraveled just before his 33rd birthday.

The Navy Medical Board discharged him honorably.

But Chance couldn't stay. Not in that little town, not around neighbors he felt ashamed to face, and certainly not under the shadow of Glenus and Eve's sisters. The humiliation was too much, the shame too heavy.

Going home didn't seem like a solution either. If anything, it felt just as bad—or worse.

They found a place, a large house with a big front porch for the boy to play, just outside Savannah a few weeks later. Chance went to work with one of the municipal police departments pretty well right away, trying to recoup his reputation and former standing with the police community.

Everything was beginning to normalize after a few months working as an agent with a multi-department anti-drug / anti-prostitution squad. Except for occasional chest pains, no more than minor inconveniences, things were actually going well. He'd work his shifts, head home, Eve acted like she was genuinely happy to see him most days, and she let him, even encourage him, to play with Dillon these evenings.

He couldn't help but wonder, frequently, to himself, *'Who here is losing their mind? Is it me, oh Lord? How can this marriage, this relationship wax to bending then wane to near break so often; so fragile, so tense, for how long? What am I missing, my God? Where do I turn but to you, Jesus?"*

God forbid – suddenly this troubled girl even insisted that he *bathe* the boy once in a while. Like there had been something unnatural about that before now.

Had he "missed" something? What happened to this over-bearing mothering, obsessive behavior?

He was cautious, suspicious, yet hopeful all at once.

The couple was now doing things married folks with a child should do. They went for walks together. They filmed the little guy and everything he did: watching TV, eating spaghetti (and making a huge mess), talking about missing daddy, playing at the park with mom.

Dillon was now right at 3 years old. He suddenly developed re-active airway disease, then asthma and had to be hospitalized sev-eral times. Eve was a nervous wreck during each of those occasions and couldn't understand the peace Chance appeared to exhibit dur-ing it all. For Chance, Jesus was looking over Dillon. He prayed for their safety, strength for their marriage, and the health of his child and wife. There was no doubt.

They made it through Hurricane Hugo later that year, un-scathed, then something happened to cause him to make a little course adjustment – again.

***

"Oh, How I Wish I Could"

Shortly after the cleanup from Hurricane Hugo, Chance and his colleagues got wind of a prostitution ring operating off I-95. At least two squads, including the Chief, had received information about this, so the team was dispatched to investigate.

On this particular Friday afternoon, with the squad commander out of town, Chance received a call. The "escort service" was now in full swing out of a specific motel near the interstate. The caller, a city council member from a nearby small town, mentioned that the "girls" would be "ramping things up" over the weekend unless some-thing was done to curb the operation. The team got to work immedi-ately.

Within a couple of hours, Chance had made enough calls using numbers provided by informants and arranged to meet one of the girls at the motel in question for some "entertainment." Normally, an operation like this would involve a full team effort with surveillance, counterintelligence, and backup officers. But tonight, it was just Chance and Detective Harold Davis.

Both were seasoned officers, more than capable of handling themselves and representing their team with dignity. With little risk involved, they decided to take on this isolated case as a two-man sting.

This pair of comic partners, reminiscent of *Starsky & Hutch*, set up their plan with their usual flair.

The motel room was a standard single, complete with a small bathroom in the back and a double bed positioned low to the floor on a wooden pedestal. This presented a minor challenge for the duo—they needed a place to hide a small tape recorder to capture the evening's events for evidence. After some debate, they placed the recorder against the edge of the bed's platform, concealing it beneath the generous folds of the bedspread.

The plan was straightforward:

Detective Davis would act as the john, the one who'd made the call. He'd greet the suspect when she knocked on the door and invite her in. As expected, she'd likely ask for identification and reassurance that he wasn't law enforcement. Davis's role was to deflect—

distracting her or saying something indirect to avoid denying his affiliation outright. An outright denial could later be used as a defense for entrapment.

Once inside, she'd probably glance around, maybe peek into the bathroom, and then get down to business. As soon as she mentioned money and suggested an act—oral sex, intercourse, or any other sexual service—it would be enough to warrant an arrest.

Chance, meanwhile, would be hiding in the shower, acting as backup. His job was to witness the interaction and step in once the arrest was made. Simple plan. Easy peasy.

With everything in place, they put the operation into motion. Davis called the number, requested a girl to be sent to his room, and gave his location. No money was mentioned, sticking to the guidelines.

The reply was short and sweet: she was on her way.

About 20 minutes went by then there was a knock on the door. Chance went to the bathroom, got in the tub, closed the shower curtain, pulled out his .45 pistol and held it at his side.

Det. Davis opened the door and Chance heard him say, *"Oh, wow."*

There was a pregnant pause.

Chance thought to himself, *"This guy doesn't usually react to women this way, she must be stunning"*.

The girl then said, *"Well, you gonna invite me in or just stare at me?"*

"Oh no, I'm sorry. It's just...you're really gorgeous".

Chance couldn't see anything, of course, but she must be something, he thought. His informant indicated the girls were a pair out of another adjacent township; one a tall, shapely blonde and the other a short, kind of pudgy younger woman. Obviously, unless he was wrong about Davis and his tastes in women, this must be the tall blonde.

As expected, she entered the room and looked around for a moment. Davis managed to get through the police questions without answering directly, she sat down at the end of the bed. He couldn't hear what they were saying for a moment, but Chance realized pretty quickly that something got her suspicious. She leaned to one side, lifted that bedspread and found the recorder.

Davis later said she moved her heel back a little and heard a clicking noise like she bumped something. That was why she looked. Either way, the shit hit the fan about that time.

She grabbed that recorder, pulled the tape out, yelled quite a few obscenities at Davis (talking about his mother and his sexual orientation and such), and stormed into the bathroom.

By now, Chance had raised that weapon to eye level and was perched behind the curtain, waiting for most anything to happen.

She threw the tape in the toilet, flushed it....

Great. There goes state's evidence #1.

....then, threw the recorder in the toilet. Too big to flush.

She turned and walked back into the room, still cursing, and he heard Davis say something about taking her hand out of her purse. Chance had information that the girls would likely be armed. He needed to make a move – now!

Chance sprung from the bathroom.....

"Man, she is a beauty!" he found himself thinking, for just a split second. Tall, probably just under six feet. Highlighted, permed, long platinum blonde hair. Well-dressed in a very attractive, very short one-piece ensemble showing a little breast and really well-shaped, incredibly long legs in platform heels. He couldn't see her face right that moment, but – hey, who cares?

Suddenly, snapping back to reality, he could see that Davis was looking down at something in front of her. Since it wasn't her reaching out for his zipper or loosening her garment, Chance assumed she must have something in her hand she was trying to remove from the purse.

He threw his left arm around her from behind, engulfing her pretty neck in the crease of his forearm, and applied pressure over her carotids. He then came around and the muzzle of his .45 struck her in the right temple.

"Metro Task Force", he said, *"you're under arrest. Drop whatever you have in your hand and put both hands out where I can see them. Right now."*

By this time Davis had his revolver out as well.

In the purse was a .25 caliber pistol she was about to take out to either threaten him with or to point in defense of this stranger with a recorder under the edge of the bed. I suspect it was much more likely the former of the two.

Within the next 2 hours the detective woke up a Municipal Court judge, obtained a search warrant for her residence, and proceeded to that location to complete the task. During the drive to that location, fully aware this time that their conversations were being recorded, she provided information that a local police officer was involved with the escort service scheme, that he was providing "protection" for their service, they would provide "a cut" from the proceeds, and that he could even help them in obtaining "substances" for their enjoyment if things worked out well and they made money.

The search warrant went down without a hitch, they arrested the suspects husband and seized pornography, videos and photographs of the couple and other men in compromising situations, marijuana and cocaine, material used in the distribution of narcotics, cash, and books containing financial records and names of clients. Apparently, they had been in "business" much longer than the informant indicated.

It's always amazing that these suspects Always have pornography in the same place as their stash.

Most surprising of all, however, the stash and the porn and their cash are most frequently in either the same room, or next door to, a tiny baby or a small child.

Two weeks later, Chance and the agent presented their care before the judge that had signed the search warrant; it was Judge Mullins.

Judge Mullins was blind from birth. Chance had been before this judge on many occasions while with the county drug squad and found him to be both objective and fair, to officers and defendants alike. And Chance had always found him to have a fairly sharp sense of humor. Occasionally this jurist and he enjoyed good-hearted humor in their interactions in the judge's chambers.

The suspect's defense attorney was a rather flamboyant jurist in the county with a reputation of outright "showmanship" in presenting his cases before the courts. The attorney was the honorable John Calhoun.

Well, they laid all that evidence out on the table in front of the courtroom. All that pornography, those self-made videos and amateur sex scenes on Polaroids, x-rated magazines, an assortment of dildos and vibrators, sexy lingerie – you get the vibe: it was extensive.

The officers laid out their case and the circumstances behind the arrest.

The Court, of course, had quite a laugh at the exploits involving the tape being flushed down in the toilet. The State then rested its case, and the Judge asked for her attorney to proceed with his.

There was a long pause while Mr. Calhoun prepared himself.

He slowly walked to the front, looked down at the table, back at his client, then turned to the judge and said, *"Judge Mullins, my client is not guilty. She was framed."*

Well of course he would, most attorneys would do the same. What he said next, though, was not a usual interaction between officers of the Court.

"Your Honor," Mr. Calhoun continued, *"This is a huge display of the most graphic filth I believe I have ever seen, especially presented in a well-respected court of law like this. I just wish you could see all this filth laid out on this table, presented by these two officers. There is no way on earth ANYONE could have this much smut in one place at one time. They must have planted this stuff, or cleaned out their*

evidence closets, to bring this much filth into these hallowed halls today." Cancun continued.

"I just wish you could see all these naked pictures, all this graphic SEX laid out, I should say 'spread out' in here in front of you, your Honor".

Without missing a beat, not a single beat, Judge Mullins leaned forward in his high-back chair, cleared his throat, repositioned his dark shades and softly said, *"Believe me when I tell you, Mr. Calhoun, without a doubt, so do I – brother - so do I."*

The gallery went into uproarious laughter for several minutes. Then Judge Mullins slammed the gavel down and declared, *"Superior Court."*

The case provided great recognition for him and he got a call about 2 weeks later asking if he'd like to come back to the county. Of course, he said "yes" right away and they re-instated him to his previous rank and position. This time the Chief issued him a new police cruiser and, by now, the county had converted all their officers sidearms to either 9mm or .45 caliber semi-automatic pistols. Chance chose a stainless-steel Smith & Wesson 9mm.

Several months went by, he settled back into his routine with the county police; he was back at home in his work and he was feeling very happy with his life and his baby boy now. Dillon was doing well, no asthma attacks and no hospitalizations for several months. Eve now had tapes of the two of them enjoying time together while

Chance was at work; a happy mama enjoying her happy, healthy baby; both talking about daddy and things to do when he got home. Normal; finally.

They were actually looking at a home they were considering across town and much closer to his folks when - he couldn't put his finger on it, something "familiar" was amiss. He'd seen Eve's aunt around a few more times than usual, a lot more than he was comfortable with. Aunt Murtice was a drunk: a drunk with a loudmouth. A troublemaker from the old school, she was someone always looking for a pot of shit to stir; frequently she would provide both.

He was also hearing a lot about Eve's sister, Donna, in upstate New York. This was the one that prompted his move years before, that didn't work out, and was always causing a stink of some kind or another between Eve's sisters all the time.

She was an instigator. Never happy unless she could see discord or discontent among the sisters.

Adding to his heartburn with her, she was implying that Chance was responsible for problems between her and her husband, Ed. You see, Ed owned a chain of businesses in New York and was frequently playing the ladies during the day when he was supposed to be working. Chance found this out, quite handily from Ed himself, very shortly after he took the job in Buffalo and started running one of the main warehouses for Ed. The guy always had an attractive, much younger, and I might add much prettier woman either in his car or be his side every time Chance saw him. Things finally came to head between them about the time Chance was leaving town.

Like I said, these were all distractions that Chance simply did not need. The wrong distraction at the right time could be dangerous - or deadly.

***

The lot is cast in the lap,

But its every decision is from the Lord."

Proverbs 16:33

Chapter Ten

Back to Chatham County

Chance and Eve were finally talking about buying a house—making a real home, something they could call their own. This baby, Dillon, was truly a gift from God to Chance, and he wanted to ensure that his mom and dad had every chance to spend time with the little guy. So, when he heard about a vacant home just down the street from his parents—in his old neighborhood, no less—he jumped at the opportunity.

Thanks to his time in the Navy, Chance was eligible for VA benefits, including special mortgages. With the VA guaranteeing the loan, they purchased the little two-bedroom house at the end of the block from his parents.

The house needed some work. The old carport in the yard was barely standing, and the fence was falling apart. It had been built around the same time as the other houses in the neighborhood, and, as Chance quickly realized, it had the exact same floor plan as the one he'd grown up in. That included the old floor furnace with the hot metal grate in the hallway. He thought about how many times he'd burned his feet on that damned thing as a kid and figured maybe he could spare Dillon the same pain. Then again, wasn't that almost a rite of passage in these old homes?

Chance had another thought that warmed his heart: with any luck, Dillon and his grandpa—whom the boy had already started calling "Pa"—would wear a path in the asphalt between the two houses over the coming years. He also knew his mama was thrilled at the idea of having everyone so close. Her excitement was almost contagious.

For Chance, this was one of those rare moments in life that he knew he'd carry with him forever. He had prayed so long and so hard for a miracle like this, and now it was here. His faith, his dedication, and his hard work were paying off. His family was happy, truly happy, and he felt a sense of peace and fulfillment that had eluded him for so long.

Was it an epiphany? Not quite. But it was pretty damned close.

For the first time in years, Chance felt like everything was falling into place. Everyone seemed happy—his parents, Eve, little Dillon. Life felt good, and his spirits were soaring.

But there was one small problem he couldn't quite shake: what to do with those magazines and drawings he had stashed away. Every time he thought about tossing them into a dumpster or trashcan, he'd hesitate. What if some kid came across them while rummaging through the trash? That would be a disaster.

"Just hold on to them," he told himself. "It'll come to ya."

So, for now, he tucked the bag into the crawl space under the house, planning to figure out a permanent solution later..

Trapped At Bay

With their home loan approval pending, his family in great shape, and everyone healthy and happy, Chance felt like he could finally focus on his work again. In police work, even the smallest distraction could prove life-threatening, and he knew better than to let his mind wander on the job.

Chance was on the day shift, patrolling the south side of the county. His beat included LaRoche Avenue, Dutch Island, Grimball Point, and all of Isle of Hope. If something urgent came up in adjoining areas like Whitfield and Ferguson Avenues, Rio Vista, or Skidaway Island, he'd handle it, though units from the station off Mall Boulevard could assist if needed. Beyond that, his nearest backup was either the unit patrolling Tybee Road or a city officer—neither very close.

Just before noon, dispatch radioed a message for him to call home. It was 1990, long before cellphones became standard, so Chance pulled over at a phone booth to make the call.

Eve answered, letting him know she planned to head down to her mama's for the weekend and might stay for a couple of weeks. Since it was Wednesday and Chance was off-duty for his monthly four-day break starting Saturday, he suggested, somewhat casually, that Dillon stay home with him instead.

Her response was curt: "No." Then she hung up abruptly.

That struck a nerve.

First of all, who the hell did she think she was, telling him he couldn't keep his own son? Secondly, his suggestion had been more of a statement—his way of saying he expected to have Dillon for the weekend while she could do as she pleased. But to flat-out deny him? That was galling.

He tried calling her back—twice—but she didn't answer. That pissed him off even more.

Standing there by the phone booth, he forced himself to take a deep breath and regain his composure. With a quiet prayer, he asked the Lord for guidance, leaving the matter in His hands. "Your will be done," he murmured. For now, he let it go.

About 45 minutes later, Chance was dispatched to a domestic disturbance in Nottingham Woods, a subdivision just off Eisenhower near Skidaway Road. According to the dispatcher, the complainant—a woman—was waiting for him at a neighbor's house across the street from the incident.

As was common during the day, Chance was the only unit sent to handle the call. That wasn't unusual for the area, the situation, or even for the county police.

Arriving at the address, Chance found the driveway positioned on a slight rise above street level. He pulled in, shifted the car into park, and opened the door to get out.

From his position in the driveway, he scanned the front of the house. A large picture window spanned the width of the living room. On either side of it were smaller, sectioned-pane windows that could be lifted for ventilation—or entry. The front door stood about 20 feet to his right, and just beyond it, near the corner of the house, was a double window that likely belonged to a bedroom. The house had no shrubs around its perimeter, leaving everything in plain view.

Chance paused for a moment, observing carefully. He didn't notice any movement behind the windows, but something seemed off. All the blinds were down, and the curtains were drawn over the large picture window. On a sunny day with beautiful mid-80s weather, that felt strange.

Where was the husband?

Chance reached down to adjust the portable radio on his side, ensuring it was turned on. Before leaving his cruiser, he reached inside, grabbed the microphone, stretched its cord behind the steering wheel, and flipped it over the spotlight mounted outside. Satisfied, he closed the door, turned, and walked across the street to meet the complainant.

She was standing in the doorway, watching him walk up. Softly she said, *"He's in the house, I think he tore it up pretty bad."* The wife wasn't injured, not bad enough to call EMS at that moment anyway: a couple of bruises on her face, holding her arm with the other hand. He asked about weapons in the home and she quickly replied that her husband did, in fact, have several – pistols, rifles, and a shotgun. Asked if he would consider using any of them on himself or anyone else her reply was quick and decisive, *"That is one crazy man right now, I don' know what he might do. He done wrecked my home and messed me up 'dis time".*

As the story evolved, something sparked his anger this afternoon and he lost control. The husband was a truck driver, he'd been on the road for about a week, just got home a few hours before. He was exhausted. A couple of small dogs in the house woke him from his well-deserved nap and he was quite upset that his wife couldn't seem to curb those mutts so he could sleep. One thing led to another, they called each other names, the usual.

At one point, though, she indicated that she slapped him because he called her a name she didn't like. He flew hot, picked up something heavy from a side table, threw it across the room right through a 50-gallon aquarium.

"Damn, this sure sounds familiar", he thought, *"must know my old man."*

He kind of chuckled. She did not see the humor.

All she wanted was someone to stand by for a moment while she went inside to get some clothes then leave for the weekend till they could work things out. Reasonable. He'd go over and talk to the husband, make sure he was alright: no problem. Pretty standard procedure, pretty common call.

Chance walked back across the street, started up the little hill, dispatch called about then and ask if everything was ok.

"10-4", he said, *"almost done here"*.

Just about the time he driver's door on the patrol car he reached over, clicked the button on that microphone over the spotlight, made the radio repeater click, then reached down and turned off his portable. He'd never done that before, never did it again.

About two feet beyond the front of the car something caught his eye in the window to his left beside the large glass. Instinctively, Chance's right hand flew back to his sidearm, he snapped the holster and nearly cleared leather damned near simultaneously. The guy was a combat master shooter, and he had this maneuver down pat. Unfortunately, not quite quick enough for this guy.

Out the window came the barrel of what looked like a large caliber rifle. Chance couldn't tell exactly what size – from his perspective that barrel looked like an elephant rifle; it might just as well have been at that point.

Chance froze.

Crouched slightly, postured in full combat stance, he was exposed to the will of this would-be assailant and at his mercy. Life flashed before his eyes; that last telephone call suddenly shot through his mind. Boy, was this bad timing (like there is a *good* time for something like this?).

The man called out to Chance about now. *"Don't clear leather with that pistol, officer. If you do I'm gonna shoot you."*

Well, that was certainly clear. His eyes scoured the surroundings again. Nope, didn't miss anything, no cover to jump to.

The lump in his throat was now about the same size as the one in the seat of his pants.

He'd learned from the wife that the husband's name was Max, so called out to him.

"Max, this is not gonna end well friend".

Not very encouraging for either of them but it did open the dialogue some. It had only been a matter of maybe a minute since the stand-off began. Chance was sweating bullets. His hand locked on the grip of his .45, he was unable to move it – partially from that straightforward threat of being shot, mostly from sheer terror.

Someone must have called headquarters and given them a report of what they were seeing in this driveway right now. He and Max could both hear the sirens getting closer.

"What are we gonna do officer? I'm afraid if I put down my gun you gonna shoot me. I really messed up. I'm sorry." Max said, now crying.

Chance stood up straighter now. Hostage negotiations. Okay, I can handle this.

"Max, lower that weapon and come to the front door with your hands up".

"But, missa, I'm scared near to def. They gonna kill me for nearly shootin' you." Max continued, now crying uncontrollably.

"Hey man", Chance said, *"shit happens".* He continued, *"We all get upsetf, I get it. Now, put that rifle down now and come to the door."*

"You gone lock me up, ain't 'cha...?"

Chance thought long and hard about it. His lieutenant on this shift was an officer from the ole school, what would he do in a similar situation.

"Come to that door, let me see your hands, I will not take you to jail. Your wife is alright, you just hurt my pride", he said.

"A'ight, I trus you."

The husband pulled that weapon inside the window. Chance dove forward about 6 feet landing on the edge of the outside wall.

Hugging it hard, he could see when the screen to the front door opened; his .45 now pointed directly at the doorway.

The police radio was abuzz, constant chatter, he could hear the Chief, his lieutenant, the sergeant all headed his way. They'd called the city police and several of their units were on the way.

Within just seconds the storm door opened out. A huge man at least 6 foot 6 or more, like pushing 300 plus pounds, muscles on muscles, came out that door with his hands well above his head.

"Max", said Chance, *"way to go. Clasp your hands on top of your head ... now, get on your knees ... good, now cross your legs one over the other ... excellent. Lay down on your stomach"*.

He got up, holstered his weapon and snapped it, walked over and hand-cuffed the man. Max stood up with Chance's help, they walked to the rear of the police care and he got in the back seat. He wasn't under arrest, Chance kept his word, he just needed to make sure there weren't any "mistakes" and the other offices came rushing in.

The lieutenant and sergeant arrived, made sure Chance was alright, and asked what happened. They walked inside the house and more than one of them nearly fainted.

The house was, in fact, demolished. This big man wreaked havoc on the entire interior, nothing they could see was either intact or unmolested. Then they found the makeshift "sniper's nest" he had constructed during the time it took for Chance to interview his wife and head back up the driveway.

At the big man's disposal was a cache a Seal would be proud to hold. Less than an arm's length away officers found a fully loaded .30-.30 lever action with high-power metal-jacketed rounds; an AR-15 with 30-round clip fully engaged; a 9mm Glock locked and loaded; a 12-gauge shotgun with 00 buckshot; a .38 Smith & Wesson revolver with armor-piercing rounds.

Praise God these two encountered each other this afternoon. How unfortunate it had been that events came together to come to even nearly this, but a much greater force than Satan took control of these two men on this day, tempered their responses, and likely saved many lives in the process. The force was not a guardian angel, or wishful thinking, or fate – it was Jesus.

Chance had no idea whether or not the man was Christian, he been praying, was saved or not, he just knew he was praying that Christ would touch this man's heart with every breath. Besides really wanting to live, Chance knew for sure he wanted to make it home to that little boy of his this evening.

By the Grace of God, he did.

What Comes Around

Chance got home about 4:00 that afternoon, Eve was busy loading the car. Several months before they bought a new Chevy Nova hatchback she really liked to drive. He could see that she'd already loaded the bassinet, stroller, and Dillon's car seat.

"What's up", he asked.

"I told you; I'm goin' to Mama's for a few days", Eve said.

About that time, Chance's mom walked up.

"Yeah", he said, *"about that. I have the next several days off. You can go wherever you want but leave the boy."*

Her face turned blood red. She started spewing out obscenities about his mama, his dad, his brother, and him. *"How do I know what you might do with Dillon, you pervert? You've got that bag of filth under the house. You going to show that to him? Tell him what kind of Daddy he really has?"*

"You are one sick bitch", he said to her. With that, he reached for the passenger's door to get Dillon's car seat out. She got in the car with the baby in her arms, reached across and slammed the passenger door shut.

"No", she said, *"this is not gonna happen. I am NOT leaving my baby with you!"*

"He is my son, you crazy bitch. You really need some help", Chance said.

"You really do, Eve", mama chimed in about now. *"What you do, the way you hover over that child all the time is unnatural. Hell, it's a wonder you don't accuse me of something when he's with me."*

Now crying, Eve said, *"When the hell was he with you?! I haven't given permission for him to visit you."*

Incensed by her tone, the implications, or just because Eve was being so abnormally outrageous toward her, Chance's mother fired back. *"Let me tell you something, you sick idiot, I am this baby's grandmother and if I wanna spend time with him I will. I don't need your permission."*

Chance now reached in the driver's side, put his arms out, and said, *"Come her buddy"*. Dillon reached over to go to his dad's arms, and she pulled him back in.

"I will call your Chief and DFACs." she said.

"Are you completely out of your mind? What the hell has happened to you?", he asked.

He reached for the child again, this time his mother by his side. His brother Alden now joined the crowd. The next-door neighbors on both side had now come outside by this time. Chance was getting quite embarrassed.

Dillon crawled across his mother's lap and jumped from the car into Chance's waiting arms.

"This is NOT over!", she screamed, now crying uncontrollably.

Eve backed out of the driveway, nearly hitting Alden who had to jump back out of her way.

Chance and Dillon had a wonderful weekend. They went to Daffin Park and then Forsythe Park to feed the squirrels. They rode down to the beach and played in the sand and water. Dillon spent time with his grandmother as well, something he hadn't been able to do recently. Eve would always find a reason the child couldn't stay with her when they'd go down to visit. Anne thought that more than just a little odd but she never said anything.

That Sunday afternoon, while Dillon was taking his nap, Chance got into the collection of VCR tapes under the TV in their living room. He found several that he enjoyed watching where Eve and Dillon were just acting silly, Dillon eating his favorite food – spaghetti – and just talkin' about daddy. For a moment his heart warmed to her and her behavior two days before. Then he found something he wished he had not.

In those tapes was one recording of a report from CBS News, a special from 60 Minutes about a plastic surgeon named Elizabeth Morgan. This doctor was involved in a bitter custody suit with her husband over their 3-year-old daughter, Hilary Fortich. The mother, Dr. Morgan, had levied accusation of child molestation and improper and sexual behavior against the husband in an attempt to force custody under the Child Protection Act. When the courts refused to grant that appeal, and the allegations were appearing to be a total fabrication, the doctor secreted her child away to New Zealand. The tape was from a show late in 1989, just less than 6 months prior.

This doctor had been warned by the presiding jurist that she was, specifically, ordered *not* to remove the child from the jurisdiction of his court under penalty of imprisonment. By secreting the child away in any manner, and thus preventing the other parent from access to the child, she was in violation of the Federal Parental Abduction Act. The child was sent away by the mother in 1987 and, as of the time of the report, Dr. Morgan had been in confinement for contempt for 750 days. The report indicated that the Court was about to release her, however, under the District of Columbia Civil Contempt Limitation Act.

In direct response to this and other similar incidents, and the nationally covered abduction of little Adam Walsh the year before, the House Missing Children's Assistance Act provided for formation of the National Center for Missing and Exploited Children. That agency had located the child in New Zealand and were attempting to bring him home.

Chance was beside himself for several moments. *"What the hell am I looking at?"*, he thought. *"Surely she wouldn't.....no way."*

Suddenly, he was stricken with the thought of that material under the edge of the house. He ran outside, pulled it out, and threw the bag in the trunk of his police cruiser.

"It'll be alright there for right now", he thought. *"I'll get rid of that shit for good now."*

He went back inside to check on Dillon. He was still sleeping. Chance got down no his knees beside the little man, now just under 3, and prayed;

"Dear God, protect our boy from the evils of this world, and my stupidity, Help me learn how I might fix this problem between his mom and myself if it be your Will. I have been faithful to this woman and my son. I know that I have fallen, I have sinned, and I have looked on other women in lust. I pray that you will forgive me and receive my repentance in earnest. I receive the power and the glory of the Father into my soul and my heart and ask your forgiveness, Jesus. Please help me look after my son, Dillon, and do what is right in his eyes and Yours, oh Lord."

They enjoyed the next few hours together. The next morning, Eve returned home. She appeared much more subdued, apologetic for her behavior and outburst. She even went down and apologized to Chance's mom. Things were good for the next few days.

***

God. My God, Why

Wednesday came, and Chance began a week of graveyard shifts, clocking in at 11 p.m. each night. The week passed smoothly, with Eve making sure Dillon stayed quiet during the days so Chance could sleep. Every evening around 8 p.m., she'd bring the little guy in to wake him up. Dillon would climb into bed with his daddy, and they'd laugh and play, sharing those precious moments as a family.

Chance went to work with a smile on his face every night that week.

When his two-day break rolled around the following Wednesday and Thursday, the three of them took a little ride down to her mother's house. Eve had forgotten something there, though she didn't say what. Chance didn't mind—he enjoyed the ride and the visit.

There's a saying, right? When it rains, it pours.

The second night after his break, Chance was back on evening shift, covering the Islands again. Instead of going home for dinner, he planned to meet Eve and Dillon at his mama's house.

Around 7 p.m., just before dusk, he pulled his cruiser up to the curb and requested permission from dispatch to take his evening break. The dispatcher approved, and Chance gave them his mom's phone number in case they needed to reach him. Shutting off the engine, he stepped out of the car and started up the little paved walkway toward the front door.

That's when something struck him as odd.

Dillon hadn't burst through the door to greet him like he always did. That was unusual. Then he noticed the curtains in the big picture window were drawn—something his mom never did.

"Mom never closes those," he thought, a twinge of unease creeping in.

Alden's car wasn't in the driveway, either. The boy rarely missed a meal, and it wasn't like he had a job or someplace to be.

Before getting out of his cruiser, Chance had taken off his portable radio and left his gun belt in the car to be comfortable during dinner. That wasn't unusual, but tonight it felt like a mistake.

He opened the storm door and tried the handle on the big wooden entry door. It was locked. He knocked and waited.

Nothing.

He knocked again. Still nothing.

Chance had a key, so he figured maybe his mom was in the backyard with the dog and hadn't heard him. He unlocked the door, turned the knob, and stepped inside.

What he saw left him frozen.

There, in the living room, were his mom and dad, both turning to look at him.

His mom sat nervously at the far end of their brown Naugahyde sofa, wearing a house dress. Her hands were folded tightly in her lap, and her voice shook as she whispered, "Hi, baby, come on in. Join the party."

His dad was seated at the opposite end of the room, slouched on the edge of a big tan corduroy lounger. He wore nothing but a wife-beater and briefs, his right hand resting on top of his left, which held his blue-steel .38 Colt revolver. The hammer was cocked back and the gun was aimed directly at his mother.

Chance's heart pounded as he slowly walked to the only other chair in the room, directly opposite his mom, and sat down.

Looking at his dad, he asked, "What's going on with you two?"

"We're not well," Bernie replied, his tone flat. "We were about to have sex when your crazy-assed mama brought up an old girlfriend's name. We argued, and now... here we are."

Confused and stunned, Chance shook his head. He asked the obvious.

"So how did we go from about to have sex to you sitting here pointing a cocked gun at her?"

His dad sighed heavily. "I'm just tired of living this way. I only have two bullets in this gun... one for her, one for myself. If I'd known you were coming...."

Seconds stretched into minutes, and minutes into an hour.

The department called the house phone multiple times, but no one answered. Eventually, they dispatched city officers to the address. A Deputy Sheriff who knew Bernie heard the call and responded as well.

Bernie allowed Chance to leave the house, then let his mom go. Finally, he surrendered the weapon and himself to the Deputy, a man who had served with him on the county force twenty years earlier.

That was the last time Chance ever saw his parents together under the same roof.

One week later, Chance was three days into a week of day shifts, working 7 a.m. to 3 p.m. Around noon, he went home for lunch. It was a quiet, pleasant meal—spaghetti for him and Dillon. Eve didn't eat. She hovered around the kitchen and Dillon, her usual neurotic tendencies on display.

When lunch was over, she made sure Dillon said goodbye to his daddy from the front porch.

Chance got back into his patrol car and pulled away from the curb, heading toward Thunderbolt. The clock read 1:15 p.m.

By 1:45, he was out on Johnny Mercer Boulevard, patrolling the islands, when the dispatcher called him on the radio.

"Signal 12," they said.

Signal 12—police jargon for "come into the Chief's office."

"10-4," Chance replied, gripping the wheel tighter. "On my way."

As he pulled into the gated enclosure behind the station, something felt off. The radio room closed the electronic gate behind him, which was unusual—typically, it stayed open during the day, except for overnight shifts.

Waiting in the parking lot were his lieutenant and sergeant.

"What the hell is this?" Chance thought, a knot forming in his stomach.

He parked the car, and the lieutenant walked over.

"Hand me your keys," he said, his tone flat, offering no explanation.

Chance handed them over, the knot tightening.

"Go to the Internal Affairs office," the lieutenant directed, motioning toward the building.

Once inside, Chance was ushered into the IA interrogation suite, where he was introduced to a Savannah Police detective. The detective wasted no time delivering a bombshell:

"I'm investigating allegations of sexual abuse and misconduct involving your son, Dillon."

It hit Chance like a bolt of lightning. A gunshot to the head. A broadaxe to the chest. None of those analogies came close to the raw pain and fury surging through him.

"Oh my God! My dear God, what is this?" he shouted, his voice trembling with disbelief. "Are you *fricking kidding me*? How utterly absurd!"

The detective continued, explaining the nature of the allegations. Child Protective Services had received complaints that Chance had, on more than one occasion—particularly during the weekend two weeks prior—touched or fondled his son unnaturally. One accusation even claimed this happened in the presence of his mother, Anne.

Chance's voice rose again, a mix of anger and desperation. "Something like this will absolutely kill my mother!" he said. "Her mother, too?"

The detective maintained his calm demeanor.

"We have to check this out," he said. "DFACS is recommending that the child and his mother be distanced from you indefinitely, at least until these accusations can be thoroughly investigated. I understand you're divorcing?"

"What?" Chance exclaimed, his shock deepening. "No, not to my knowledge. We sure as hell are now, bet your ass on that."

As the conversation progressed, the accusations grew more outrageous. Chance felt sick to his stomach. Fear, humiliation, confusion, and fury churned together in his head.

"They asked her," the detective continued, "if you had any films or videos of the child, or of you doing anything unusual or unnatural with him—or with other children, or by yourself. She said no to those questions but claimed you kept a stash of pornography in the trunk of your patrol car."

Chance froze. *The bag.*

He'd put that bag in the trunk on Monday, after Eve returned. How could she have known about it? Unless... she must have looked under the house, found the bag gone, and made an assumption. Maybe she had even searched his trunk in the last few days.

Like the calculated risks she had been taking lately, this one had paid off in her favor.

For now, Chance wasn't being charged with anything, but the detective emphasized the seriousness of the allegations. Contact with Eve and Dillon would have to be limited until the investigation was completed.

But his position with the county police was another matter entirely.

Unknown to him, when Chance was reinstated, the Chief had placed him under a six-month probationary period per county policy. This was Chance's third—and final—reinstatement. His benefits wouldn't become active until the probation expired. It was a detail buried in the fine print, one Chance hadn't been made fully aware of.

They ushered him into the Chief's office.

On the desk sat *the bag*.

The Chief gestured toward it. "This yours?"

Chance's heart sank as he saw its contents laid out in plain view. Stacks of magazines, loose-leaf photos, detailed drawings, and penciled illustrations of women in all kinds of poses—graphic, nude, and professional in quality. There were no images of children, animals, or anything deviant. Just a collection of work that hinted at an unhealthy but harmless hobby.

He realized, with bitter clarity, that this discovery would overshadow everything else.

Chance stood there, silent, as the weight of the situation bore down on him.

From the Chief's perspective, it was cut and dry. The items found in Chance's trunk—this "contraband"—were in clear violation of county and department rules. Having such material in an official police vehicle, under normal circumstances, would already raise concerns. But in the context of the allegations leveled against Chance by his wife, the situation became untenable.

The Chief, a man Chance had come to trust and respect, was now in an impossible position. He had no choice but to make the only decision available to him.

"We found this in your trunk, Chance," the Chief said, pacing as he spoke. "What the hell were you thinking, son? This is conduct unbecoming a police officer. You're still within the six-month probation period. And with these allegations against you? This looks bad—really bad."

Then came the words that shattered him.

The Chief stopped pacing, turned to face Chance, and said, "I need you to surrender your badge and gun. You're relieved of duty."

It was a death blow.

"Just let me fire it one more time—into my head," Chance thought bitterly.

As if twisting the knife, they handed him a paper to sign on his way out. By signing it, he acknowledged that he could never return to employment with Chatham County, whether in the police or sheriff's departments.

He would have preferred they drove that pen straight through his heart. It crushed him. His spirit, his soul—everything he was—felt destroyed.

The pieces were coming together now.

Eve's erratic behavior. The tape. That weekend he insisted on keeping Dillon. Her threats. How much of this had been orchestrated by her crazy sister Donna, that drunk Aunt Murtice, and the rest of the halfwits in her family?

Chance's lieutenant drove him home in silence. Neither man spoke a word. Chance sobbed openly in the passenger seat, the weight of his world crumbling around him.

When they pulled to the curb, Chance stepped out of the car and saw Eve and Dillon standing in the doorway, behind the screen door.

Something about it seemed off. If she was supposedly so afraid for Dillon's safety, why were they standing there like nothing had happened?

He walked inside.

"What happened? Where's your police car?" Eve asked, her tone sharp and almost accusatory.

For the first time in their nearly 13 years together, Chance looked at her with nothing but utter contempt. A lesser man might have reached out and taken her life right then and there.

Dillon reached for his daddy, his little arms outstretched. But Eve tightened her grip on the boy, refusing to let go.

"You know full well what's happened today," Chance said, his voice low and his teeth clenched tightly.

"Okay," she said casually, as if she were discussing the weather. "I think we need to go now. DFACS says I need to take Dillon and get out of the house."

And there it was. Another gut-wrenching blow, cutting straight through his soul.

She was leaving. Taking Dillon. The one thing that meant more to him than anything else in the world.

It was clear she'd known this was coming. Someone must have called her shortly after he left for work, giving her enough time to pack. The car she was taking was already loaded. She was leaving him behind—alone. No family, no job, no transportation.

Good thing they took my service revolver, Chance thought, *not because I'd use it on myself, but....*

She had taken everything. His career, something he had worked tirelessly to build, was gone in an instant. She was taking Dillon. And to add insult to injury, she had leveled criminal accusations against him—claims so heinous that he would never, could never, even entertain the thought of doing such a thing.

"Oh my God," he prayed silently, his mind swirling with grief and anger.

*"I know Thou hast not forsaken me, yet this is such a heavy load to bear. Why, Lord, why this? I have been faithful to You. You blessed me with this son after years of barrenness. We endured his malformed head and his illnesses, and we saw only Your mercy through it all. You were patient with my transgressions. You forgave my weaknesses and blessed me so many times. And now—now, when I thought my blessings were multiplying beyond my expectations—this.

Dear Jesus, my Father, this is more than I can bear. I pray, my God, that You take mercy on my soul again and show me how to restore my life and my faith in this time of trial. Protect my son and his mother, and, if it be Your will, my soul as well. Amen."*

Days stretched into weeks, and weeks into months, each passing moment a reminder of how much Chance's life had changed. Eve moved frequently during that time, often making it a challenge for Chance to locate her and Dillon. It was as if she wanted to keep them one step ahead, out of reach, making him feel like a stranger to his own son.

The divorce case was assigned to Superior Court Judge Frank Cheatham, a man known for his no-nonsense approach and razor-sharp sense of fairness. Judge Cheatham made it clear from the outset that he had little patience for manipulative behaviors from either party. His rulings reflected a deliberate attempt to safeguard the child's well-being and ensure that neither parent could exploit the court system for personal vendettas.

The judge ordered a full evaluation of Dillon to check for any signs of abuse—physical or psychological. Until the results came back, Eve would retain custody. However, the court mandated that Chance's visitations be supervised. This wasn't just for the child's protection but also for Chance's, shielding him from any additional false accusations or unfounded allegations that could arise during the ongoing proceedings.

Sitting in that courtroom, Chance felt equal parts humiliated and grateful. *"This must be the will of God,"* he thought. *"This man is wise where I am lost. Thank you, Lord, for his discernment. Give me the patience to endure this trial."* He clung to his faith, even as his world seemed to crumble around him.

Judge Cheatham didn't stop there. Both Chance and Eve were ordered to undergo rigorous psychological evaluations by independent specialists. A psychiatrist was also assigned to investigate the allegations against Chance and determine whether Eve's claims were genuine or fabricated—possibly as a calculated attempt to alienate Dillon from his father. The court left no stone unturned, ensuring that the truth would come to light.

Through those agonizing months, Chance bore witness to the toll the situation was taking on Dillon. His once-vibrant, happy boy was beginning to show signs of distress.

When Chance left their shared home that fateful day in May, Dillon had been a bright, cheerful toddler. His dark brown hair had been long and straight, and his head had nearly fully recovered from its earlier deformity. But now, whenever Chance saw him, the changes were stark and heartbreaking. Eve had hacked away at Dillon's hair, leaving it uneven and clumped, with some sections cut down to the scalp as if to punish him for something. His once-neat clothing was now perpetually disheveled, and the boy's little frame was thinner than before. It was as if every part of him—his body, his spirit, his joy—was being neglected or stifled.

By July 1990, the investigations were nearing their conclusion. The reports were submitted to the court, and the findings were clear: supervised visitations were no longer necessary or justified. The police department had never filed charges against Chance, and the allegations were officially deemed unfounded.

Eve, unsurprisingly, was livid. The evaluations had been damning for her. The reports painted a troubling picture of her behavior and psychological state, revealing her to be the parent more likely to endanger Dillon's safety or emotional security.

Meanwhile, Chance struggled to rebuild the life that had been torn apart. He took on whatever work he could find, hustling to make ends meet. At one point, he was delivering slushy mixes to retail stores—a physically exhausting job that paid pennies on the dollar. When that wasn't enough, he picked up bartending shifts at local restaurants, scraping by on tips.

But even in the darkness, there was a glimmer of light.

Chance managed to land a gig at the city's biggest adult pop music station, hosting oldies shows on the weekends. The return of Jay Hanson to the airwaves brought him more than just income—it brought a sense of purpose and normalcy back into his life. That job helped him save his mortgage, keep his car, and preserve a sliver of his sanity. Through it all, he never stopped thanking God for His blessings, even when the trials seemed insurmountable.

Every Friday evening, Chance picked up Dillon for the weekend. They'd head straight to his mama's house, where the little boy would be showered with love and attention. Those two and a half days became a sanctuary for them both—a time when life felt joyful again.

Chance's mama took special care of Dillon, bathing him every night and making sure he felt safe and loved. The house would fill with laughter, and for a while, it felt like nothing else in the world mattered.

But Sunday afternoons always loomed like a dark cloud on the horizon.

When the weekend came to an end, Chance would kneel down, look into Dillon's big, tearful eyes, and say, "Come on, buddy, it's time to get ready to go back to Mama."

The boy would cry, his small shoulders shaking with heartbreak. And Chance, unable to hold back his own tears, would weep with him.

They'd cry together all the way to wherever Eve was staying that week. By the time they arrived, Chance would wipe his eyes, kiss his son goodbye, and pray silently for God's protection over Dillon. Each goodbye felt like a piece of his heart was being ripped away, and each drive back home left him lonelier than before.

Parental abduction cases had become a grim backdrop to Chance's personal nightmare. That year, the media was filled with stories of children being taken by one parent, leaving the other in a relentless search. *America's Most Wanted* dedicated weekly segments to these heartbreaking cases, sometimes featuring two at a time. The faces of missing children stared back at Chance from every corner—flyers in post offices, grocery stores, and even on milk cartons. Names like Flores, Blackwell, Martinez, Chin, Khan, and Khalid became etched into his mind as haunting reminders of what could happen to Dillon. Whenever Chance saw one of these posters, he would stop, trace the faces of those lost children with his fingers, and imagine what their parents were enduring. Each time, his heart sank further, wondering if Dillon's face might one day end up among them.

In late August 1990, as the world watched the first Gulf War unfold and the Berlin Wall crumble after 30 years, Chance's own life shattered completely.

The court had ordered evaluations of both parents' housing situations to assess the suitability for joint custody. The intention was clear: Judge Cheatham wanted to ensure that Dillon would have a stable and secure environment, regardless of who retained custody. But Eve was furious. She opposed anything that could limit her control or autonomy as a parent, and her anger boiled over during the court hearing. She didn't just disagree—she openly threatened the court.

"If you try to make me share custody," she spat, "I'll leave this state. You won't find me or Dillon. Ever."

Judge Cheatham didn't flinch. Fixing her with a steely gaze, he replied firmly, "If you leave the jurisdiction of this court, I will invoke the Prevention of Parental Abduction Act. You will be brought back here, jailed, and permanently stripped of custody. You will lose all parental rights. Do not test me."

Eve's defiance, however, was unshakable. Less than a week later, she disappeared—taking Dillon with her.

Chance died that day.

It wasn't the kind of death that comes with a final breath or a heartbeat stopping. It was the slow, agonizing kind, where the very essence of who you are is stripped away, leaving a hollow shell behind. Losing his career had been devastating, a blow to everything he'd worked for and built. But losing Dillon? That was unbearable.

He had thought he'd endured the worst when Eve's false accusations cost him his badge and his career. The humiliation of that day—being stripped of his position, his reputation tarnished by baseless claims—still burned in his memory. The carefully crafted character assassination had been her masterpiece. She knew exactly what strings to pull and what accusations would destroy him. And they had. But even that, as devastating as it was, paled in comparison to what she'd done now.

When Eve vanished with Dillon, she took more than his son. She took his purpose, his anchor, the one thing keeping him grounded in the storm of his life.

The man of faith, the man who had clung to God's promises through every trial, was now broken beyond recognition. He sat alone in Dillon's empty room, holding one of his son's favorite toys, inhaling the faint scent of baby powder that still lingered. Tears streamed down his face, but there was no relief in them. Only an endless, aching void.

"My God," he prayed, his voice cracking, "what is my son suffering for my sake? Protect him, Lord. Keep him safe when I can't. Don't let my failures fall on him."

But his prayers felt hollow. The silence that followed each one was deafening.

The world outside seemed indifferent to his pain. Neighbors mowed their lawns, children played in the street, and the seasons shifted as if nothing had changed. For Chance, time stood still. The days blurred into an endless gray haze of grief and longing.

Parental abduction was no longer just a headline—it was his reality. The fear that Dillon was out there, somewhere, scared and alone, consumed him. The thought of what Eve might be telling their son about him was almost too much to bear. Every moment was filled with questions he couldn't answer: Was Dillon okay? Was he being cared for? Did he think his daddy had abandoned him?

Chance began searching immediately, reaching out to anyone and everyone who might have a lead. Eve had family scattered across several states—sisters, cousins, aunts—and any one of them could be hiding her. He cast his net wide, following up on every rumor, every whisper of a possible sighting.

Sometimes, the leads seemed promising. He'd feel a flicker of hope—a name, a location, a clue—but it always led to another dead end. Eve was always one step ahead, moving Dillon before Chance could catch up.

Weeks turned into months, and the weight of it all began to crush him. Dillon was just three years and two months old. The milestones Chance would miss haunted him: the way his voice would change, the new words he'd learn, the way his laugh would evolve.

But Chance refused to give up.

He realized that if he was going to survive this, he had to change everything about his life. His faith, his perspective, even his understanding of endurance had to transform. Nothing about this journey would be easy, but Chance held onto the belief that God's love, even if it felt distant now, would guide him through.

To a father searching for a lost child, the quest becomes a sacred mission. Every shred of information, every rumor, every whisper of hope is a lifeline. It consumes you, filling every waking moment and haunting every dream. The hole it leaves in your soul is vast, and no amount of tears can ever fill it.

But there is a moment—a rare, precious moment—when the search ends. When the child you've longed for, cried for, and prayed for is returned to you, and your souls are reunited. That moment is the closest thing to heaven on earth that a father can know.

Chance held onto that thought like a lifeline. It was the only thing keeping him moving forward—the hope that one day, Dillon would be back in his arms, and the world would finally feel whole again.

"The tragedy in a man's life is what dies inside of him while he lives."

-Albert Schweitzer

Roberts Essex

About The Author

Roberts Essex is a pseudonym for the living man who is the character of Chance Brogdon. He continues to write about how his missing son's abduction was handled and the ensuing turmoil of that period. His actions and enduring faith during those times of tremendous emotional strain resulted in miracles of faith and redemption neither he nor his son could imagine. His character will win a rebirth of spirit, bringing new life to himself, his son, and the lives of three other unsuspecting souls struggling in their existence and awaiting their just redemption.

This work, and two additional works to come, chronicle over six decades of a man's life; the decisions he had to make, the results of those actions, and how his life and actions affected so many others.

Now in his late 60s, Roberts can reflect on the great wealth of his experiences and the resolve of persistent faith. He and his wife of over 30 years are coasting into his forecast retirement, at peace with their four children, five grandchildren, and two new great-grandchildren. Together, they enjoy photography, motorcycles, gardening, and traveling at their own pace around the country and overseas. He continues to live in rural Georgia, enjoying the tranquility and quiet of their quaint country home.

www.ingramcontent.com/pod-product-compliance
Lightning Source LLC
Chambersburg PA
CBHW080944120626
46546CB00010B/2836